Verne Sankey

Verne Sankey

America's First Public Enemy

by
Timothy W. Bjorkman

University of Oklahoma Press
Norman

Library of Congress Cataloging-in-Publication Data

Bjorkman, Timothy W., 1956–
Verne Sankey : America's first public enemy / by Timothy W. Bjorkman.
  p. cm.
Includes bibliographical references and index.
ISBN 978-0-8061-3853-4 (hardcover : alk. paper)
1. Sankey, Verne, 1891–1934. 2. Gangsters — United States — Biography.
3. Kidnapping — United States — History. I. Title.
HV6248.s328b56 2007
364.15′4092 — dc22
[B]

2007009852

1 2 3 4 5 6 7 8 9 10

For my father, who endowed me with the love of a good story well told, and for my soul mate, Carol Kay. If not for your tender frankness, persistence, and love, this book would be a pale shadow of itself.

Contents

Illustrations

Preface

A small boy sat in a dusty barbershop chair, feet dangling above the metal footrest. He listened in unblinking silence as the two old barber brothers wove a tale about a brassy local hustler who had one day long ago kidnapped a wealthy Denver man and held him for ransom. They told of the kidnapper's free-spirited nature, of the bullet-ridden car he drove into town one day, of his untimely demise.

I was the boy who heard the story as one of the pair performed my customary buzz cut. The story lay dormant for decades, dwelling in the foggy recesses of my mind, among the myriad tall tales and half-myths of boyhood. After I married, began the practice of law, and started a family, I recalled that story of my youth from time to time. Because it was one I never heard or read about elsewhere, I began to question whether it had really happened, like many a childhood yarn.

Then one day, a road trip with one of my young sons took us past the hamlet of Gann Valley, South Dakota. I found myself drawn off the highway and into the decrepit village. Before long, I was leafing through dusty, yellowed editions of the 1933 *Gann Valley Chief*, the town's now defunct weekly newspaper. As I did, the story came alive before my eyes. I could not know then that I was about to embark on a journey that would extend well over a decade. The effort was more excavation than research, demanding the removal of layers of figurative earth and sod, a shovel full at a time, in search of the truth of that kidnapping and the lives of the people it changed. In many instances, it was history that did not desire recovery, too tender for some, even generations later. The unearthed result, though, is a story much richer and more poignant than I had imagined.

It is a fascinating, largely forgotten story, and it is all true. This is how it happened.

Verne Sankey

1

The Best of All Possible Worlds

At half past three in the morning, Verne Sankey and Gordon Alcorn eased into the sleepy city of Greeley, Colorado. Hours earlier, they had fled Denver in a hail of police gunfire. Bullets had pierced the windshield of Sankey's performance-enhanced 1932 Ford V-8, narrowly missing each man's head. Now they breathed sighs of relief. A club bag containing sixty thousand dollars in ten- and twenty-dollar bills lay safely near Alcorn. The men helped themselves to some local gas in the slumbering city then rolled north toward its outskirts, bound for Dakota. When a solitary patrol car approached, they turned east a block ahead of it. When the patrol car also turned, Sankey cut his lights and sped away, screeching around corners, turning first north again, then east. The patrolmen raced closely behind.

Suddenly Sankey's Ford sputtered. He swung off the street alongside a warehouse. The police appeared to have the men checkmated. Alcorn panicked. He bailed out of the car, tossed his gun onto a Greeley street, and disappeared into a nearby field. Unwilling to surrender or to follow his partner on foot, Sankey hopped out of the Ford sedan and, using it as cover, trained his .32-caliber pistol on the police car as it pulled to within twenty yards of the warehouse and stopped. He exchanged several shots with officers who also exited their Terraplane. As Sankey fired, his Ford slowly rolled down the gentle knoll on which he had stopped. Now exposed, Sankey chased after the moving auto. When he reached it, he jumped in and fired it up. The Ford restarted and Sankey roared away, cornering at times on two wheels, driver's door open as he fired back at pursuing officers until he outran them.

It was the beginning of what would be labeled the most exhaustive manhunt in the history of the West.

The life that Verne Sankey had forged throughout the Prohibition years presaged what transpired that February night in 1933. Sankey roared through the 1920s with the best of them—adorned in a raccoon coat, diamond rings on his fingers, flashing large bills, tipping grandly.

He was born Reo Verne Sankey, the product of German and Irish ancestry, in Avoca, Iowa, on July 18, 1891. As a boy, he moved with his family to a farm near the tiny town of Wilmot, in South Dakota's northeastern corner. There, the Sisseton-Wahpeton tribe had negotiated an agreement with the federal government that entitled each tribal member to a 160-acre tract, a deal that permitted the government to open the remaining land to homesteaders. On a spring day in 1892, five hundred hopeful homesteaders breathlessly waited at the starting line. As a bugle sounded, the homesteaders raced onto the newly opened sod, feverishly staking out sites for farms, homes, and businesses.

The boy Verne Sankey—the youngest of three sons born to Joseph and Wattie Sankey—arrived at this frontier soon after with his family. Joseph Sankey worked at turns as a farmer, a railroad engineer, and a rural mail carrier, but it was railroading that flowed through his veins. Mesmerized by the train's whistle and the thunderous roar of its massive engines, Joseph's youngest son loved the rails too. The boy stood fascinated as the iron horse's steel wheels slowly began their rhythmic turn, gradually gaining in momentum and speed. He grew accustomed to the smell of the sooty, black smoke trailing the engine.

Wilmot folks knew Verne Sankey as a convivial boy, full of life, neither more nor less mischievous than the average turn-of-the-century American lad. He was soft spoken and polite, particularly toward women and elders—the kind of youngster good parents hoped their daughters would bring home but also the kind to which other young men were drawn. As Verne Sankey grew he worked as a farmhand around Wilmot but he dreamed of engineering a train.

In the spring of 1914, Sankey, twenty-two, married his Wilmot sweetheart, nineteen-year-old Fern Young, whose own parents homesteaded a mile or so across the prairie from the Sankeys. Fern was petite and pretty with a gentle personality that easily won friends. The heritage of a good family showed in her quiet but distinct dignity and bearing. The two seemed a good match.

Around the time of their marriage, Verne took a bold step toward attaining his childhood dream. As war broke out in Europe, he left with Fern for Saskatchewan and the promise of a railroading career. Settlers were flooding Canada's Great West, and railroad companies were building track as fast as they could to accommodate the westward push. As Sankey left for the Saskatchewan town of Melville with his young bride, the editor of the *Wilmot Enterprise* wrote, "We have yet to meet a man who did not say he liked Verne Sankey and enjoyed his friendship and company.... He loved children, too, and it was a bad day for him when he didn't have a word of cheer or greeting for the young folks about him."

Once in Melville, Sankey landed a job on the Grand Trunk Pacific Railway, which was built to allow the Grand Pacific to compete with the Canadian Pacific Railway for the robust passenger business spurred by settlement of Western Canada. Its main line from Winnipeg, to Melville, to Edmonton, to Jasper, to Prince Rupert had opened in April of that year and there were jobs aplenty. Sankey began as a lowly watchman in the railroad yards, vigilant for freeloaders and thieves. Before long, he was promoted to fireman. Verne wrote his parents that first Christmas, bursting with pride over his new job feeding coal to the steam engine's fire. He earned good money — November's pay had totaled well over two hundred dollars, about a fifth of what the average worker earned in an entire year. He sent his parents a photograph of the check to prove its amount. For Verne Sankey, money was already the chief measuring stick of his success in the world.

Melville was a frontier town. Established only six years before the Sankeys' arrival there, the town was strategically located as the second divisional point of the railroad west of Winnipeg. It served as the intersection for trains running north-south and east-west. Within a year of its founding, the town claimed one thousand inhabitants. By the time the Sankeys arrived there in 1914, Melville boasted a power plant, a fledgling hospital, a milling company, Luther College, and the Queen Street Arena, home of the semipro Allan Cup champions, the Melville Millionaires. It was hockey lover Verne Sankey's kind of town.

In 1919, Fern gave birth to a daughter, whom they christened Echo, and Verne busied himself establishing a reputation as a solid railroader. He briskly climbed the employment ladder, eventually reaching his goal of becoming an engineer. Sankey's steam locomotives often pulled their load from Melville southwesterly to Regina, ninety miles away — passenger cars brimming with optimistic immigrants bound for the West. Each town along the way, often little more than a whistle stop, boasted its own personality.

There was, in the life of the railroader, something that appealed to Verne Sankey's wanderlust. Whatever problems he encountered at home seemed diminished amid the vast expanses of land spreading across the horizon. In the restaurants and bars, the railroader, especially the engineer, held a position of status and authority. He was a local celebrity of sorts, seldom staying long enough to wear out his welcome. There was, too, the camaraderie he shared with fellow workers on the rails and the seemingly endless track, that ribbon stretching across the vast, treeless prairie.

The long hours on the rails provided Verne Sankey with idle hours to fill. He passed his time reading true crime magazines, mocking the hapless criminals foiled by police, confident he could do better. Games of chance also beckoned him, especially cards and dice. The railroad was a natural environment for refining his skills in both pursuits with its long, unoccupied hours and forgiving salaries. Sankey bit the gambler's hook. Early success spurred him on, and he plowed harder and harder. On good nights, he spent lavishly, tipped big. Neither the money nor the luck lasted long but what never abandoned him was his zest for the good life.

Sankey was stocky and rather short — no more than five feet, seven inches tall. He often covered his receding hairline with a Stetson hat set above intelligent, rather sensitive blue eyes, the hallmark of his cherubic face. His inviting smile revealed mildly bucked teeth. He possessed midwestern charm, conversing confidently and easily with people.

Sankey's colorful, good-natured personality made him one of the best-known trainmen on the line. Betty Champagne fondly remembered the day she made Verne Sankey's acquaintance as a fifteen-year-old high school girl. Sankey came to see her father, a fellow engineer. She considered Sankey a "nice looking man. You wouldn't call him terribly handsome. He was fine looking," she recalled. "He [was] the sort of man you'd be attracted to because he had a very pleasant personality." Almost everyone who met Sankey shared Champagne's impressions of him, but there were exceptions among fellow railroaders, some of whom got a larger helping of him than they desired. Unlike most people who found the trainman disarmingly soft-spoken and fun, some fellow rail workers witnessed a braggadocio that rubbed them wrong.

By 1923, Sankey's insatiable urge for money and what it could buy led him into the illegal but widely tolerated bootlegging industry. He began hauling Canadian whiskey south across the border at handsome profits, sometimes in train cars. It was easy money. If Fern objected, her protests did not cause her to decline the fruits of her husband's endeavors. The Sankeys lived a cut above their neighbors. They owned a charming home on a corner lot in Melville, which still stands. They went places and owned things beyond the reach of others around them. Fern wore fine clothes and expensive jewelry. Sankey "always had the . . . smartest and newest Nash car in the Melville district," one Melville old-timer recalled. "And he was the envy of the youngbloods of the town. He always spent his money liberally, and he rarely drank." This latter observation was not entirely accurate. Others who knew him were aware that he frequently imbibed, although he seldom seemed affected by it. Sankey became something of a legendary figure to those young Melville men seeking adventure, some of whom he reportedly employed on his liquor runs.

Sankey's bootlegging was no secret to Melville residents. He loved to recount rollicking tales of his exploits with police that were full of color, drama, and vivid humor, sometimes including dramatic escape scenes.

Despite his Prohibition law-breaking, though, Verne Sankey was a hard man to resist. As Betty Champagne explained it, "You couldn't admire his bootlegging, but at the same time, you couldn't help but like him."

By the mid-twenties, Sankey's bootlegging operation generated large sums of money — far more than he could earn on the railroad. As a consequence, his dream job began to lose its luster. To accommodate his budding liquor enterprise, Sankey, by then a naturalized Canadian, took leaves-of-absence from the Grand Trunk Pacific, which had by then merged with the government-owned Great Canadian Railway. When he traveled, he stayed at luxurious resorts, bought the finest tailored suits, and returned home with expensive presents for his young family. He ran liquor to Minnesota, Michigan, Wyoming, Colorado, North and South Dakota — to small towns, cities, and to "boom towns" like Casper, Wyoming, where oil and liquor both flowed freely. Sankey's marketing strategy was to sell high-quality Canadian liquor at below-market prices. He transported his product in a rickety automobile, portraying himself as a railroad man traveling to his farm in the States for respite. Sankey often took his daughter, Echo, on these trips. He loved her company and found her an unmatchable decoy at border crossings. On a single trip, Sankey hauled twenty-four cases of liquor placed in a concealed compartment underneath his rear car seat, and sold them for an average of $125 per case.

Alas, Sankey's huge rum-running profits were eroded by occasionally devastating gambling losses. While cards and dice were his preferred forms of chance, he bet on anything. One-time Sankey poker partner, Raymond Bailey, Sr., recalled a time the local dray man pulled up outside Ernie Thomas's Melville barbershop for a haircut. The shop had a pool room in the back, where Verne Sankey and a friend engaged in a friendly game. The two began discussing the dray horses outside, one a bay and the other black. A debate arose over which horse would defecate first. Soon each man dropped one hundred dollars in one of the pool table's pockets, and watched through the pool room's window to see who the winner would be.

In 1924, Sankey's commodities market losses nearly broke him. Two years later, he made a huge windfall from liquor sales in Casper, then embroiled himself in a no-limits poker game at a resort on the town's outskirts. The game dragged on for five days. When it was over, Sankey had lost virtually all his profits. He seldom held his cash tightly. Sankey once found himself in the café of a North Dakota town with a car full of booze when he noticed two men he suspected were Prohibition agents watching his movements from across the street. Sankey calmly ate his lunch, then quietly slipped out the back door to the train depot and boarded a train to Minneapolis, abandoning his contraband-laden car parked in front of the café.

Sankey was an avid sportsman. He bowled competitively and loved to watch the Melville Millionaires play hockey, befriending and assisting members of the team. "The beggar had a lot of good points," remembered old friend Bailey, referring to Sankey's hallmark kindness. "Sankey heard about Clint Head's young teenage daughter who was dying [after being struck by a hockey puck] and so went to her home. He insisted her parents take her to a Regina hospital to save her life and tossed $800 in rolled up bills on the dresser. But the parents refused, knowing the money was tainted. The girl died."

Sankey's gambling reputation and his penchant for flashing money — he frequently dropped five-dollar and ten-dollar tips — drew ire from more than a few in the bustling new town. "Women in Melville used to hate the sight of Mrs. Sankey because Sankey took all their husbands' money for gambling or liquor," recalled Sankey contemporary, Wilmarie Spearey.

By the fall of 1930, Sankey had developed a particularly lucrative trade in Denver as a gentleman rumrunner, catering to the exclusive banker and broker trade. That took him to Denver's Seventeenth Street where the city's most powerful men kept offices. By this time, Sankey's work absences had increased; he claimed Fern did not tolerate Canada's cold winters well. The family moved to Regina for a time, and from there Sankey continued his rum running venture. "He operated two big Nash cars equipped with truck springs to carry a heavy load without a noticeable sagging," Regina resident Clark Zimmerman remembered. "With these cars he ran big loads of liquor to Denver during the summer months. During the winter months he operated over the Mexican border."

Sankey's Denver business was robust. He would call at his customers' offices and take orders but never left a phone number. He sold nothing but high-end booze such as Baccardi, with prices ten dollars to twenty dollars a case lower than his competitors. Sankey was a born salesman; how many other bootleggers sent Christmas cards to customers? One Seventeenth Street customer recalled Sankey's delivery of an order to the fashionable Denver home where the customer's wife was hosting a bridge party. Sankey carried his shiny leather suitcase to the front door, was shown in, unloaded the liquor in the kitchen, and bowed himself out with apologies for having interrupted the gathering.

For all Sankey's bootlegging, his record was remarkably spotless, blemished only by a solitary bootlegging conviction in Fergus Falls, Minnesota, where he posted bond and never returned.

As the thirties dawned, however, Sankey's bootlegging business faltered. Syndicates controlled more and more of the trade and ran him out of some cities, finding his considerable competition unwelcome. As the Depression wore on, moreover, people had less money to spend for the contraband. Sankey, like other bootleggers, began to seek easy money elsewhere.

From around 1929 to 1931, Sankey also spent large amounts of time in Winnipeg, where he set off a craze in the area by introducing Manitoba to miniature golf through a business he operated known as The Mall. Sankey frequented a local hotel there, where he established himself as a generous and good-natured wheeler-dealer and kept a sweetheart on the side — Beth Earhardt, who waitressed at the Silver Slipper Cafe. An old Sankey friend who tended bar in Winnipeg commented, "You get to know a man pretty well when you're tending bar." He knew Verne Sankey as a jovial, straight shooter, a "square guy." He ran a card game in town, frequently paying his bills with the coins he raked in — his vigorish, the 10 percent the house kept from each bet.

In February 1931, the same day Sankey delivered a train to Regina bearing the Melville Millionaires for a hockey game, the Royal Bank on Albert Street in Regina was robbed. Two masked men thrust guns into the chests of the bank's manager and a teller and heisted thirteen thousand dollars of government payroll. Stories abound about the return trip. One version posits that Sankey threw his trainman's club bag in with the team's equipment. "Here," Sankey supposedly told the athletes. "Take this home for me and I'll pick it up later." As the story went, the hockey players knew of the bag's contents, but out of fondness for Sankey, remained mum.

Within a month of the Regina robbery, the railroad granted Verne Sankey a leave of absence, and he never returned. The Sankeys left Canada shortly and returned to the state of their youth — South Dakota — landing in Kimball, a south-central town of about nine hundred on the Chicago, Milwaukee, St. Paul and Pacific Railroad. There they rented a house close to the school Echo attended while Fern cared for the couple's young son, Orville, born in February 1929. Within a few months, Sankey bought 320 undeveloped acres of farm-ranch land twenty miles northwest of Kimball. He paid fourteen dollars per acre for the farm along Crow Creek, which drains into the Missouri River ten miles to the west. Sankey paid $2,000 cash, and he and Fern signed a mortgage for the balance of $2,480 at 6 percent interest, placing title to the ranch in Fern's name.

The Sankey farm was remote, almost eleven miles southwest of the nearest town, the tiny hamlet of Gann Valley. The last mile to the ranch was a grassy path over knolls and across a meadow. Crow Creek sliced across the farm's northern end, its tree-lined ravine ideal for carrying out activities below the radar of local attention. Sankey built a three-room house on the land, complete with an elaborate basement. He situated the house near the middle of the half-section, a little to the north of a knoll. The land beyond the house sloped to the ravine. This meant that, even after traversing the mile of grassy path, one had to negotiate a final half-mile of short-grass prairie to get to the simple white clapboard, single-story structure. That it was built at all in the pit of the depression was a marvel to neighbors. Sankey raised grain and corn on the land, and grazed 75 head of purebred beef cattle along with some 150 turkey hens and 30 gobblers.

If Sankey's neighbors wondered how he could buy and build in such times, their curiosity did not distance them from him. Like people in his hometown of Wilmot and in Melville, too, citizens of the Gann Valley and Kimball communities found Verne Sankey to be an affable fellow. When he came to Kimball, he loved to juggle and perform tricks to entertain the kids gathered around. He bowled competitively. He drank constantly though seldom appeared inebriated. He found plenty of company in the community and easily fit into the fabric of life in the Gann Valley and Kimball communities. At the farm, Sankey shared labor and chores with his neighbors, the closest of whom were about three miles away by roads.

Though the world would soon know Sankey chiefly as a crook, he was an honest one to the extent that is possible. Woodrow Wentzky, then a nineteen-year-old student at Yankton College, recalled a time when he worked at a Gann Valley grocery store. Sankey ordered a large supply of food and left after paying the bill. He returned half an hour later and handed Wentzky forty-seven cents, telling him he'd been given too much change.

"Honesty is the best policy, buddy," Wentzky recalled Sankey telling him. "Always remember that."

Sankey continued to flash his money, paying for a haircut and a shave at the barber shop out of a roll of large bills. He suggested to local friends that his cash came from his gambling. "I sure am a lucky devil," he would grin. Sankey's 1932 Model 18 sedan—Ford's first V-8— attracted more than a little attention in the community, purchased as it was amid depression and drought.

While Sankey's affability and wholesome rural demeanor held him in good stead with most of his South Dakota neighbors, his frequent displays of cash and long absences from home had begun to raise eyebrows. Neighbors noticed other oddities. The occasional plane would land at the ranch. Some grew even more suspicious after an incident in November 1932 in which Sankey fired a gun at four men who, he claimed, were attempting to steal turkeys from his ranch. He winged one intruder. All four were jailed but Sankey refused to press charges against them. Curiously, the four—whom *The Kimball Graphic* characterized as "police characters" from Iowa and Nebraska—escaped less than a week after their capture. The local publication observed that their departure coincided with the arrival in Gann Valley of a woman named Kohler, who was suspected to have assisted their escape.

The presence of the Iowa and Nebraska men at the Sankey farm coincided with another incident. On October 4, 1932, the Bank of Vayland, a town north of Gann Valley, was robbed of nine hundred dollars. Witnesses said two well-dressed young men entered the bank, while a third stood guard outside. The men sped away south. Immediately after the Vayland robbery, State Sheriff Bruce Barnes was contacted and picked up the outlaws' trail south of Vayland, as they entered the Crow Creek Indian Reservation. The sheriff called ahead to block all roads leaving the reservation, but this tactic proved fruitless. Within about ten miles of the Sankey farm, the trail was lost. The next day a bank in Winner, southwest of Gann Valley, was also robbed.

Even if some had their suspicions about Sankey — and as time passed, more and more did — he was mostly among friends in Kimball and Gann Valley and on his neighbors' farms and ranches. If Sankey made extra money bootlegging, it was not, for many, a morality issue; he was simply doing on a larger scale what many of their other neighbors and their relatives had been doing on a smaller scale for years.

For all of Sankey's affability, he was not without a healthy measure of shrewdness. His relationships often bore strategic significance. For example, he befriended not only Buffalo County sheriff's deputy Armour Schlegel, but also the county prosecutor, Harold Brown, who served as Sankey's personal lawyer. Sankey counted as good friends a number of leading businessmen and ranchers in the Gann Valley community. The cynical view that these sorts of relationships served Sankey's criminal behavior has much to commend it. The greater weight of the evidence, however, leads to a more complex conclusion.

Sankey undoubtedly made friends with those likely to convincingly vouch for his character when lawmen from other jurisdictions asked about him. Yet aside from that, and the cover that the remote ranch provided, he relished the sorts of connections with people rural life afforded. In small Depression communities such as Gann Valley and Kimball, people depended on each other of necessity.

Although a criminal, Sankey was also a South Dakotan. He had grown up in the rural lifestyle, had known the hard work common to all who shared the hardscrabble existence, and had, to some degree, returned to it. He mingled with townspeople and attended church services; he danced at barn dances, cried at funerals, and celebrated at festive summer gatherings. He was drawn to the rural life, where he could easily impress others and gain the seclusion the ranch could provide him. It was for Verne Sankey the best of all possible worlds.

By early 1932, Sankey had made plans that went beyond bootlegging or even the occasional bank robbery. He began to approach his old railroad buddies to solicit their assistance. One was Sankey's one-time fireman on the railroad, Gordon Alcorn.

Alcorn was born in the tiny Saskatchewan village of Welwyn on December 1, 1905, into a respected family of railroaders. He was the third of eight children. His father, a Grand Trunk Pacific Railway section foreman, moved the family to Melville, Saskatchewan, when the railroad came there shortly after Gordon's birth. Alcorn attended rural schools, completing eighth grade at fourteen, then went to work. At sixteen, he caught on with the Canadian National Railroad as a fireman, a job he held until 1932 when he was laid off, a victim of the Depression. He and a railroad friend named Arthur Youngberg labored briefly for Dominion Construction Company in Cochran, Ontario, but both were laid off that job as well by the fall of 1932.

Having grown up in a family of Melville railroaders, Alcorn had known of Verne Sankey from the time he was a boy. The two men became friends in about 1927 when Alcorn began to "fire" for Sankey on the Canadian National. Spending long hours crossing the prairie on various runs to and from Melville, the shy Alcorn was naturally drawn to the story-telling high roller he had admired as a youth. The easy-going bachelor stood an inch over six feet and weighed a slender 180 pounds. He had earned good wages working for the railroad, averaging about two hundred dollars per month. He neither drank nor smoked. His only brushes with the law had resulted from a freight train incident as a teen, and for abusive language in Melville, for which he was fined two dollars.

Alcorn was a follower — and malleable; it was this latter personality feature that Sankey exploited.

In April 1932, Sankey divided his time between the Buffalo County farm and Minneapolis, trafficking liquor across the Midwest. One day he looked up Alcorn in Winnipeg. In the course of the conversation, Sankey mentioned that he had been thinking of kidnapping someone there. With all the publicity the Lindbergh kidnapping had generated, Sankey was dissuaded from executing an abduction in the States. He had some Winnipeg prospects, however; he had even explored renting a house to hold the victim. When Alcorn declined Sankey's invitation to join him, Sankey returned south of the border.

While he looked for work in Winnipeg, Alcorn got a letter from Sankey, inviting him and Arthur Youngberg to come to South Dakota to tend to Sankey's farm. Alcorn showed Youngberg the letter. The offer appealed to them both, as they considered their bleak employment prospects. Unlike Youngberg, who was a northern Minnesota native living in Canada, Alcorn, as a Canadian, could not work legally in the States. So Sankey came to Winnipeg, picked up the pair, and smuggled Alcorn across the Canadian border into North Dakota a few miles east of Walhalla. The three arrived at the Sankey farm on Armistice Day 1932, and Youngberg and Alcorn assumed their duties as farmhands.

Arthur Youngberg was born in 1898 and grew up on a family farm that straddled the international border near the small towns of Baudette, Minnesota, and Rainy River, Ontario. Like Alcorn, he was the third of eight children, born to hard-working Swedish immigrants. Youngberg's father farmed and worked in a sawmill and died of an accidental gunshot wound when Arthur was thirteen. His mother raised the family alone until she remarried six years later. Arthur's brothers all grew up to be miners or railroaders. None, including Arthur, had ever been in trouble with the law.

Youngberg ended his schooling after the fourth grade — about the time his father died — to help on the farm. At nineteen, he landed a brakeman's job with the Canadian National Railway and held the same job for the next thirteen years, based in Melville, Saskatchewan, where he met Verne Sankey and Gordon Alcorn. In 1931, the railroad laid Arthur Youngberg off, and he struggled just to feed himself. He found the Dominion job, where, along with Alcorn, he helped build an Ontario power plant, but by early 1932, he was again jobless. By the time he came to work on Sankey's South Dakota farm that fall, Youngberg was nearly penniless. He reasoned that Sankey's farm job would feed and shelter him until something better presented itself.

Youngberg, like Alcorn, was single. He had an engagingly direct manner and a homespun nature. He came from Swedish Lutheran stock but attended church only occasionally. He enjoyed close relationships within his family. Though an eligible bachelor, his relationships with women tended decidedly toward liaisons with those who cared little of their reputations. He ran with the "sporting class" — gamblers, drinkers, carousers — drinking moderately; on occasion, excessively. He loved to skate, swim, and run. Youngberg was a *big* Swede. Reliable records place him at around six feet, two inches tall, but his enormous frame made him seem larger. Youngberg's size, combined with his dark complexion and movie star looks, drew attention in a crowd. Testing showed him to be of average intelligence but he was callow and unschooled in the ways of the world. His naiveté made him an easy mark for manipulators, talkers, dominating figures, and con artists, like the one who had invited him to South Dakota.

Even though the Sankeys had just finished building their modest ranch house, they spent part of the spring and summer of 1932 in Minneapolis–St. Paul and vacationed in Canada's Lake Victoria area. With hands to care for the turkeys and cattle through the winter of 1932, Sankey and Fern told friends they wanted to spend the winter months in a milder climate. The night of the 1932 Congregational Church Christmas program, Verne Sankey and Echo performed a saxophone duet. Shortly after the program, the Sankey family left for Denver.

They rented a handsome bungalow at 2922 South Emerson, a few miles east of Denver's Capitol Hill district. They obtained it through a contact of Sankey's Denver friend, Carl Pearce, who would come to play a significant role in Sankey's Denver sojourn. Pearce was a tortured soul, tall and well built, but with droopy eyes. He had suffered shell shock in World War I and still carried its effects fifteen years later. Psychiatrists called his war condition psychoneurosis: His head shook continuously; sometimes his hands shook, too. The symptoms grew more noticeable around groups of people. At times, his voice cracked.

After he graduated from high school in Burlington, Colorado, Pearce attended a business college until he ran out of funds. He served in the army just long enough to suffer his traumatic injury. Honorably discharged, he returned to Burlington where he worked in an abstract office, his salary supplemented by a modest disability pension. In 1921, Pearce married an attractive hospital secretary named Elizabeth Flemina. They moved to Denver in 1923, where Pearce sold insurance. Employers considered him a steady, competent, and reputable worker. He made good money — as much as five thousand dollars a year — but things began to unravel for Pearce as the Depression lingered. Elizabeth witnessed his behavior become increasingly bizarre. Unable to endure, she left him in September 1930. It was an enormous setback for Pearce, accelerating his downward spiral. Early the next year he was hospitalized for two months. Although he had never cared for liquor, he began to drink, often to excess, which only exacerbated the problem.

Pearce tried to sell insurance again after his hospital release but the worse his shaking got the more difficulty he had approaching people and in turn the more nervous he became. Noises and crowds became intolerable. Eventually, his employer let him go. He was fired from three successive jobs. He drank more and more and hung around others who also had too much time on their hands — bootleggers and men and women who operated on the fringes of society. Among them were a rumrunner named William Ellsworth and his wife, Frances. In November 1931, Pearce was rehospitalized for three months for psychoneurosis. In July he was sentenced to ninety days in jail for issuing bad checks a year earlier. He was released in October 1932 in time for Sankey's return to the Denver area a few months later.

Through the Sankeys, Pearce met Fern's sister, Ruth Kohler, and the two fell madly for one another. They were a pair of lost souls, she a widow and he an outcast. Pearce passed his time with Ruth and the

Ellsworths. The women cared for him and cooked him meals, and Ellsworth provided him bootlegged liquor.

When the Sankeys arrived in Denver in December 1932, Verne Sankey paid three months advance rent for the Emerson Street bungalow, signing the name "Sykes" to the rental agreement. Meanwhile, just after New Years' Day 1933, Alcorn and Youngberg got into a rip-roaring fight at the ranch. Youngberg, the taller and heavier of the two and seven years Alcorn's senior, got the better of the bout, which turned vicious, finally ending when Youngberg broke a chair across Alcorn's face. Days after the fight, Sankey returned to the ranch and found Alcorn still hurting, so he offered to get Alcorn medical care in Denver. Alcorn left the ranch with Sankey and stayed with the Sankeys in Denver, leaving Youngberg alone to handle the winter farm chores.

Once back in Denver, Sankey again floated plans for a kidnap to Alcorn. He had scoured every available record, including a book of insurance ratings of the city's wealthiest citizens. From those sources, Sankey developed a list of about thirty prospects, which he pared to four or five serious candidates. Among them were beer magnate Adolph Coors; Charlie Boettcher, the son and grandson of Denver empire builders; and Charlie's young daughter, Ann. For weeks, Sankey — often with Alcorn in tow — drove throughout the city, casing the homes of kidnap prospects, observing, planning.

In the end, Sankey rejected the idea of kidnapping a child and instead settled on Charlie Boettcher as the most promising prospect. Sankey decided it would take at least three men to do the job: a driver — him; a guard in the car; and one or more at the ranch. He asked Pearce to type the ransom notes in the basement of the Emerson Street house. Sankey wanted to demand $100,000 for Charlie Boettcher's ransom; Alcorn thought $25,000 was plenty. They settled on $60,000.

2

Rogues' Gallery
Denver, February 12, 1933

The timing of the kidnapping was serendipitous. Driving around the snow-dusted city on a Sunday evening in February — Lincoln's birthday — Sankey and Alcorn noticed Charlie and Anna Lou Boettcher pass them in their car. The two men quickly turned around and followed the Boettchers to the elegant Brown Palace Hotel, which the Boettcher family owned. They watched the couple park their car and enter the hotel.

Sankey and Alcorn then drove back to the Sankeys' Emerson Street home. While Alcorn waited in the living room, Sankey grabbed two revolvers, one of which he handed to his confederate. "Leave the safety on so you don't shoot anyone," Sankey told Alcorn. Then he turned to Fern. "We're going to try to kidnap Charlie Boettcher tonight. If they shoot me, don't identify my body."

Sankey directed Fern to listen to his short-wave radio for news that the kidnapping had been successfully staged and for signs the Boettcher family had notified police. If there was any trouble at all, Fern was to dispose of the typewriter and anything else that might be evidence. Verne kissed her and left the home.

Thirty-two-year-old Charles Boettcher II — Charlie — was the product of one of Colorado's richest and most prominent families. His grandfather and namesake, Charles Boettcher, made his fortune selling hard-

19

ware to Leadville miners during the 1870s silver boom. After moving to Denver, the patriarch led development of the state's sugar beet and cement industries. Charlie's father, Claude, expanded the family's businesses, their profits, and their reach.

It has been observed that a family dynasty often declines in the third generation. The phenomenon manifested itself in the Boettcher family. An almost insoluble bond existed between Charlie Boettcher's hard-driving father and his octogenarian grandfather, the patriarch Charles. It became evident to Charlie early in life that he would never measure up to their standard. A family friend observed, "Young Charlie was a very bright boy. But he was not a very demanding fellow. He realized he couldn't invade the world created by his father and grandfather and he went his own way."

Charlie was Yale educated, Class of Twenty-four. After graduation, he returned to Denver where, together with a friend, he formed a financial company known as Boettcher and Newton. After just a few years, the overbearing Claude decided he did not enjoy competition from within his own family and bought a controlling interest in the operation. Allowing this to happen was an act of subservience toward his father that Charlie would often repeat. But then, few stood up to Claude Boettcher, so his only son's submissiveness hardly set him apart from others. Despite his father's overbearing presence, by name alone Charlie Boettcher commanded unmistakable respect in and around Denver.

As the quintessential caricature of the period's businessman, Charlie Boettcher could have strolled grandly out of a Sinclair Lewis novel: he kept his well-oiled hair slicked back, and his arching eyebrows perched above almond-shaped eyes that turned slightly inward. Thin lips underlined his prominent nose. Photographs of him suggest a somewhat jaded persona but Charlie Boettcher was a character. He loved to party and reveled in playing the jovial jokester, often armed with a sharp quip or comment. While work propelled his father and grandfather, Charlie generally spurned it. He was not without his passions, however; baseball was among them. He frequented the home games of Denver's Class A Bears and closely followed major league baseball.

In 1926, Charlie married a young blonde Montana beauty named

Anna Lou Piggott in an elaborate Helena wedding. Anna Lou was the graceful daughter of respected social climbers. She was first groomed at Miss Spencer's renowned finishing school in New York City then matriculated at Vassar College, eventually graduating from Montana State as a popular member of the Kappa Kappa Gamma sorority.

Anna Lou differed from Charlie in that small talk and high society did not enthrall her. She could mix with people and she involved herself in community activities, but she did not relish social gatherings, preferring the comfort of her own home and close friends. There was about her an almost ethereal radiance. Gleb Ilyin, the world-renowned portrait artist, observed that she had been perhaps the most beautiful subject he had ever painted. Her facial features, framed by her honey-colored hair and highlighted by deep blue eyes, evoked an aura of warmth and caring. Anna Lou was not just beautiful, she was bright and energetic, though a discernable vulnerability hovered beneath the surface.

After the couple's marriage, Anna Lou did her best to immerse herself in the role expected of her as a leader in Denver's civic and social circles and in fashionable St. John's Episcopal Church. She was elected to the Junior League and hosted social gatherings, but her greatest interest lay in national affairs and social causes such as the anti-Prohibition movement. She chaired the Denver branch of the Womens' Organization for National Prohibition Reform.

In 1931, the seemingly charmed couple moved into an elegant two-and-a-half story Normandy chateau, which Claude built especially for them as a wedding gift. Designed by a German architect, the mansion at 777 Washington Street in Denver's exclusive Capitol Hill district was constructed of the finest handcrafted wood and stone. Charlie christened it *Les Trois Tours* for its three towers, or turrets. The chateau contained twenty-one rooms, massive carved beams, vaulted ceilings, and crystal chandeliers that illuminated lead glass windows during long evening hours. The mansion's walls were of brick and stucco, eighteen inches thick; an equally thick concrete slab topped the basement ceiling and supported the main floor. Claude expected the home to help the young couple establish their place in society.

For a time, Charlie and Anna Lou tried to do just that. The Washington Street mansion quickly became known for its gala atmosphere. Charlie's friend and fellow flight enthusiast, Charles Lindbergh, who had captured the nation's attention with his solo flight from New York to Paris in 1927, was a prominent house guest at *Les Trois Tours*, reputedly having stayed there on a Denver visit following his transatlantic flight.

As 1933 dawned, the Boettchers were weathering America's financial calamity, but Charlie Boettcher drank too heavily and he caroused, sometimes gambling away family money. Yet, by all appearances, the young Boettchers and their five-year-old daughter, Ann — a second child was due in early March — were archetypal Americans blessed by wealth, beauty, youth, and happiness. Their well-connected lives were facilitated by chauffeurs and maids. Their weeks were peppered with frequent travel and black-tie dinner parties. Their relationships were populated by the wealthy and socially prominent. Awash as they were in the finest of material goods, Charles and Anna Boettcher lived lives far different than those of most Depression-weary Americans.

And then suddenly, two men emerged from the shadows, snatched Charlie Boettcher at the garage of *Les Trois Tours*, and sped away into the Colorado darkness.

The *Denver Post*'s February 13 "night extra" trumpeted the news in enormous bold print:

CHARLES BOETTCHER II HELD
FOR RANSOM OF $60,000.

Charles Boettcher II, 31, prominent broker and a scion of one of the west's wealthiest families, was kidnapped from his fashionable home, 777 Washington Street, late Sunday night by dapper desperadoes who are holding him for $60,000 ransom.

Young Boettcher and his beautiful wife, Anna Lou Boettcher, an expectant mother, had just driven into the driveway of their home when the abductors suddenly appeared, forced Boettcher into their machine and whisked away after handing Mrs. Boettcher a note demanding the ransom."

As Charlie got out of his car, Verne Sankey's voice pierced the darkness: "Come here, Charlie, and stick up your hands."

Anna Lou nudged him. "This is a holdup," she said. "Don't resist." Charlie complied.

"Do what you're told and everything will be all right," Sankey told him. The lights of a passing car shone onto the Boettcher driveway. "Put your hands down until that car gets by," Sankey ordered. After the car passed, Sankey handed Anna Lou, still in the car, an envelope, with a polite bow. "Mrs. Boettcher," he said, "open that envelope please." When she did, a smaller envelope fell to the floor. "Now open that one," Sankey calmly directed as she retrieved the inner envelope. Enclosed was the ransom note. As she opened the envelope, Sankey bade her goodnight and disappeared with her husband. Anna Lou sat stunned and motionless. When she regained her composure, she read the straightforward note that, like all of Sankey's correspondence, was riddled with grammatical errors:

> Do not notify the police. If you do, and they start making it hot for us, you will never see ——— alive again. We are holding ——— for Sixty Thousand Dollars. We are asking you to get this money in Ten and Twenty dollar bills and they must be old bills only. When you get this money ready and are willing to pay as above for the safe return of ———, then insert the following add in the Denver Post, personal items. . . .
>
> (Please write, I am ready to return) SIGN (Mabel). . . . .
>
> We will not stand for any stalling thru advise that police may give you. You are smart enough to know what the results will be if you try that. You know what happened to little Charles Lindbergh through his father calling the police. He would be alive today if his father had followed instructions given him. You are to choose one of these to courses, Either insert add and be prepared to pay ransome, Or forget it all.

With its blanks, the note was written like a generic-form ransom note, containing no names save "Mabel." Anna Lou immediately called Charlie's father. Despite the kidnappers' admonition that the family not notify the police, Claude immediately did so.

The first police cruiser arrived at the Boettcher home within three minutes of Charlie's abduction. Within five minutes, the dispatcher blared: "Attention, all cars! Pick up — any car — small, black sedan. Three men in it. License unknown. Last seen going east on Seventh Avenue. Two of these men are armed, desperate. Use caution. This is a kidnapping case!" Denver police chief Albert T. Clark and Manager of Safety Carl Milliken with a cadre of detectives raced to the Boettcher home.

Police pressed Anna Lou for clues, but few were available. The kidnappers had not touched the Boettcher car. Sankey had taken away the envelope he had touched. Both kidnappers wore handkerchief masks but Anna Lou could describe one of them — Caucasian, around forty-two, about five feet, seven inches tall, a stout build, and a sandy tweed overcoat and a cap. Anna Lou recalled the man's sandy complexion and smoothly shaven face but had been particularly struck by his eyes: they were peculiar, almost round.

Despite little to go on, Denver Police chief Albert T. Clark announced the next day that he had positively concluded that Charlie Boettcher's abduction was the work of professionals, a couple of racketeers who had recently been seen in Denver. Clark assured Denver citizens that Charlie Boettcher would be safely home and the kidnappers in custody within forty-eight hours. "By checking on the associates of these two we hope to be able to determine who the others in the plot were," explained the chief. It was the first of many such authoritative but unfounded pronouncements.

Among the authorities' early suspects were several rogues recently seen in the city, including Chicago gangster Louis "Diamond Jack" Alterie and Capone-crony Mike "Bon Bon" Allegretti. Alterie had already cemented his name into gangland lore by allegedly shooting a horse that had thrown and killed fellow gangster, Samuel Morton, an event immortalized on the silver screen in 1931's *Public Enemy* starring James Cagney. But on January 31, Alterie, on orders to leave the state, had checked out of a Denver hotel and disappeared.

Al Capone was serving time in a federal prison for income tax evasion but his empire was alive and well, thanks in part to Allegretti. The Capone cousin had recently shot and killed two of his enemies in a gunfight, one in the presence of a U.S. marshal, but a jury had absolved him. Both were prime police suspects — but when authorities pursued the leads, each fizzled.

As Charlie's father, Claude, deliberated whether to place the ad Charlie's abductors had demanded, police combed apartment buildings and rooming houses throughout the city, particularly those lodgings that the police and press referred to as "known police characters." The search was so exhaustive that virtually all the city's speakeasies simply shut down during the investigation. Bootleggers complained, "Too much interference and too many suspicious people."

Of course, bootleggers faced other, larger problems in February 1933. As Prohibition's long day waned, so did the bootleggers' profitable thirteen-year run. It had helped some to survive and made others rich: Capone reportedly made $60 million off the illegal sale of alcohol in a single year. Many also made their own hooch for private consumption. California grape growers, no longer permitted to produce wine, sold a grape juice known as Vine-Glo. The product's literature provided detailed instructions of what not to do, because if one did those things, the juice would turn to wine in sixty days. Predictably, sales grew exponentially. By 1932, with polls showing that nearly three-quarters of Americans supported repeal, Prohibition's twilight neared. As a result, bootleggers sought to replace revenue with bank robbery or kidnapping. Charlie Boettcher had just become the first of 1933's highly publicized kidnap-for-ransom victims.

The *Denver Post*, calling kidnapping the most damnable of crimes, proposed commissioning vigilante forces to nab the kidnappers and string them to the nearest tree, much as they had brought horse thieves to justice in the West a generation earlier. Governor Edwin Johnson, speaking from his Capitol office a few blocks from *Le Trois Tours* condemned kidnapping as "the most reprehensible of crimes." He warned that if not sternly addressed, such crimes could result in the "complete collapse of law enforcement."

Colorado's little-used kidnapping law then carried a maximum punishment of seven years in prison, the lightest of any state. The Colorado legislature rushed a bill to the governor that would make kidnapping a capital crime punishable by life in prison—or if the victim was killed, by death. Other states and the District of Columbia quickly enacted similar laws. The outrage was not universal, however.

Throughout much of the twenties and early thirties, the public's attitude toward its colorful criminals was schizophrenic. The wealthy and politically conservative reviled the gangsters and their deeds but day laborers and poor farmers held more ambivalent views. After all, what was it to them if some fat cat was lightened of a little excessive wealth? Because the robbers primarily targeted banks—and kidnappers, the wealthy—the multitudes expressed noticeably little outrage. Many throughout the Depression saw their meager—and for some, not so meager—life savings vanish from the repositories once considered secure. Others lost their land and homes to foreclosure. To such bruised Americans, those who stole from bankers were not necessarily the bad guys. This fertile breeding ground produced myths of robbers who helped poor farmers satisfy loans or who, when robbing a bank always destroyed or stole mortgages. These stories built the legend of the midwestern bandit as the common man's antihero.

Still, by the early 1920s, influential citizens became increasingly convinced that bootlegging and disrespect for law generally was out of hand. Their reaction took many forms, the most ghoulish of which was the revival of a dormant agency of terror—the Knights of the Ku Klux Klan.

The Klan's resurgence originated in the Deep South but, because of still-smoldering Reconstruction issues as well as the Klan's favorable depiction in the movie, *Birth of a Nation*, it quickly spread to other parts of the nation. Reaction against bootleggers was particularly fervent in Denver where in 1922, the KKK movement reached the city and swept across the state.

The Denver Klan's mayoral candidate, Ben Stapleton, strolled into office in 1923, eventually appointing ardent Klan member William Candlish, a newspaperman with no law enforcement experience, as the city's chief of police. A year later voters elected Denver Klansman and local judge Clarence Morley the state's governor, and city attorney and

Klan member, Rice Means, won the short-term Senate seat. Incumbent Lawrence Phipps, though not himself a Klansman, won reelection to a full term in the Senate with Klan backing, giving the Klan a complete sweep of the governorship and both U.S. Senate seats.

In the end, the Klan's reappearance produced but a few isolated acts of violence, a rash of cross burnings, and precious little legislation. Klan leaders quickly overplayed their hand and embroiled themselves in a series of scandals. In 1928, Denver voters eliminated Klan members from the city council. Stapleton survived but his power was diminished. By the time of Charlie Boettcher's kidnapping, the Klan had ceased to exist as a political force, though the attitudes and biases that fostered its rise remained. They simply returned to the crags and clefts of the secret societies, country clubs, and other power cliques.

So Denver was far from a united community that held its collective breath as the Boettcher family awaited a reply from the kidnappers.

Denver police established a continuous guard around the homes of both father and son. Multitudes of vehicles coming and going from Charlie's Washington Street mansion and Claude's palatial home a few blocks away carried the occasional courier but more often brought newspapermen, photographers, representatives of the national press, and even movie newsreel cameramen. Each maintained a vigil, seeking a new angle to cover or photo to shoot. Claude's home, with its iron-grilled fence and massive gate appeared to reporters a guarded fortress, armed as it was with machine-gun toting police. The press soon dubbed it "Camp Claude" and Charlie's *Les Trois Tours*, "Camp Charles."

Three days after the abduction, police summoned Anna Lou Boettcher to Denver's City Jail for a lineup that included Kansas City mobster Red Mitchell. Denver citizens pressed against one another along the sidewalk in front of the jail and watched as Anna Lou stepped from her chauffeured sedan, wrapped in a luxurious mink coat, collar turned up to ward off the February chill, and a dark hat stylishly tilted to the right. As Anna Lou, accompanied by Claude and his second wife, the elegant society maven Edna Boettcher, strode past the jail's bull pen and into its viewing room, a *Denver Post* reporter captured the scene.

For many years the women of the Boettcher family have made triumphal entrances at theaters. Box number one has usually been set apart for Mrs. Claude K. Boettcher or Mrs. Charles Boettcher II and their guests. . . .

Never before had either of the society leaders touched even the rim of the life that oozes in and out at city jail. As they crossed the wagon way, filled with official cars, the younger Mrs. Boettcher drew her collar close about her, as tho to shut the strange sights from her eyes. Mrs. Claude K. Boettcher lifted her chin as tho to defy anything to touch her. Behind, walking like a grim, determined image of vengeance, came Claude K. Boettcher.

In three sentences the reporter had captured the moment and hinted at what lay deep in the hearts and minds of each of the three.

Police led the Boettchers into the shadow room where Anna Lou viewed the suspects. She could say only that Mitchell resembled one of the abductors. Chief Clark again expressed confidence that he had the right man but Mitchell was soon quietly released.

As they scoured the city for evidence, police revisited an earlier extortion attempt against Charlie Boettcher. Family and friends recalled the strange events that had transpired on a business trip to Chicago, in which Charlie had visited a cabaret club and was accosted at gunpoint, only later to be graced by the delivery of a case of champagne — bootlegged, of course — delivered at the offender's order to his hotel room. Charlie Boettcher had just returned from a Kansas City trip, where he had been seen in the company of other women, and rumors flowed that his abduction might somehow be related to his activities there. Other reports leaked information that Charlie had unsatisfied gambling debts.

And then on Valentine's Day, forty-eight hours after Charlie Boettcher's kidnapping, J. Edgar Hoover, the Federal Bureau of Investigation's youthful director, thrust his agency into the case.

In February 1933, the bureau was still a fledgling, rather insignificant entity within the Justice Department. From its beginning twenty-five years earlier, the bureau's authority had been largely limited to the investigation of crime on Indian reservations and white slavery cases. In the years following Russia's Bolshevik Revolution, bureau agents arrested thousands suspected of fomenting communist revolution in America in what came to be known as "the Red Scare," though few were ever prosecuted or deported.

The bureau's political espionage did not cease once the Red Scare subsided. The agency continued to collect information on people whose ideas or speech seemed revolutionary; in some instances, people became suspect merely because they espoused positions adverse to the government. Amid the Harding administration's early 1920s Teapot Dome scandal, the Justice Department became heavily embroiled in the investigation of political enemies of the administration. When President Coolidge appointed future Supreme Court chief justice Harlan Stone attorney general, Stone was appalled to find graft and agents with criminal records at times employing brutal and illegal procedures. Stone fired bureau director William J. Burns and appointed Hoover, Burns's youthful assistant, to replace him on an interim basis.

Hoover had come to the bureau in 1917, fresh from law school and led the Attorney General's task force assigned to address the Red Scare problem. Stone imposed on Hoover and the bureau a series of strict but basic ground rules that redirected bureau activities, improved enforcement, and strengthened morale. Hoover reduced graft and incompetence and dramatically increased conviction rates by standardizing the training and qualification of agents. He required all agent applicants to possess either a law or accounting degree and implemented uniform procedures in the bureau's many field offices.

Yet, despite Hoover's successes, his enemies from the Red Scare and Teapot Dome days had not forgotten him. The most formidable among them was Montana senator Tom Walsh. Walsh had learned that Hoover had investigated him during the twenties when Walsh had challenged the scandal-ridden Harding administration. When in late February 1933 president-elect Roosevelt named Walsh as his attorney general designate, Hoover's bureau career hung on the most tenuous of threads. On February 28, Senator Walsh announced plans to conduct a massive overhaul at Justice. The implication was clear: Hoover would go. With his bureau career in doubt, Hoover sent two agents from the bureau's Salt Lake City office to aid Denver police in the two-day-old investigation of the Boettcher kidnapping. It was the first time the bureau had entered a kidnapping investigation.

The bureau's entry into the Boettcher case was neither the boon it may now appear, nor even authorized by law. The Lindbergh Law — enacted in March 1932, shortly after Charles and Anne Lindbergh's child was snatched from their New Jersey estate — had marked another expansion of the bureau's investigative powers. It granted the federal government jurisdiction in kidnapping cases — after a seven-day waiting period — where there was evidence the victim had been transported across state lines. The waiting period had not expired, and no evidence of interstate transportation existed at the time of Hoover's order. Nor was the bureau the crime-fighting force it would soon become. By 1932, its numbers had been pared to about three hundred agents nationwide, perhaps sixty of whom were accountants. Bureau agents had no authority to carry firearms or even to make arrests. More than a few suspects escaped while an agent searched in vain for a telephone to summon local authorities for assistance. The bureau's crime lab was still in its infancy.

For these reasons, the bureau's entry into the case was hardly crucial to the investigation at that point but Hoover, already attuned to the benefits of free publicity, was more than happy to cultivate the bureau's image and aid his own sinking prospects by sending his men into Colorado. The bureau's initial investigation failed to produce a single solid lead. After five days — with no real suspect and no verifiable response to Claude's ad from the abductors — the tension at Camps Claude and Charles was palpable.

3

"Bumped Off"?

The kidnapping case mesmerized Denver. Citizens could not resist a trip past Charlie's home. Streets of the Capitol Hill neighborhoods became so laden with drivers focused on viewing the Boettcher homes that more than a few accidents resulted. Calls came to the Boettcher home, purportedly from the kidnappers, stating they had reduced their demands and suggesting payment arrangements.

The family was inundated with hundreds of letters and telegrams, many from Boettcher friends and business associates around the country, but mostly from people they did not know. Some were encouraging, some spiritual in tone, others threatening, still others contained pleas for money. Some were downright weird. Several offered theories about the abduction. Together, they displayed a cross section of Depression America.

A woman who had supplied the family with eggs and chickens years earlier, wrote: "This depression has robbed me of my home and I might say every earthly possession." She said Charlie might remember her as the "egg woman." One helpful sort suggested the name of an astrologer, who, for a dollar, would answer any three questions the Boettchers might wish to pose.

A woman wrote, "I know how I would feel if one of mine was to be kidnapped, but we are real poor people and in no danger don't think."

Letters arrived airmail from England and Germany. Often they contained newspaper clippings of the story. R. M. Tierce, of Millsap, Texas, had an invention that, with just a little financial backing from Claude, could become an enormous success. Mr. E. Hermanson, of Leavenworth, Kansas, asked for a job. A Miss Griffin said she had never asked anyone for a penny, but she needed "a change of living for health reasons," and sought aid.

One industrious twenty-one-year-old from Commerce, Texas, enclosed his photograph that bore the gaunt look of poverty. "I am a Half-orphan trying to go further in my education. Will you loan me about $10,000 for at least ten years?"

Sister Gratiana of St. Mary's Hospital in Emporia, Kansas, informed Claude that the Boettcher family was in their daily prayers, then added, "Now Dear Mr. Boettcher please, aren't you going to help us, as we need it so badly, . . . May the 1st is near here and we have to pay $5,000 interest. . . . Our Dear Lord will sure repay you in some other way. The patients have no money but they need care in every way."

Were they beggars, panhandlers, charlatans, chiselers? Some undoubtedly were. Even as the Boettchers experienced deep distress, hoards beseeched them for financial aid. But the letters also represented a nation whose ordinary citizens had become so desperate they grasped for any potential help.

Dozens of other letters arrived from purported kidnappers but none could be authenticated, presenting Claude with an entirely separate quandary: Which, if any, of the multitude of communications from the purported abductors was genuine? Police convinced themselves that Charlie's abductors must have known him, since they had not searched his person for a gun before they shoved him into their car. Based on this thread of deductive reasoning, the investigation focused more intensely on Denver's mob-affiliated culprits. By week's end at least seven suspects had been jailed. Time would demonstrate none of them were involved in the crime.

Meanwhile, Charlie Boettcher sat blindfolded in the basement of the Sankey ranch house. He had experienced a rough few days. The night Sankey and Alcorn abducted him, Charlie was compliant. The problem was, as he began to walk toward the car, apparently drunk, he reeled as if he were about to fall. Alcorn caught him and placed him into the back seat and they were off, down Eighth Avenue and out of town. Alcorn taped his eyes closed and tied his wrists with ropes, telling him if he behaved they would get along fine.

When Sankey stopped for gas, Alcorn set a pair of glasses over Boettcher's blindfold and got out of the car with Boettcher some distance away. The two men remained prone alongside the road until Sankey again picked them up. Sankey drove the back roads the 570 miles to the farm, arriving there early the next evening. When Sankey and Alcorn appeared with a blindfolded man in dark glasses, they caught Arthur Youngberg entirely by surprise.

Until then, his farm job had demanded little of him apart from tending to Sankey's livestock and turkeys. Most of the time, Youngberg had laid around reading Sankey's true crime magazines. "Take care of this new boarder," Sankey told him, as they appeared at the door with Charles Boettcher. Youngberg's initial response to Sankey was that he and Alcorn should take Boettcher back where they got him. According to the *Denver Post*, Sankey and Youngberg had the following exchange:

> "You big lummox, do as you're told!" Sankey commanded. "Take this fellow downstairs and put him in the little room. When you've done that, fire the kitchen stove and get things a little warmer. I'll make it right with you."
>
> Youngberg protested. "They'll have us all in jail."
>
> "Don't worry," Sankey reassured him. "This is as safe as sitting in an armchair."

Youngberg thawed when Sankey promised him a "nice fat share of the proceeds."

The pair whiled away the time. Youngberg prepared Charlie daily breakfasts of toast and coffee, lunches of sandwiches, soup and coffee. He gave Charlie cigarettes and shaved him. Occasionally — careful to stand behind him — Youngberg removed Charlie's blindfold to allow him to read magazines and write the letters to his family, which Sankey took to Denver. During those times, Charlie was told that if he turned around, they would "bump him off." Boettcher and Youngberg chatted about Anna Lou and Boettcher's folks and made other small talk. And so they spent the slowly passing hours as the city of Denver and the nation buzzed with the question, "What happened to Charlie Boettcher?"

Over the last two weeks of February, Sankey shuttled between the ranch and Denver three times. At the farm the men discussed their possible capture. Sankey "swore he would die by his own hand" before giving police the pleasure of arresting him. He suggested the others do the same. "Don't give those bulls the pleasure of capturing you. Why don't you just bump yourself off?" The others each assented.

On Wednesday, February 15, Claude, having heard nothing from his son's captors, placed the ad in the *Denver Post* as the kidnappers had directed. He and Anna Lou awaited the abductors' reply. Actually, the kidnappers had already written before they saw the ad on the sixteenth, sending a letter addressed to the Rev. B. D. Dagwell, the young pastor of St. John's Episcopal Church, where the Boettchers were members. Dagwell received it the day the ad appeared. Inside the envelope were two other letters, each separately sealed; one to Claude, the other to Anna Lou, both from Charlie. Sankey wrote Dagwell that Charles had asked him to write to the reverend "as he believes you will do as we ask you. Thru the laws of our church, I belive I can trust you to secrecy. Be sure no dicks see you hand these letters over, as that will stop the whole deal, and endanger the life of Charles."

The letter to Claude scolded. "So far you have not done as I requested. . . . If you are ready to keep this a secret and pay the 60,000 Dollars in small bills as I wrote you first, then insert this ad in the Post. . . . Charles is very nerves [*sic*] and frightened, He often asks if we will release him if you pay and I keep telling him we will, but he lives in fear of being bumped off."

Claude was willing to deal, but Charlie had to first be returned safely before Claude would pay up.

That same day, Sankey walked into a Denver Ford dealership and, using the name of Roy Carlson, bought a 1932 Ford Model 18 two-door sedan. The car would soon get a hard workout.

The next day things got more complicated when unknown assailants shot Joe Roma to death. Roma, originally from Brooklyn, was a chieftain in Denver's bootlegging industry who fronted as a grocer. The day before his death he had met with Chief Clark and offered his services to help solve the kidnapping. He was gunned down in his home, his body so riddled with bullets, police could not count them all. The *New York Times* colorfully recounted the murder.

> Someone came in. The door was locked so Roma must have let
> them in, . . . Roma, practicing on his mandolin with a stand of music
> before him and one eye on a steaming pot of spaghetti in the near-by
> kitchen, must have returned to his chair to talk.
> There was friendly conversation. Apparently the callers then arose,
> pressed close to Roma and, in the language of his craft, "let him have it."

The authorities' chief suspects were two North Denver gangsters who, police theorized, killed Roma out of fear he would turn them in for kidnapping Boettcher. For extra measure, though, Captain Armstrong ordered police to arrest "every known 'police character' " and bring them to headquarters for questioning.

On February 18, the second ad the kidnappers requested appeared in the *Post*. It stated that a wallet containing sixty dollars had been lost, but no correspondence was exchanged for three days because Sankey had returned to his ranch. The silence was painfully mysterious to the authorities and to the Boettcher family. On February 20, Claude issued an open letter to the kidnappers in the morning *Rocky Mountain News*, accompanied by a story with bold headlines and alongside Claude's photograph. Part of it read:

> I have received many ransom notes, thru the mail and otherwise —
> most of them obviously spurious. Some of the notes received,
> however, I am convinced, by certain inclosures, among other things,
> came from the persons who have my son in custody.
> The contents of these notes I have not divulged to the police or the
> press. The conditions and method of payment of ransom contained in

these notes were such that they cannot under any circumstances be carried out. Furthermore, no assurance was given of the safe return of my son when the ransom was paid. . . .

Obviously the police, the press, myself and family are each actuated by different motives — the police primarily to apprehend the culprits, the press to print all the news, myself and family to accomplish the safe return of my son. I appreciate and am confident of the sincere motives of both the police and the press, but in this situation I feel that I must and will act independently if the opportunity is presented.

Claude K. Boettcher

There was no doubt that Claude Boettcher was in charge of negotiations: Chief Clark publicly supported Claude's pledge to act independent of police, saying regretfully that, due to the Boettchers' standing in the community, Claude's guarantee would be "strictly observed."

Fifty-eight-year-old Claude Boettcher was indeed a man of standing both in Denver — where many considered him the city's First Citizen — and nationally. Born in 1875, he spent his earliest years in Boulder, then moved with his parents to Leadville, where his father ran hardware stores, and later to Denver, in 1890. Although Claude grew up amid wealth and privilege, his parents imbued him with a sense of obligation and an appreciation for hard work, honed in part by the militarily regimented boarding school he attended.

His parents were not content with the education the western universities offered, so they sent Claude to Harvard. After he graduated from its rudimentary engineering program, he returned to Colorado. One after another, he led the exponential growth of the companies his father had established: Ideal Cement; Potash Corporation of America, which grew into the largest potash fertilizer maker in the world; and American Crystal Sugar Company, which became the third largest sugar beet producer in the nation. Claude established an investment banking house in Denver which grew into the largest investment house between Kansas City and the west coast.

In 1900, Claude married De Allan McMurtrie, a marriage that produced one child, Charles II, but failed. In 1920, Claude married Edna

Case McElven. She was beautiful, gracious, and extremely society savvy. Together, she and Claude became Denver's social leaders. Episcopalian and Republican, they immersed themselves in the city's most prominent fraternal, civic, and business organizations, with a guest book that boasted the names of famed actors, political leaders, and power brokers.

Claude made the Fifth Avenue Tailors' list as one of America's ten-best dressed men. He served as a delegate to the 1928 Republican National Convention that nominated Herbert Hoover for president. *Time* magazine called him one of the nation's most influential men — among the sixty-four, it said, who ran America. In time he would develop a personal friendship with President Dwight Eisenhower, a frequent guest at Denver's elegant jewel, the famed Brown Palace Hotel, which Claude bought in 1931.

Work obsessed Claude; it supplied much of the satisfaction and self-esteem he drew from life. He called it "the great pleasure." It also fueled his domineering nature. If Claude was a leader in Denver's business circles, Edna was his societal counterpart. On her return to Denver after several weeks in New York, the *Post* commented that she was likely to "pull the smart set out of their doldrums." The *Post* applauded Edna's personality, graciousness, and what it termed her thorough kindliness, asserting that she could have won the host of friends she claimed in any walk of life she graced. At least that was her public persona. She had no children of her own and little use for them in general, but she loved jewels, the kind found only in New York's finest Fifth Avenue stores.

Claude's open letter to the kidnappers prompted a reply when Sankey returned to the city that day.

I see by the Post where you say it is impossible to comply with instructions. Why then did you answer the two ads . . . ? You answered them thru police advise just to try and trap us. . . . If you do not make this payment on receipt of next instructions from me, We are going to stay with that statement of Friday and make you pay the $100,000. . . . We may be killed at this end collecting the money, but if we are the agrement [*sic*] is that they shall even the score and make there get away leaving no evidence behind. . . . P. S. Charles is suffering as we keep his eyes taped all the time and at times he is in very bad condition, but if you want more evedence he is alive it will take me a few days to go and get it."

Late on the afternoon of the next day, Tuesday, the twenty-first, a worn, seemingly frustrated Claude Boettcher summoned newspapermen to his home. He issued this statement published in a "night extra" of the *Post*:

> Since Sunday I have received many more ransom notes. . . . All of the notes demand substantially the same procedure — call off the police — go alone to some designated remote spot — leave ransom — and return home — with no assurance whatever that my son would be released.
>
> It is very obvious that I am powerless to call off the police and under present conditions it would be absolutely impossible for me to go to any designated point alone without being followed by the police and representatives of the press, even if I was willing to do so. Hence I am powerless to act on the instructions received up to this time. . . .
>
> Claude K. Boettcher

Claude was not ready to simply deliver the ransom; Sankey's letter provided the best argument why he should not do so. He still feared the kidnappers would trick him into delivering the money and then fail to produce his son. Claude's concerns about being duped were not solely the product of his cautious business nature. They arose in part from the unsolved Lindbergh kidnapping eight months earlier, which had seared the nation's consciousness. When the purported kidnappers had given instructions as to payment, the Lindberghs complied but the child was not returned. The boy's lifeless body was discovered months later in a wooded area near his home. To the Boettchers, Lindbergh was not only a national hero — he was Charlie's friend and his loss was personal to them. Claude refused to be victimized in the same fashion.

Meanwhile Chief Clark further strained his credibility by continuing to profess unwarranted optimism that police were close to solving the case. In reality, although leads poured in from across the nation — some preposterous, many plausible — all proved unfounded. The police were lost.

In fairness, like most of the nation's law enforcement, Denver police had little experience investigating kidnap-for-ransom. When kidnappings occurred, they more often involved gangsters kidnapped by other gangsters — rarely reported to police — or child kidnappings, like Lindbergh's. That was about to change. In June 1932, St. Paul businessman Haskell Bohn was abducted, the first ransom kidnapping executed in the wake of the Lindbergh Law's enactment. A few other less noteworthy kidnappings had occurred nationwide in the ensuing months but Charlie Boettcher's would serve as the catalyst for a crime epidemic that was about to sweep the country.

4

Undoubtedly Desperadoes

Whatever else one could say about Claude Boettcher, he loved his only son and worked incessantly for his return. The ordeal, now into its second week, was taking a physical as well as mental toll on him; he shed some twenty pounds over its course. Its effects were even more pronounced on Anna Lou. As the murky negotiations sputtered and stalled, Anna Lou, almost to full term with her second child, struggled to maintain her composure and at times wilted under the strain.

Aggravating matters were the nagging rumors of marital discord. Anna Lou refuted them in an interview appearing in the *New York Journal*. "We have always been happy together," she told reporter Dorothy Battle. "The idea that because my husband has been at some entertainments without me or with a woman friend indicates any lack of harmony in our marriage relations is absurd. After all, you know, I have not felt like going about much lately."

Battle characterized the relationship as a "'modern' marriage, with freedom of companionship for both" spouses. "What Mr. Boettcher does is his business," Anna Lou told her, "and what I do is mine. I do not select his friends for him. . . . He also respects my rights as an adult individual. Our love is unaltered — indeed, strengthened by this terrible thing that has happened."

Whatever the state of her marriage, this expectant mother summoned all her strength to endure until her husband's return. Yet, as time passed, she found it harder to hide her increasing anxiety from those around her.

Anna Lou did her best to stay occupied with daughter, Ann, and crossword and jigsaw picture puzzles, the crazes of the day. On occasion, she wandered downstairs to chat with the patrolmen on duty. She anxiously anticipated each day's newspapers for the latest development, like everyone else following the story. "I've got to see it thru, till Charlie comes back, for the baby's sake," she pledged, between tears. "Then everything will be all right." Part of her problem was sheer physical exhaustion. She sometimes went twenty-four hours at a stretch without sleep, a challenge to anybody, let alone for one about to give birth.

Day after day, new developments in the Boettcher kidnapping saga captured the nation's headlines. The *London Daily Mirror*, unsatisfied with wire service accounts, conducted an extensive interoceanic telephone interview of Anna Lou.

There was plenty for reporters to write about, as police arrested new suspects almost daily. Authorities did not discriminate. Any whiff of evidence pointing to one's potential involvement in the crime might result in arrest and jailing. In all, authorities jailed no fewer than twenty innocent suspects.

Meanwhile, back at the South Dakota ranch, Sankey, still armed with data he had gathered from the thirty Denver prospects, schemed about other human heists, hoping to make half a million dollars before he quit the business. As Alcorn later recalled, "Sankey thought his South Dakota ranch . . . was an ideal place to hold victims and would never be found."

He had trailed wealthy Golden, Colorado, brewer, Adolph Coors, whom he considered a prime candidate and carried on his discussions at times in Charlie Boettcher's presence, floating three other Denver names as targets. Charlie conceded one of the men would be an easy prey but told Sankey the other two were then in New York. Sankey brushed off the remark with defiant bravado. "Miles make no difference to us," he told his victim. "When we want someone we get them, and when we get someone we will collect." Charlie Boettcher was impressed.

On Thursday, the twenty-third, with no resolution in sight, Claude issued the kidnappers an ultimatum. He insisted that the kidnappers release his son by midnight February 25. "Upon the return of [my son] unharmed, I will personally guarantee the payment of $60,000 ransom demanded." Claude then addressed reporters, with rage. "If the abductors of my son harm one hair of his head, I will spend five times $60,000 — or 10 times that sum — to track them down and bring them to justice." His frustration and fatigue were evident.

As the police and the Boettcher family and friends waited impatiently for the kidnappers' reply, strange messages surfaced. Claude received twenty notes in a single day, all spurious, some laughably so, but the deadline approached without any word from the kidnappers. Then a letter arrived by hand delivery to Claude in which the abductors promised to release Charlie Sunday if Claude first dropped off the ransom at 7:30 that evening. Claude refused.

> "I am going no place at no time to deliver money on their word to release my son later," he said. "Public opinion may condemn me as a heartless man. . . . But I feel if I paid that money before I got my boy, I would be signing his death warrant. Men who will kidnap will murder. . . . Understand, it is not a question of money. The amount does not mean a thing to me. Surely these men must know that I realize that my life and the life of my son would not be safe if the ransom was not paid as promised. We could not step out on the street without fear of our lives if we did not keep our word."

Anna Lou was crestfallen. Dean Dagwell issued a pledge from the Episcopal bishop that if the kidnappers released Charlie, the money would be paid promptly and secretively.

Then on February 28, after Claude stated that he would not reveal the contents of the notes to the police, officers abruptly ended their sixteen-day vigil at Camp Charlie and Camp Claude, ostensibly leaving Claude at liberty to negotiate more directly and freely with the kidnappers.

The *Denver Post* that day condemned Denver authorities for their failure to solve the case.

Absolutely nothing has been accomplished by the police to restore
[Charles Boettcher II] to his distracted family, apprehend his
kidnappers and avenge their monstrous crime. . . . THEY DON'T
KNOW ANY MORE ABOUT THIS CASE THAN THEY DID
WHEN IT WAS REPORTED TO THEM. . . . . Police activities
seem to have been confined to guarding the homes of the kidnapped
man and his father — Claude Boettcher. Perhaps this was on the theory
that the kidnappers might return and steal the two houses. . . . Are the
police so in awe of great wealth that they are going to allow the Boettcher
family to dictate how the Boettcher kidnapping case shall be handled?

The editorial tapped into deep veins of anger and frustration that
fomented not only in Denver but across America in the early days of
1933. The people's anger was rooted in the sense that there were two
vastly different Americas, one for the rich and powerful and another for
the rest of the nation. Their frustration questioned whether government
lacked not just the power, but the soul to fight the criminal elements that
seemed to hold America's true power. Will Rogers quipped: "The government floated an $800 million loan the other day and Al Capone took
most of it himself. There is the guy that should be Secretary of the
Treasury. Just turn the country over to him and split the profits."

As proposals circulated for a more national approach to the crime issue,
Herbert Hoover's administration balked. Attorney General William
Mitchell expressed the administration's attitude in words to Congress in
1932: "You are never going to correct the crime situation in this country
by having Washington jump in. . . . Unless we can stimulate public
opinion to get the right kind of men in our local governments, and to see
that they do their duty and clean up those conditions, they will not be
cleaned up."

Almost immediately after Chief Clark announced his decision to
withdraw from the case, another ransom note arrived.

If you are agreeable to have the ransom of $60,000 delivered tonight at
8:30 P M at the same place you have had the two letters delivered we
will have Charles home safe at 7:30 P M tonight. There must be no

police interference and every thing must be as you have promised. If you are agreeable to the above have a letter left at the same place at 6:45 this evening advising us of your intentions.

The bandits had given in. Claude had won a major battle: first Charlie Boettcher would be released; only then would the ransom be delivered.

In reality, Sankey and Alcorn had by then concluded that whether or not ransom was paid, they needed to get Charlie Boettcher out of the ranch house basement. Their fears centered around their Buffalo County neighbors, who often came to the door and entered the house without warning. They would likely become suspicious soon. They also called Alcorn and Youngberg by name, which the men feared Charlie could use to later identify them.

On February 27, Pearce returned to Denver from the ranch with Sankey's handwritten note, which he typed after he reached the city. Sankey and Pearce arranged to meet at a designated place north of Denver on highway 81 on March 1 at 7:00 P.M. They worked out a system of signals by which each driver would flash his lights several times on the highway. In the meantime Sankey directed Pearce to mail the final instructions to Claude Boettcher and to retrieve Claude's reply at a designated site. If Claude Boettcher did not provide a positive response, the men decided they would take Charlie to the Emerson Street home and hold him there while negotiations continued.

Sankey and Alcorn left the ranch with Charlie Boettcher at 2:00 A.M. on March 1. They arrived north of Denver at the appointed time. Pearce flashed his headlights and the men pulled off the highway. Pearce handed Alcorn a note and told the men everything appeared in order for Charlie's delivery and collection of the ransom, which could be picked up at 8:30 P.M. if they had released Charlie. Around 7:45 P.M. Sankey and Alcorn released a still blindfolded Charlie Boettcher in East Denver, three miles from his home.

The men waited within a few miles of the location where the ransom was to be paid. Around 8:30, a car appeared with two taillights specially rigged in accordance with Sankey's directions, indicating it was the car with the ransom. At a designated bridge one of the car's occupants tossed a package into the dry creek. On seeing the specially rigged car, Sankey drove to the drop-off site in his Ford, hustled down the ravine, and grabbed the package.

As he and Alcorn drove on toward Denver, Sankey looked at his mate. "Better open it and see if it's real money," he instructed. It was, in ten- and twenty-dollar bills, which Secret Service agents had marked with indelible ink.

When Charlie Boettcher got out of Sankey's car, he stood for awhile, then removed the bandages from his eyes, and scurried to a nearby drugstore. From there he made a call not to his wife but to his father. Soon, two of his father's confidants appeared and whisked Charlie away. Shortly after he left the drugstore, people began to flood it, already having read about his release at that same corner in the *Denver Post*'s special edition.

Crowds also quickly formed outside Camp Charlie. To avoid them, Claude's retinue took the ransomed son across the alley to the home of Sidney Sinsheimer, the president of American Sugar Beet Company and Claude's business partner. There Charlie met with his father, several family confidants, and the *Denver Post*'s Charles O'Brien — the only re- porter admitted to the house and one who had covered the story from its inception. Chief Clark arrived late, after first smashing up his car and obtaining a replacement. A visibly shaken but healthy Charlie described his ordeal to O'Brien.

> Sixteen days and nights of blackness, discomfort and threats! Thank God it's over!
>
> Where I was held and by whom I do not know. . . . I am thankful that they treated me as gentlemanly as possible under the circumstances. They even shaved me when I complained that my beard was growing so long.
>
> Desperadoes? — undoubtedly. But that's all over now unless I dream about it. . . .
>
> I had a cot to sleep on and only one blanket for cover. The room felt damp as a basement would. It was a small room. There was a bed on

which my guard rested and two chairs, a coal oil lamp and a small table. . . .

My captors appeared to be sober men, very intelligent and serious in the business in hand, which was me. . . .

I am certain that the place I was held was isolated. At no time during my imprisonment did I hear the sound of an automobile or a train whistle. . . .

The first I knew that I was going to be released was the night the kidnappers told me we were all going back to Denver. . . . We finally began to get into traffic and I judged we were in town. I could hear cars passing us. Eventually the car stopped and they told me to get out. They said to count 150 before removing the blind and that within a block or two I could find a place to call my father. They said to be sure to call because my folks were worried. A moment later I heard the car pull away. I waited what seemed to me like a reasonable time and tore off the adhesive tape. . . .

You can't guess how good my father's voice sounded to me.

O'Brien was a hustler. He had joined the *Post* in 1916 as a fourteen-year-old copyboy and worked his way up the journalistic ladder despite only eight years of schooling. He was covering the biggest story of his career and later boasted that he had been the only newspaperman allowed to interview Charlie that night, a claim that was inaccurate: the *New York Times* reached Charlie that same night and ran its interview of him on its front page the next day.

After Charlie talked to his father, Chief Clark, and the press, his keepers secretly escorted him from the Sinsheimer home in a car across the alley into his driveway, where at the sound of a horn, policemen guarding the way quickly opened the garage door and Charlie disappeared inside, his handlers outwitting the throngs who awaited his return. Charlie reentered the home at the point from which he had been abducted seventeen days earlier to the hour.

Anna Lou, bedridden from exhaustion for days, was, it seemed, about the last person to learn Charlie had been freed. Police and reporters knew. The chase for the abductors was already underway. Masses of people who heard the news thronged her yard. While Charlie met with his father and others, reporters finally broke the news to Anna Lou that her husband had been released. Charlie's reunion with Anna Lou was less than romantic. His first words were, "I'm back and don't worry." Yet, when she heard what he said and saw her husband, her eyes lit up, and she leapt to her feet, smiling joyously. It was one year to the day after Charles Lindbergh's curly-haired infant son was abducted. "Fate was cruel to the Lindberghs but kind to the Boettchers," one observer noted.

It soon became apparent that the reported break between Denver police and Claude Boettcher was a ruse calculated to promote the appearance that Claude was operating without police involvement. With his son safely home but sixty thousand dollars lighter, Claude brimmed with indignation and disgust.

"I met every obligation and fulfilled every promise that I made thru any source in the efforts to get my son back," he bellowed. "But, this play is not ended; the first act is completed and we will see what the second act brings forth." Filled with righteous vengeance, he vowed that he would pursue his son's kidnappers "as long as I live."

When Claude Boettcher returned that night to his Eighth Avenue Mansion more reporters greeted him but Claude already had his fill of the media. He drew from his overcoat an automatic pistol and waved the journalists off his front steps with it. "Get back. Get away from here, every damn one of you," Claude exploded. "All I have to say is to clear away from this gate." A policeman among the suddenly startled crowd saw Claude's gun and drew his own in reaction. Seeing him, Claude restored the pistol to his overcoat pocket, walked through the gate, and into his house, leaving in his wake a cadre of dumbfounded reporters.

With their advance notice of the ransom's delivery point, Denver police had been poised to pounce on the kidnappers as soon as they picked up the money. Early that afternoon, the department had assigned officers to cut off all entrances into and out of the city, but police failed to execute properly. When the report of Charlie Boettcher's release arrived at police headquarters, Captain Armstrong assumed Chief Clark had also been notified and so did not alert officers to speed to their stations. Thirteen crucial minutes elapsed before the error was rectified — enough time for Sankey and Alcorn to avoid the dragnet.

When he was about to pick up the ransom, Sankey had noticed a troubling detail: The delivery car blinked its lights. He immediately became suspicious that it was signaling police patrolling the area. He and Alcorn first worked their way toward Denver to the Sankey home on the city's east side, but as they approached Brighton, on Denver's northeastern outskirts, they encountered a Brighton posse. The posse exchanged gunfire with Sankey's fleeing Ford, as it raced toward Brighton.

Sankey's Ford resurfaced at a Brighton roadblock in a scene that could have been filmed for a Keystone Cops picture of an earlier era. The officers assigned at the roadblock, Deputy Williams and a posse member named Ingram had been told to stop only cars going west; so when a Ford sedan matching the description of the kidnappers' auto whizzed past them in the opposite direction, they just watched it fly by. An instant later they decided to pursue, but instead of chasing in their car, they leapt out of it and fired on the fleeing Sankey auto. Sankey swerved, then screeched, almost turning the Ford on its side as he reversed course then veered again, this time northbound at the intersection. The officers kept firing. Two bullets pierced the Ford's windshield, one narrowly missing Alcorn's head. As the Ford skidded past the officers it nearly struck Williams. Sankey suddenly stopped, then kicked into reverse, stirring dust up around his sedan. Just as suddenly, Sankey again changed course, this time speeding forward, nearly taking the Ford over an embankment. The turbulence, combined with abnormally heavy vehicle flow created a minor traffic jam as the fleeing Ford passed the other vehicles frozen in place. Sankey returned gunfire at the officers, then sped away north, his Ford's flanks perforated by a hail of gunfire from Williams's rifle and Ingram's sawed-off shotgun.

The exchange clinched it for Sankey. He was certain that the blinking lights were a signal to law enforcement, who, he figured — correctly — must have been tipped in advance of the ransom's delivery point. The problem for police was their delay in closing all exits from the city. The presence of police vehicles infuriated Sankey, who felt that Claude had violated his "sacred" promise that the men would have a half an hour head start before police were notified.

Long after the Brighton gunfight, when even Chief Clark should have realized that the kidnappers were fleeing northeast of the city, Denver authorities finally called out the dogs. Clark blanketed the city with law enforcement. He dispatched more than thirty-five police cars, each loaded with several officers, who inspected all cars entering and exiting the city at all points. It had little effect beyond enraging hundreds of innocents, inconvenienced by the frisking.

Driving on gravel roads without lights, Sankey and Alcorn finally reached Greeley, Colorado, eight hours later—at half past three in the morning—and drew some relaxed breaths. They gassed the Ford and drove the city's main thoroughfare, Eighth Avenue, where they encountered Greeley police officers. It was then that Alcorn bailed out of the car, tossed his gun on a Greeley street, and ran toward a nearby field. Almost miraculously, Sankey again eluded his pursuers, and as he had done so often, worked the back roads to the ranch. Youngberg greeted his return there the next night.

As federal authorities hastily convened a grand jury in Denver, bureau agents confiscated all of the ransom notes and other evidence. On March 4, the day Franklin Roosevelt was inaugurated in Washington, Claude increased his reward for the abductors' arrest and conviction to twenty-five thousand dollars and appointed Denver's mayor as the arbiter of who would be entitled to claim it.

Although blindfolded throughout most of his ordeal, Charlie provided police with a wealth of useful information about his prison. He knew there were four steps up to the house; he heard no telephone bell. Charlie could identify the color of the basement walls; he discerned that the basement floor was cement, covered with linoleum and carpet into which he had accidentally burned a cigarette hole. He recalled a basement window with green curtains held in place with narrow strips of wood. There was, Charlie said, a clothes closet in one corner of the room, a bed in another and a dresser, stove, and a cot. On his return ride to Denver, Charlie had slipped the tape off his eyes long enough to spy the word "Torrington," a southeastern Wyoming town, painted on a service station. His attention to detail well served authorities.

It also fueled the press. For more than two weeks, Charlie Boettcher had been the subject of conversation across the country. The *Rocky Mountain News* called Charlie the most discussed man in America, "hunted by the police of every city from coast to coast." So it is not surprising that legends stemming from Charlie's incarceration transformed him into a folk hero of sorts, elevating his exploits beyond reality. A story gained currency soon after his return. It was that he had deliberately left marks to identify the place of his keeping. As it went, he used a cigarette to burn a hole in the rug of his basement prison and plastered the walls with his fingerprints, to someday prove it was where he had been kept. The *New York Times* praised Charlie Boettcher's resourcefulness. "The authors of the Arabian Nights would have been delighted," the *Times* wrote. It was, alas, a simple case of the media misconstruing Charlie's words on the night of his release; while he had marked the walls with his hands Charlie went out of his way to acknowledge that the cigarette burn was accidental.

Another later, more enduring tale survived Charlie's lifetime: while in captivity Charlie detected the sound of an airliner flying overhead at a certain hour each day and that he utilized this information to assist officers to pinpoint the location where he had been held. The evidence disproves the fable. Charlie himself told the press the night of his return that he had not heard even "the slightest sound which might indicate where I was being held."

At first, police directed their attention to northern Colorado and southern Wyoming but both areas were far closer to Denver than the eighteen hours Charlie said he had traveled. By the end of the day following Charlie's release, authorities directed their search for the captors' hideout further east, into the Dakotas. The Torrington tip brought George Carroll, sheriff of nearby Cheyenne, Wyoming, into the investigation. Carroll, along with Denver detective George O'Donnell and Wyoming's commissioner of law enforcement, George Smith, trekked through Wyoming to the Lead-Deadwood area in the northern Black Hills of South Dakota.

Because of factors beyond poor communications, the "Three Georges' " multistate pursuit of Boettcher's kidnappers into other states was not unique. Few police training academies existed, resulting in an uneven quality of law enforcement. A local officer might be extremely competent or a buffoon. Worse yet, there often loomed the troubling question of whether a given locale's law enforcement could even be trusted, an issue that would constantly plague the Boettcher investigation.

Police corruption manifested itself most strikingly in what became known as "safe cities," those in which organized crime had infiltrated the police departments. The most notorious were St. Paul; Kansas City; Hot Springs, Arkansas; Cicero, Illinois; and Newark, New Jersey. Although each safe city's relationship with gangsters was unique, the common denominator was that, so long as gangsters refrained from committing violent crime in that city, it would harbor them from authorities in other jurisdictions. These limitations handicapped the Denver posse.

Also, the *mode* of crime had begun to change at least a decade earlier, due largely to the advent of the automobile as an instrument of crime. The last train robbery by horse occurred in 1923; the trend was to rob banks rather than trains and flee in cars. Culprits could rob a bank in the morning and be two states away by mid-afternoon. Once having evaded the law's initial pursuit, it became virtually impossible to identify, let alone apprehend the thieves.

This new mode of crime required an adroit and coordinated law enforcement capable of changing with the circumstances. Unfortunately, America's law enforcement had no organized national network that could either promote change or coordinate programs to implement it. This lack of coordination was the most pernicious problem American law enforcement faced in its burgeoning efforts to combat the new crime wave, and it plagued the kidnap investigation from the start.

The press did not suffer the same lack of agility as the law. Its ability to constantly stay on top of the case was its great strength — even if it did say so itself. The *Denver Post*, by its own admission, was the nation's best newspaper, its motto, "First in Everything." The day Charlie Boettcher was released the paper credited itself with "another scoop," proclaiming that it had been the first to give the world the news of his

release. It had published its first extra only minutes after Charlie Boettcher walked into the drugstore. Altogether, the news team issued "three
Denver Post Extras. . . . before any other news service knew anything
about the release of the kidnapped man." The editors exclaimed that its
coverage of the story "was one of the biggest and most complete in
Denver newspaper history."

Unarguably, the *Post* had been on top of the Boettcher kidnapping
story from its genesis and had saturated its 300,000 paid subscribers with
daily doses of the latest kidnapping news. On many days during Charlie
Boettcher's captivity, the *Post* not only led with the story, but filled its
front page with any detail it could glean about the case. Anything — even
tangential tidbits — was fair game.

The *Post* reached the Boettcher family patriarch at his Denver office
early on the morning following Charlie's release. Eighty-one-year-old
Charles Boettcher answered the phone himself, the switchboard operator
having not yet arrived. Yes, he was joyful and relieved that his grandson
had safely returned home. No, he had not yet seen nor talked to Charlie
and would likely not do so that morning, he said, as he had a business
conference that would engage his time. The *Post* told its readers:

> On the morning when wires were sizzling, headlines screaming his
> family name from coast to coast, telling the entire nation about the
> release of his namesake for a $60,000 ransom in one of the most
> sensational kidnapping crimes in American history, Charles Boettcher,
> the elder, was at his desk conducting "business as usual".

To his friends, the patriarch's response was fully in character. He had
come to America in 1869 from Prussia, as a seventeen-year-old only to
visit his older brother, but eventually built a fortune selling hardware. In
1875, his young wife, Fannie, gave birth to Claude, in Boulder where the
young couple then lived. A daughter followed. Charles later moved the
family and his business to Leadville. In the midst of silver prospectors
seeking riches, Charles Boettcher established a solid business of selling
those prospectors hardware supplies.

When the silver boom waned, the Boettchers left rough and tumble

Leadville for Denver, where in 1890, Charles built a grand brick home on Grant Avenue in what was to become Denver's prominent Capitol Hill district. The nation's largest city not built on a river, Denver was in the midst of tremendous growth.

In 1900, Charles, then almost fifty, decided to retire, embarking with Fannie on an extended trip to Europe, where, by chance he met German businessmen engaged in the production of sugar beets. Seeing potential in this crop, he decided to employ German methods in Colorado. The venture thrived, and the sugar beet industry proved a good compliment to Colorado's already established livestock industry. Today, Charles Boettcher is remembered as a pioneer in the development of the Colorado sugar beet industry. He later noticed that the cement used to construct one of his sugar factories had to be shipped from Germany, which to him was absurd, since all the minerals needed to make the cement existed naturally in Colorado. The result was the Portland Cement Company, which he founded.

Regrettably, after the couple's premature return from their European trip, Fannie and Charles gradually drifted apart. Their marital problems culminated in 1919 as their only daughter prepared to wed. Fannie desired to add a sunroom to their Grant Street home; Charles chafed at the idea. He told her that if she built the addition he would leave. Fannie built the sunroom and Charles kept his word. Charles had built a lodge on Lookout Mountain, west of the city during an earlier separation around 1915. He began to spend his weekends and summers at the lodge, which still stands, now known as the Boettcher Mansion. During the week, he kept quarters in the Brown Palace Hotel's ninth-floor suite.

Charles Boettcher was a world-class tightwad. Brown Palace employees watched nightly as he negotiated the elevator and crossed the street to a drugstore, where he bought a bottle of Coca-Cola. When once asked why he did not simply order from room service, he replied, "And pay these prices?" Frugal indeed, considering he owned the hotel. Employees noticed him in a run-down tailor shop having his trousers pressed because he considered the Brown Palace's valet fees excessive. Once asked why he was not chauffeured in a limousine like his son, Claude, the patriarch replied, "I didn't have a rich father."

In 1933, past eighty, Charles could have served as the model for the old man with the mustache on the Monopoly Board games first sold that same year. As he demonstrated that morning of his grandson's release, work still governed and framed his life.

While authorities pushed their search for the fleeing kidnappers into Wyoming and the Dakotas, J. Edgar Hoover's fortunes took a dramatic turn.

Several days before Roosevelt's inauguration, Hoover's nemesis, Attorney General designate Walsh traveled to Havana to wed his young, Cuban-born love. Walsh planned to return to Washington for Roosevelt's March 4 inauguration, but on the couple's train back to Washington, the seventy-four-year-old Walsh fell suddenly ill and died. Apparently anxious to quell any suspicions of foul play, Hoover dispatched senior bureau officials to meet the Walsh train in North Carolina and accompany Mrs. Walsh and the senator's body back to the Capitol for his funeral, after which it was taken to Helena for burial.

Also on March 4, as Chief Clark pressed the investigation for Charlie Boettcher's captors, he issued his standard pronouncement that he had definitely identified the kidnappers, and authorities announced they expected arrests within forty-eight hours. On March 6, police again announced that they were questioning all the city's known and suspected gangsters in hopes of locating those involved in the abduction. They appeared no further along than they were the night Boettcher was freed, but this time they were about to catch a break.

Although Arthur Youngberg was at the ranch to greet Sankey on his arrival on March 2, the night after Sankey's adventurous Greeley shootout, Youngberg and Sankey must have wondered whether Alcorn would ever return. Alcorn, forced to find his way on foot, traversed fields, walked gravel roads, and eventually came to Eaton, Colorado, fifteen miles from Greeley, where he hopped a train that took him to Cheyenne, Wyoming. Around noon, he boarded a Cheyenne bus to Alliance, Nebraska. He took a room in Alliance for the night. When he awoke, he anxiously scoured the next day's papers to see whether Sankey had been captured. He found nothing about it, so he set out for the ranch, finally arriving there two days after Sankey.

The trio believed themselves safe and thought authorities would never find them. But, on the afternoon of March 3, Miss Lucille Fletcher entered the Denver offices of U.S. Attorney Ralph Carr and revealed what she had overheard from her dress shop co-worker, Frances Ellsworth, the wife of Carl Pearce's bootlegger pal. When they learned of Fletcher's visit, Ellsworth and her husband, William, came in to Denver police headquarters and provided Chief Clark with the same information that Mrs. Ellsworth had shared with her friend, Denver patrolman, John Wells. Mrs. Ellsworth had told Wells that while imbibing, Carl Pearce had bragged to her that he'd had "a hand in the kidnapping," claiming that he had been promised two thousand dollars for typing the ransom letters. He would, he said, soon be "sitting pretty." Mrs. Ellsworth connected Wells to Pearce and Wells won his confidence. Anxious for attention, Pearce took Wells into his home and shared his life story, including the details of the kidnapping—even the names of his fellow operatives.

Early on Sunday morning, March 5, Denver police brought Pearce in for questioning. They also questioned Fern Sankey and her sister, the widow Ruth Kohler, who was Pearce's lover, and Ruth's sixteen-year-old daughter, Merelyn. Police grilled each woman and the child separately, questioning Kohler until six the following morning, when she finally admitted that she knew the identity of the kidnappers and the approximate location of the ranch hideout that had served as Boettcher's prison. Kohler denied any involvement, but allowed that, days before Boettcher's kidnapping, she had overheard Pearce and her sister's husband, Verne Sankey, talking about a kidnapping at the Sankeys' South Emerson home in Denver. The day after the kidnapping she claimed to have fainted, only then realizing the men had been serious.

With this information, authorities arrested Fern Sankey at the couple's home, where they found fourteen hundred dollars cash and pencil drafts of the ransom notes among men's underclothes. Fern Sankey's account tracked her sister's. After first denying any involvement, Pearce rolled when interrogators convinced him that his lover, Kohler, had implicated him. Pearce claimed that, because Sankey knew he could use a typewriter, Sankey had asked him to type ransom notes Sankey had written out. He claimed that Sankey never told him he had kidnapped Charlie Boettcher, but from the letters, he suspected it.

Pearce also identified Sankey's helpers — Gordon Alcorn and Arthur Youngberg. He told authorities that he had known Sankey for about a year and a half. Sankey, ever the salesman, had, Pearce said, convinced him he should move to South Dakota and buy Sankey's Buffalo County ranch. Sankey had promised Pearce a new car and some cash as payment for his limited typing services. Pearce had met Alcorn only a few times, and met Youngberg only on his sole trip to the Sankey ranch shortly before Charlie Boettcher was released.

"Sankey showed me all around the place, pointing out the features of the house and other improvements," Pearce told authorities. "I didn't know Boettcher was there." What Pearce did *not* tell police is that he had driven a car to meet the kidnappers outside Denver shortly before they released Charlie Boettcher.

The *Denver Post* did not widely circulate in central South Dakota but Sankey obtained a copy and learned that police were pressing their search for Charlie Boettcher's abductors into South Dakota. So on March 5, as police interrogated Pearce, Kohler, and Fern Sankey, Fern's husband, unaware that the three were being questioned, drove his bullet-riddled Ford into the deep ravine north of his farmhouse to hide it. He thought he was in the clear and needed only to wait for it all to blow over, as in all his other escapades. Youngberg reacted differently to the news. "I got nervous and wanted to 'blow' right away," he later recalled. But Sankey calmed his fears. "Never mind — they'll never find this place." It was a grand miscalculation.

When police began questioning Fern Sankey, she asked that her attorney be present. Ben Laska was a Denver attorney who had defended the Klansman Dr. John Galen Locke in a highly charged kidnap case a decade earlier. When Laska appeared at the police station, the authorities asked him if they could now question his client. In his laconic manner Laska replied: "Sure she can talk. She can cut her throat and pull out her tongue if she wants to."

Born in Russia, Laska immigrated to the United States with his family as a small child. As a boy, he toured America, Europe, and the Orient with his father, who trained and marketed him as a boy magician. In Russia, he performed before the czar. Laska was a proficient magician, having, as he later recalled, almost learned the rope trick. As Laska grew older, he graduated to hypnotism, operating "Professor B. Laska's School of Suggestive Therapeutics," which promised to cure all sorts of ailments, from epilepsy to paralysis and addictions to "the Liquor" and tobacco.

In his late twenties, Laska enrolled at the University of Michigan's School of Law, working his way through school by staging magic performances. Graduated in 1907, Laska returned to Denver to ply his new trade but never forgot his old one. While trying a case in Denver's federal court, a hostile witness offered testimony that was particularly damaging to his case. Laska drew a white handkerchief from his pocket and gently waved it. Suddenly, it became an American flag; he waved it some more and it turned solid red, then green. The next day's *Rocky Mountain News* noted the judge's admonition to Laska that he not attempt to hypnotize the jury. When Laska saw the story, he treated the editorial staff to an impromptu magic performance to "re-pay them" for the advertising value of the paper's suggestion that he could actually hypnotize a jury.

Laska, who was Jewish, had experienced prejudice up close and knew both sides of the crime of kidnapping. In 1924, Denver Klansmen kidnapped him at gunpoint, administered a severe beating, and departed with some advice: "Don't get these bootleggers off. Don't defend them." Laska got the message. A year later, when Klan leader John Galen Locke was charged with kidnapping and forcing the marriage of a recalcitrant fornicator, Laska successfully defended him. The case never went to trial. Laska simply orchestrated a series of venue changes until he secured for his client a Klan judge, who promptly dismissed the charge. The Jewish Laska even joined the Minute Men, a Klan offshoot Locke formed after he broke from Denver's Klan. The Klan kidnapping case enhanced Laska's notoriety in Denver. Before long, he commanded hefty fees. Sometimes clients simply could not pay but Laska represented them anyway, faithful to his attorney's oath.

Police were skeptical of Fern Sankey's account of the kidnapping, but teenaged Merelyn Kohler appeared unaware of the plot. She had been to the South Dakota ranch hideout — it was, after all, her aunt and uncle's home — and described its remote location. Her information led officers to the Sankey ranch. Clark directed the Three Georges to fly to Mitchell, some sixty-five miles east of the ranch — far enough removed, he thought, that their arrival would not attract local attention. At Mitchell, they were to meet other police who would fly there from Denver, supplied with additional machine guns. That, at least was the plan. When Clark reached the Three Georges with news of the investigation's turn, however, they were preoccupied with an entirely different and potentially more lethal enemy: a fierce March blizzard.

Unable to commandeer a plane in the storm, the Three Georges fought their way across plains covered by four feet of snow with drifts to eight feet. Conditions became so immobilizing the men abandoned their car in a snowdrift. They set out on foot with snowshoes, leaving behind most of their arsenal. The trio plodded through the deep drifts amid the brutal Plains wind until they finally reached O'Neill in north central Nebraska. There another officer joined them, and together the men boarded a train bound for Chamberlain, the Brule County seat, about twenty miles southwest of the Sankey ranch. They arrived there at midmorning on Monday, March 6.

Once at Chamberlain, the exhausted group contacted the local sheriff's office. Fearing their revolvers and the two machine guns they had hauled through the snow would prove inadequate for the monumental encounter they anticipated, the men secured a 300 Savage rifle in Chamberlain and three more rifles from Kimball's American Legion club, twenty miles east.

Because the ranch was situated just inside Buffalo County, Brule County deputy sheriff Charles Farnsworth invited Buffalo County sheriff Lars Rasmussen and his deputy, Armour Schlegel, to meet them in Kimball, twenty miles south of the ranch. These men knew the area, the trio reasoned, and might prove valuable in the confrontation for which officers braced. The Three Georges may not have known it, but Schlegel and Sankey were friends. Schlegel thought Sankey was a "good guy," had cared for Sankey's turkeys, and had helped Sankey with finishing work on the very ranch house to which the group was now proceeding.

On the way to Sankeys' isolated ranch, the group stopped at the farm of Sankey's closest neighbors and friends, the brothers Andrew and Mike Chopskie, for information. When they got to the Chopskie ranch, to their surprise, Arthur Youngberg, Sankey's hired man, was there helping the Chopskies butcher. They arrested Youngberg on the spot, without resistance.

The band of officers then stormed the Sankey ranch, poised for a shootout. As the AP reported it, the officers "pounced on the gang's lair in a wild, isolated region 50 miles from Chamberlain, South Dakota, late Monday, and captured one of the suspects there." Actually, the geography was off, and so were the details. When the officers got to the ranch no one was there. The house was in disarray: two chairs had been smashed and a window broken. The officers speculated that the kidnappers had fought over the ransom money. The reality was the bachelors Alcorn and Youngberg had apparently not repaired the damage resulting from their January fight. The lawmen's search of the house confirmed it was indeed the "four-step" ranch house Charlie Boettcher had described to Denver authorities.

When the *New York Times* banner proclaimed: "Ringleader Caught in Boettcher Plot" it referred to Arthur Youngberg but, again, the statement was hardly apt. When they questioned Youngberg, authorities mistook his pronounced Swedish dialect for a Scottish brogue. Youngberg was pleasant with police, but he refused to talk about the kidnapping or any involvement he might have had in it, saying only that he was a turkey farmer and a former railroader who had come to the Sankey ranch to work for Sankey.

That night in the Brule County jail, Youngberg, acting on Sankey's suggestion that they end their lives in the event of capture, took a razor blade and slashed his throat and wrists. Authorities rushed him to the hospital with injuries that were serious, but not life-threatening. Youngberg's action created an unexpected problem for police: they had hoped to keep his arrest secret until Sankey and Alcorn returned to the ranch. Now Youngberg's apparent suicide attempt and hospitalization forced the police to release information of his arrest, fearing the papers would learn of it anyway. Youngberg's actions and the authorities' response to it carried far-reaching implications for the manhunt the press was now casting as the greatest in the history of the West.

Denver authorities continued leading the investigation in South Dakota as they transported Youngberg back to Denver and housed him there while they awaited the filing of kidnapping charges. As he stepped off the train at Denver's Union Station, Youngberg appeared every bit the sporting gentleman, clad in a navy blue suit, black oxfords, a blue shirt, and newsboy cap. The detective who accompanied him from Chamberlain on the train quipped: "He may be a kidnapper, but he is a model prisoner."

In Denver, Chief Clark brought Youngberg to his office. Charlie Boettcher was there and Clark seated Youngberg across a table from Charlie, only a few feet away. When the chief asked Youngberg if he recognized Boettcher, Youngberg replied, "I never seen him in my life." At that, Boettcher lunged at Youngberg. Police separated the two, but Youngberg's accent had confirmed for Boettcher that Youngberg was indeed the man who had held him captive.

Still, Youngberg kept silent about his involvement in the case until he received a telegram from an older brother back in Winnipeg. "So finally Sankey got you hypnotized into this after trying for a year and a half. He took advantage of you being sick and out of job. He said all you do is look after farm. Tell the truth. There is a petition following. Don't worry. Friends are with you."

The telegram moved Youngberg, encouraged him, broke him down, so that he unfolded for authorities his role in the plot.

Youngberg told police his response on seeing Alcorn and Sankey at the ranch house door with their captive had been, "Oh, my God. Why didn't you pick out somebody that wasn't so hot?" Youngberg recounted that immediately after Charlie Boettcher arrived, Sankey forced him to write letters to his father and his wife and provide hair samples, all of which Sankey took with him as he shuttled back and forth between the ranch and Denver.

Youngberg gave his own account of the food service he had provided

Charlie Boettcher at the ranch. It was much different from Charlie Boettcher's account to the *New York Times*, which reported that he had eaten only sandwiches but in line with what Charlie had told the *Denver Post*. According to Youngberg, Charlie Boettcher was a guest not easily satisfied. He complained so mightily about the cuisine that Youngberg twice butchered turkeys for him. "Charlie was a good guy, but he demanded a lot of service," Youngberg said. "One time, Charlie made so many requests for different things that I asked him, 'Where do you think you are? At home?' He was as hard to wait on as a woman."

As soon as police identified Verne Sankey as one of Boettcher's kidnappers, rumors swirled around Denver that he had been the "official" bootlegger for the Denver 400, the city's elite business leaders. Sankey was, the *Post* reported, well-known to many of the men who donned fine suits and drove, or had driven for them, their Pierce Arrows to their Seventeenth Street suites each workday to conduct business. Sankey's trade with Seventeenth Street financiers aroused speculation that he had actually sold liquor to Charlie Boettcher. The Boettcher family quickly dispelled the rumors. Eventually Charlie himself denied them. In truth, almost certainly the two men did not know each other, as facts would later show. Whatever the case, though, the revelation that Charlie Boettcher had been kidnapped by Verne Sankey startled Sankey's old Seventeenth Street clientele, who pondered whether they themselves were candidates for a Sankey snatching. Many began to arm their chauffeurs and some armed themselves.

The investigation's forgotten agency was the Bureau of Investigation. The case had been solved not by bureau efforts but by the work of lowly patrolmen Wells and others in the Denver police force. No bureau agents were involved in the Denver arrests, and none were invited to join the group who eventually arrested Youngberg and stormed the Sankey ranch. The slight stung. This major crime generated such extensive publicity that it had presented a prime opportunity for favorable press, yet J. Edgar Hoover and his men were on the sidelines.

Undoubtedly mindful of his still tenuous job status, even as Senator Walsh's body was being laid to rest, Hoover was not about to forego a golden opportunity for publicity for the bureau and for himself. He authorized a press release that appeared on March 8 alongside his picture, which recounted the bureau's "vital role" in solving the Boettcher kidnapping case.

According to the release, the bureau had eliminated several suspects in Kansas City, Los Angeles, and other cities. Most incredulously, though, the bureau claimed that its operatives "developed confidential informants" who, the article stated, gave bureau agents "the same information concerning the suspects as police obtained." The article punctuated the striking coincidence. "The remarkable feature of their work was the fact that from these sources came the same clews that police obtained at exactly the same time." Hoover pledged to employ all bureau resources to pursue Sankey and Alcorn. The article concluded: "The bureau's reputation of 'always getting its man,' regardless of obstacles, began to be demonstrated Wednesday in the countrywide manhunt now underway for the two other suspects, Verne Sankey and Gordon Elkhorn [*sic*]."

Although Hoover's agency had not generated a solitary valid lead, Hoover shamelessly claimed credit for "solving" the case. He was proving himself more than able to utilize the press to serve the bureau's ends — and his own — even if it meant competing with local law enforcement.

5

"Charge It to Mr. Hoover"

While the continuing manhunt for Sankey and Alcorn captivated newspaper readers, each day also brought new stories chronicling an increasingly bleak human drama.

In March 1933, a Chicago father brought home a dead pig he found in an alley. Although he worked four days a week as a street cleaner for the city of Chicago, the man had not received a paycheck in months, and the pig was his children's first full meal in weeks. The family feasted on the pig for two days and even invited neighbors and relatives to share in their good fortune. Then one of the man's eleven children fell violently ill and died the next day.

Ashamed to reveal the truth about the pig, the father told physicians the boy had probably become ill from macaroni. But soon a second child died and then two more. Eventually, the father and six of the other children became sick. Near death, the father finally told physicians about the pig, shamefully explaining that because he was employed, he was not permitted to accept relief; yet, with no paycheck, he could not afford to buy food.

The news was rife with such anecdotes, yet Americans needed no anecdotal evidence to gauge the severity of conditions. They were experiencing them. The Depression's grim effects on a nation desperately trying to feed itself helped blur the lines between right and wrong for many struggling Americans. Otherwise honest men and women were drawn into crime's web. Still others, like Verne Sankey, were able to operate on the law's outer edge — and often stray outside it — without being shunned by their neighbors.

By March 1933, one in four American wage earners was out of work; one in three were, as Franklin Roosevelt declared, "ill-housed, ill-clad, ill-nourished." Men roamed the countryside, rode trains, slept in camps outside towns and cities, working for food along the way, sometimes begging for it. In New York, a couple moved into a cave in Central Park and lived there for an entire year, unable to afford other shelter.

October 24, 1929, had begun without hint of what would follow. By day's end, panicked stockholders had sold more than 12 million shares, the largest single-day sell-off in history. The country's most influential bankers emerged late in the day to prevent a further slide. The press hailed their efforts, but it turned out that the bankers had bolstered prices only long enough for them to withdraw their own sizeable assets from the market. When stock prices again collapsed the following Tuesday, the result was staggering: the market lost $9 billion — roughly 10 percent of its value — that day alone. The market's tailspin continued with little respite, for three more years, so that the composite of stocks listed on the New York Stock Exchange eventually lost more than 80 percent of their total value.

While the lasting popular image of the Great Depression is the collapse of stock markets in America and around the world, working families and farmers were more likely to entrust their small holdings to their local banks. Fear soon gripped the banking industry as well. The blows their customers suffered were often the cruelest. More than five thousand banks across the nation, unable to satisfy all their investors' demands, closed in the last three years of Hoover's administration, often leaving investors with no recourse to recover their losses.

Stories were heart-rending: an elderly woman was found pounding her fists on the closed doors of a midwestern bank, screaming and sobbing uncontrollably over the tormenting reality that she had just lost her life's savings — some three thousand dollars she had saved from her deceased husband's life insurance proceeds and from more than twenty-five years of weaving rugs.

The situation for farmers such as the Sankeys' South Dakota neighbors was unique. They had not basked in the economic roar of the twenties. Between 1910 and 1920 commodity prices had been sustained by war in Europe but the nation's postwar prosperity inflated industrial wages which, in turn, increased prices the farmer paid for the goods and services he purchased. Worse still, overproduction caused crop prices to decline, so that by the close of the 1920s the typical farmer, despite the long hours he labored and the entrepreneurial risk he assumed, earned less than an entry-level industrial worker.

Conditions got so desperate that crops sometimes went unharvested because the cost to do so exceeded the price the product could command. By 1932, America was overflowing with corn, wheat, and other commodities its people could not afford. This resulted in a striking anomaly of poverty amid plenty.

A witness told a congressional committee of a woman hugging a dead chicken under a ragged coat. "When I asked her where she had procured the fowl, first she told me she had found it dead in the road, and then added in grim humor, 'They promised me a chicken in the pot, and now I got mine.'"

The Associated Press reported from Boise, Idaho, that

> A woman with five children tagging at her skirts entered a cash and carry grocery store took a basket and began to fill it with things to eat. In appearance the family was decidedly ragged. Depression had written lines in faces, worn tattered clothing thin.
>
> All packages were carefully inspected. It was a heavy laden basket by the time the woman reached the cashier's stall, smiled and said.
>
> "Just charge it to Mr. Hoover."

Equally devastating to the farmer was the severe drought that gripped much of the Great Plains, beginning around 1930. The effects of cultivating marginal ground, in defiance of warnings about the perils of soil erosion, worsened this decade-long run. This problem was especially acute in central South Dakota, where the land allotted to the settlers by the Homestead Act was simply not enough to support a family through-out the vicissitudes of dry cycles and rising and falling commodity prices. As a result, massive numbers of farmers faced foreclosure.

By the time of the Boettcher kidnapping, the Depression had reached such depths that it noticeably affected even America's elite. In March 1933 Yankee owner Colonel Jacob Ruppert offered the "Great Bambino," Babe Ruth, $50,000—half of his previous contract. Ruppert reasoned the thirty-nine-year-old Ruth's new contract offer was worth as much as $100,000 had been two years earlier. The typical physician of the day earned about $3,400; the typical lawyer, $4,200. A public school teacher could expect annual income of around $1,200, a textile worker, $435, a farmhand a mere $200.

Compared to any of the so-called average Americans—compared even to Ruth—the Boettchers were fabulously wealthy and flourished financially, even in the Depression's bleakest hours. A contested federal income tax assessment yields a glimpse of their wealth. A Boettcher family trust appealed an assessment on $485,000 of income received from just one of their several companies. The Boettchers were in a financial league to which few others belonged, and ideal kidnapping targets.

As spring arrived, Sankey and Alcorn remained at large, but a picture of Verne Sankey began to emerge as Denver police searched Sankey's Emerson Street home.

Sankey aroused no suspicions in next-door neighbor Carl Satt, a Denver patrolman whose children played with Orville Sankey. It was an oversight Satt would never live down. Sankey's landlord, D. W. Johnson, however, remembered the image of a high roller. "Sankey carried a large amount of money on his person in a leather money belt." Another neighbor, Mrs. Donney, was perhaps one of the few people who saw through the Sankeys—although it is equally plausible that she simply brought out the worst in them. Mrs. Donney recalled going to the Sankey home for some dishes she had left there. When no one answered her knock at the door, she simply let herself in and encountered a startled Fern Sankey in the kitchen. Fern scolded Mrs. Donney for "nosing around," Donney later related. After the Sankeys were implicated in the Boettcher kidnapping, Mrs. Donney reported that she always thought they were suspicious-acting people. "We had a mind to turn them in," she later said. "I'll never forgive myself for losing the reward which my unemployed husband and I might have got if we had used our heads."

When police searched the basement of Sankey's South Emerson home, where Sankey reportedly had slept with a revolver under his pillow, they found a tiny black book of biblical verse. It was opened to the quote from Psalms 22:11: "Be not far from me; for trouble is near and there is none to help." A check mark appeared alongside the verse.

The window above Sankey's bed afforded a view of the street — and of anyone who approached the home. True crime magazines were strewn around the home. A rear door to the house allowed quick access to an alley garage, and a waiting car provided a ready means of escape.

If police sensed that Verne Sankey had selected his Denver house with criminal motives, the officers who searched the Sankey ranch house on March 6 reached that same conclusion. They were immediately struck by its remoteness, situated miles from a paved road and reached only by negotiating rutted gumbo paths through treeless plains, the last mile across a rolling hayfield.

The design of the ranch house increased officer's suspicions that it was built to serve as a lawbreakers' lair. It contained only one entrance; in order to enter the house, one had to pass completely around its rear. When *Denver Post* photographer Edward Eisenhand drove to the hideout, he noted that his car was within a hundred feet before even the chimney was visible. "Anyone watching from the crest of a little ridge that screens the house from the road could have picked us off with a rifle without the slightest risk to himself," he marveled. "We had to circle the ridge and pass halfway around the house to get in. On the other side of the house there is a view for miles across a country unmarked by roads."

One entered the little frame house through its twelve-by-fourteen-feet kitchen. Beyond it was an adjoining bedroom, ten feet square. The basement stairs, to the right of the kitchen, opened to a storage room, which in turn led into the room that had served as Charlie Boettcher's prison.

Meanwhile, the Colorado legislature became the nation's first to repeal prohibition and to permit the sale of 3.2 percent beer, echoing Congress' own recent action. The law change brought satisfaction to Charlie and Anna Lou Boettcher, who had fervently supported an end to Prohibition. There was cause for joy in *Les Trois Tours* that exceeded even Prohibition's repeal, when on March 8, 1933, a week after Charlie's release Anna Lou gave birth to a healthy five-and-a-half-pound baby girl. They named her Claudia in honor of her grandfather.

But all was not well in the Boettcher home. In the weeks that followed Charlie's release, he suffered bouts of extreme nervousness — anxiety attacks in today's idiom — which became so severe that they triggered stomach problems requiring hospitalization.

Days after his release, Charlie entangled himself in another bizarre altercation — this time, as the aggressor. Driving on a Denver street he noticed someone who appeared to be following him. Charlie decided to force the issue and stopped the other car to investigate. When Charlie approached its driver, he flashed a revolver. The startled motorist soon convinced him that he bore Charlie no ill will and had not intentionally tailed him. Charlie apologized, got in his car, and drove away. The motorist, however, was not willing to let the matter rest. He reported the encounter to police. Days later, when Charlie applied for a concealed weapon permit, this incident surfaced in the press.

The fallout that Charlie and his family as a whole experienced after the kidnapping did not end there. One might assume that the victims of such a crime would be a source of universal sympathy, but that was not the case. Since the kidnapping, the Boettcher family had become the targets of death threats. They were usually directed at Claude, often delivered via mail; more than a few were dropped on his doorstep. While most appeared to be the work of harmless cranks, some had a more sinister feel. They evinced Depression-era America's underlying resentment toward the wealthy. It was as though the crime against Charlie Boettcher had highlighted the family's fabulous wealth to an impoverished and often angry people, some few of whom vented their frustrations with the missives. Some harbored the opinion that there were far worse calamities in life than money taken from a rich person, even by means of kidnapping. It was a sign of the times.

In the midst of it all, the government was investigating the Boettchers, questioning whether the sixty-thousand-dollar ransom Claude paid was subject to the federal gift tax laws. The IRS reasoned that since the money Claude paid was unearned, it must constitute a gift and therefore Claude owed a tax!

6

A New Deal for the Desperadoes

From the outset of the 1932 campaign, Herbert Hoover stood little chance of reelection. When the Republicans had gathered for their 1932 convention, they promised to turn things around in America. Will Rogers jokingly came to their defense. "In the Republican platform at Cleveland they promised to do better. I don't think they have done so bad. Everybody's broke but them."

Events in March 1933 transformed the world. In November of 1932, voters had elected Franklin Roosevelt by the largest margin of any candidate since Grant, and now in March, after surviving an assassination attempt, Roosevelt began the first of his four terms in office. That same month, Adolph Hitler ascended to the chancellorship of Germany, immediately suspending its legislative body and initiating action that would lead to the expulsion of all Jewish people. At the same time, Japan asserted its militant sovereignty over the Pacific waters. By Inauguration Day, every state in the nation and the District of Columbia had partly or entirely suspended banking operations, declaring what became known as "bank holidays." The new president acted quickly to nationalize the bank closings, allowing banks to reopen only after they could establish solvency.

In the wake of Senator Walsh's death — even before Walsh's body was laid to rest — Roosevelt asked Homer Cummings to give up his new post as governor general of the Philippine Islands and assume Walsh's place as attorney general on an interim basis. Walsh's death and Cummings's appointment provided J. Edgar Hoover a reprieve of sorts, and he made the most of it. He issued a series of memos designed to impress on Cummings that whatever other problems might exist in the Justice Department, the Bureau of Investigation was operating efficiently.

At the time of Roosevelt's inauguration there were as yet no nationally known midwestern gangsters. America's infamous criminals were Prohibition mobsters such as Capone, Legs Diamond, Bugsy Siegel, and Dutch Schultz; the Lindbergh kidnapper had not been caught or identified and the nation had not yet been introduced to Arthur "Pretty Boy" Floyd, George "Machine Gun" Kelly, or Bonnie and Clyde, each of whom would emerge on the national scene later that wild summer. John Dillinger and "Baby Face" Nelson would leap onto the stage the following year. So, when police identified Verne Sankey as leader of the Boettcher kidnapper gang, he instantly gained a national notoriety and became the first in a parade of notorious Depression era gangsters from the nation's heartland.

Sankey's ill fame was further enhanced when authorities identified him as the suspect in the 1932 abduction of St. Paul banker, Haskell Bohn. Bohn had been held for thirty-five thousand dollars' ransom, but his family eventually negotiated his release for twelve thousand dollars. After Sankey was identified as Boettcher's kidnapper, Minnesota authorities investigated his whereabouts during June 1932 and learned that he had lived in Minneapolis with Fern and the children that summer. Additional evidence there further incriminated him, and a search of the Sankey ranch uncovered more facts implicating Sankey in Bohn's abduction.

In reality, Sankey's singular — albeit involuntary — rise to the status of a nationally known criminal in the spring of 1933 overshadowed others whose illicit ventures were at least as lucrative as his own. However, bandits like Harvey Bailey, Frank Nash, Verne Miller, the Keating-Holden Gang, and the Barker-Karpis Gang operated their automobile-oriented bank robbing enterprises so fluidly that authorities had not yet gathered sufficient information to realize the significant roles they each played in the spate of bank heists plaguing the Midwest. An even greater blight on the country than Sankey and other budding midwestern outlaws were the Prohibition mobster organizations that controlled entire cities.

As an astute politician, Homer Cummings knew that the public increasingly viewed each new unsolved crime as added evidence of law enforcement's impotence and government's general inability to solve the myriad problems it faced. Cummings decided to spend some of the currency the new administration had earned with its resounding election victory and take the fight to the increasingly glamorous image of the gangster. His first target was Hollywood.

The box office success of *Little Caesar* (1930) and *Public Enemy* (1931) had ushered in the era of the gangster movie. In 1931 alone, some fifty gangster movies played in America's theaters and 1932 brought still more. The movies lionized gangsters, often portraying police as ineffective, almost irrelevant buffoons. Cummings lobbied Hollywood's executives to deglamorize the role of the gangster and to portray law enforcement more positively. He was aided by the American Catholic bishops, who that year launched a drive against movies they considered objectionable, usually because they included scenes of nudity, drug use, or violence. The bishops' campaign culminated in the formation of the Legion of Decency, in which Catholics pledged to boycott movies that glorified vice or crime. As other denominations joined the cause, Hollywood grudgingly agreed to enforce its Production Code — standards the industry had drafted years earlier but largely ignored.

Cummings next set about to create public support for law and its enforcers in what he characterized as the nation's "war on crime." Unlike the Hoover administration's attempt to strengthen *local* law enforcement efforts, Cummings believed meaningful transformation could occur only through an expanded *federal* crime-fighting role. He proposed vesting the federal government with the necessary authority to fight the war, winning FDR's support for a twelve-point program that authorized bureau agents to carry guns and make arrests and extended federal authority to bank robbery, racketeering, kidnapping, and a variety of other crimes.

To promote this twelve-point program, Cummings launched a largely radio-based publicity campaign advancing the idea of a federal "super police force," with the powers he sought in the twelve-point program. While Cummings's efforts were unwittingly aided by the epidemic of kidnappings and high visibility bank robberies later that summer, still not all Americans accepted the notion that such criminals were the worst scourge the country faced.

Even though colorful coverage of criminal escapades like Sankey's splashed across newspapers, America was more intently focused on her economic woes. The country reached the pit of the Depression that spring, and few places in America were more depressed than Buffalo County, South Dakota — a place where residents had warmly received their well-off newcomer, Verne Sankey, a few years earlier.

It was not by chance that Sankey chose to locate there. Buffalo County comprises about five hundred square miles of semiarid, isolated, and mostly treeless rolling hills along the mighty Missouri. The county, near the geographic center of the continent, straddles the imaginary divide between the fertile plains to the east and the westward Great Plains. Gann Valley never experienced overcrowding. As one longtime resident put it during the 1930s, "If I started counting, I could come up with over fifty people." But what the village lacked in numbers it made up for in heart and vigor, quickly establishing itself as a center for the area's farm and ranch families.

When one views the terrain around Gann Valley, the question that presents itself is: what possessed people to settle in such a bleak land? The most obvious draw was the free ground. Some were mesmerized by the freshness of the wide, unsettled prairie. Many sought a new beginning. The tiny town is nestled in a valley among a generous cropping of trees, but the undulating prairie surrounding it is imposing. Not far from town, one can look in every direction and not see a solitary tree, indeed, nothing at all but grass and sky.

The temperature is subject to extreme variations. On the hottest day in the state's history, in July 1936, the thermometer reached 120 degrees here; five months earlier, to the north at McIntosh, the mercury dove to a state record low of 58 degrees below zero. It was to this sort of country that pioneers came, forsaking the tree-filled hill country of Ohio, Pennsylvania, New York, and Indiana.

The deadly 1888 blizzard was soon followed by a particularly devastating drought. North at Aberdeen, a young newspaper publisher named Frank L. Baum dreamed away the drought-dreary parched soil and dry brown growth, conjuring in their place images of an emerald city. Years later, he turned his imaginings into a novel, *The Wizard of Oz.* Although many gave up and left the land, the robust homesteaders who persevered grew stronger. When they socialized, they often gathered at a home. Someone would bring a fiddle, others food. Pushing aside the furniture, they danced away the Depression, at times into the early morning light, often fueled by a little moonshine.

They needed each other to survive. The hot, dry summers, and windswept, treeless prairies created an ideal environment for fires. The land could be thick with rattlesnakes. Disease and pestilence also lurked. Anthrax posed a threat to livestock like that of a mass murderer, skulking about in deadly silence. The diseased animal contaminated the ground it touched, the anthrax spore retaining its killing capacity for generations. Entire herds were often decimated.

A diphtheria epidemic hit the town during the Sankeys' sojourn there. Typhoid fever also swept through the area, killing parents as well as beloved children. In nearby Chamberlain, the disease first appeared in late 1932, as the Sankeys left the area for Denver. Soon people were dying every week—some 223 cases in all, leaving nearly three dozen dead. Just as the worst of the Depression hit, and with it the typhoid and dust pneumonia, angelic beings descended on the town in the form of Pastor Ralph Keithahn and his physician wife, Mildred. While her husband tended to the community's spiritual needs, Dr. Mildred vaccinated for typhoid, whooping cough, scarlet fever, and small pox; conducted eye, ear, and nose clinics; tonsil-removing clinics; and whatever else circumstances demanded. She refused to accept pay from her patients, most of whom had little with which to compensate her.

In 1933, Gann Valley supported a blacksmith shop, a cafe, hotel, service station, ice cream parlor, two general stores, a law office, and a scattering of other small businesses that provided the most basic necessities. The Frasers operated the "Quality Store." The Hughes Store was "Headquarters for everything on earth." A person could buy there, it was said, anything from a mousetrap to a casket. Electricity would not come to the area for years; homes had no potable running water. The town witnessed the arrival and departure of several banks, small upstarts, usually undercapitalized.

The town's lawyer, Harold Brown, doubled as the county's part-time state's attorney. Brown's practice kept him busy drafting deeds, examining abstracts, rendering title opinions and tax advice, holding the hands of county officials struggling with continuous budget shortfalls. He prosecuted few crimes, more rarely tried a case to a jury.

Buffalo County holds the unofficial national distinction of having elected the most widely divergent sheriffs, at least in height and within just a few years of one another. Miniature Morris Nelson, who served as the county's sheriff in 1935 and 1936, stood barely five feet tall and weighed 125 pounds. His successor by a few years, August Klindt, stood seven feet, three inches tall or, as he liked to say, "six feet, fifteen inches," in his prime, and weighed in the vicinity of 450 pounds. Circus audiences paid to see the "Buffalo County Giant" pass fifty cent pieces through his gigantic ring.

Nobody though — not even the Gann Valley Giant — loomed larger in 1933 America than its new president, Franklin Roosevelt.

Roosevelt's action to address the banking crisis altered Verne Sankey's efforts to "launder" the ransom money, which he correctly assumed to be marked in some way. He and Alcorn needed to exchange it quickly but because the banks were closed, they had to find other means.

Before Alcorn had returned to the ranch, Sankey and Youngberg counted the ransom — Sankey had been suspicious it was not all there, but it was: exactly $60,000 in tens and twenties. The ransom was to have been divided $30,000 to Sankey, $18,000 to Alcorn, and $12,000 to Youngberg, but Sankey deducted $1,000 from each of the other men's shares, telling Youngberg that he had "taken care of another fellow or two." Sankey gave Youngberg his $11,000 share and also Alcorn's share, telling Youngberg to hold it for Alcorn. Along with Alcorn's share was a note explaining that Sankey had deducted $500 toward Pearce's share, $250 each for expenses, and another $250 for "amusement, liquor, etc."

When Alcorn returned to the ranch, he was visibly miffed at being shortchanged but appeared to get over it. The next day, Sunday, March 5, Alcorn threw his gun and his ransom share on the table and announced that he planned to bury his cut on the ranch. He and Sankey then agreed to take four thousand dollars with them to Minneapolis. Then, along with Youngberg, they buried the rest. Each man knew the general area where the others had hid their shares.

Sankey prevailed on his older brother, Frank, to come in from Clark, South Dakota, and drive him and Alcorn to the Twin Cities, where Sankey used his bootlegging connections to tap into the thriving money laundering operations there. Verne gave Frank $350, part of which was reimbursement for Verne's share of the cost to have their mother's body moved from Miami, where she had died only days before the Boettcher kidnapping, to the family plot in Watertown. While in St. Paul, Sankey wrote a letter to Youngberg — postmarked Monday, March 6, at 6:30 P.M. — instructing Youngberg about the care of the farm and telling him he would return in five or six days.

Police intercepted the letter and learned of Frank's assistance. When authorities left the abandoned ranch and interviewed Frank Sankey, he claimed to know nothing of his brother's role in the Boettcher kidnapping. He recounted for agents that when he drove Verne and Alcorn to Minneapolis, they carried a handbag that they studiously guarded. Frank figured it was bootleg money.

While in Minneapolis, Sankey and Alcorn stayed at the Hotel Sheridan, where the clerk recalled Sankey as a salesman from Clark, South Dakota. The pair stayed at the Sheridan until Tuesday evening, the seventh. On Sunday night, the fifth, Sankey wrote to Fern and the kids in Denver, unaware that she was then in the custody of Denver police.

Dear Fern + Kids -
Arrived here O.K. everything fine only car is in not very good
condition. So Carl better by a car at a price of around $300, in his own
name. License and all and leave for the farm as soon as possible. If they

have to much to haul he will have to repair trailer tongue and get the two tires and all nuts and lugs are in a white can in the basement together with tires. You can give him the price of his car, license Etc. And about $50 or $60 for there expense money on the road. We are leaving for a few days so here is what Carl and Tut are to tell Chopskies if they arrive here befor I get back to farm. Verne went with Gordon east as Gordon was returning home and Verne is then going to Watertown to help make arrangements to bring his mother back to her old home for burial. But he will return to the farm soon. Or if I arrive back to the farm ahead of Carl it will be the same and O.K. Carl must follow Hiway No. 16 to Puckwanna and then straight north to Shelby. Then east about 5 miles to Hoffmans corner and then north 1 mi. then N. W. 2½ miles. I thot it best to keep your car at home. Will write more when I hear from you.

    With Love to all,

    Verne

At the top of the letter he added a postscript:

I Left two good letters for you 60 ft. east of spot where I left you the letter last year.

The reference was to a point between two marked fence posts west of Sankey's ranch house, where Sankey had buried his share of the ransom money.

The letter arrived while Fern was in custody and it was given to Chief Clark. He questioned Fern about the two "spots." When she asked to read the contents of the letter, Clark tore off the postscript, thinking she might try to destroy the letter before he could stop her. With a picture of the ranch in hand, Clark had Fern identify the location of the fence posts, then relayed to his men at the ranch what Fern told him. They searched furiously but fruitlessly. They were most likely given wrong information.

By March 7, police decided to simply wait for Sankey and Alcorn to return to the ranch. But after Youngberg cut himself, and the story of his arrest broke in the nation's newspapers the next day, Sankey and Alcorn headed the other way, for Chicago, carrying five sets of stolen licenses.

Alcorn settled in Chicago under the name Walter Thomas. Sankey assumed the name William E. Clark, but shortly after he arrived in Chicago a pressing matter required his return to the ranch. Most of his money remained buried in two separate cans roughly a hundred yards from the ranch house. Sankey had to return to the ranch: Youngberg knew the approximate location of the buried money and worse, the authorities might find Sankey's letter to Fern.

So it was a desperate Verne Sankey who boarded a Chicago westbound to Council Bluffs, where he bought a secondhand car and motored west. He traveled at night with lights off, taking gravel roads. A few miles north of the ranch he parked and walked the rest of the way. Machine-gun armed officers kept watch over the property around the clock to keep sightseers and even the press at bay, while they searched for ransom money and poised for Sankey's return.

Sankey reached the ranch after dusk. Lights were on in the house as the armed law enforcement officers loitered away the early evening hours. Sankey crept low as he approached the farmyard. The bark of the German shepherd he had bought for Alcorn froze Sankey in place, and he waited for the ring of machine-gun fire. He could see officers inside the well-lit house, but no one moved. Minutes passed. The dog's barking subsided.

Sankey again crept forward, finally reaching the ravine where his buried money lay. Frantically, he dug into the frozen March soil, his only tool a pocket knife. When it broke, Sankey continued with his hands. The digging seemed to take forever. The lights of a police car appeared in the distance. Slowly it rounded the ranch house and rolled to a stop. Fearing he would be seen, Sankey jumped behind a tree. The officers exited their car and walked into the well-lit ranch house, oblivious to Sankey's presence. Sankey resumed his digging and finally reached the cans. He removed their bounty along with most of Alcorn's hidden funds as Alcorn had asked, then dashed away in the dark. Retrieving his car, he retraced his route back to Chicago, carrying with him about forty thousand dollars.

Sankey's timing was exquisite. Soon afterward, authorities came across one of the holes Sankey had dug. Denver Detective Sherman

Turner, assuming there were other holes, searched the ground around a hole where cattle had been fed. Kicking aside corn husks and stalks, he uncovered most of Sankey's broken pocket knife. Turner and Buffalo County sheriff Rasmussen excitedly dug to elbow's depth where finally they struck three tobacco tins. Like kids in search of buried treasure, they grasped for the tins, flipped off their lids, and found all were empty. Sankey had beaten them to the stash.

Fern Sankey remained jailed in Denver, where her lawyer, Ben Laska, admonished her not to talk. But she talked anyway, if not with complete candor, to Denver police. Now, she consented to an interview with the *Denver Post's* Frances Wayne as well. The reporter described her interviewee as "small, dark as a Spaniard, with nicely waved black hair and wearing a black crepe house frock" and characterized her as poker faced during most of the interview. She noticed at one turn "a faint first smile [that] warmed her face and parted her lips over even white teeth."

Fern professed utter ignorance of her wayward husband's illegal conduct. "There are thousands of others like me — just home wives. Our husbands are good providers. We take their goodness and honesty for granted. They tell us nothing of their affairs, whether they are in debt or have money in the bank. They give us jewels, automobiles and new fur coats. We say thanks and never think to ask where the money came from. . . . Is it any wonder we are surprised when something unusual happens?" she plaintively asked. Her emotions finally surfaced at interview's end. "Why are we here[?]"

In reality, as time passed, authorities had more reasons to hold Fern Sankey. Because of the similarity the crime bore to Haskell Bohn's kidnapping in June 1932, St. Paul investigators had been interested in the Boettcher suspects from the time they were first identified. Bohn was the adult son of a wealthy, well-connected St. Paul family. As in Boettcher's case, the Bohn ransom notes made liberal reference to the Lindbergh abduction. Abductors in each case corresponded with the father of the victim through the mail. When St. Paul authorities examined the handwritten ransom notes recovered from Sankey's Denver home, the resemblance to the Bohn notes was striking, even to an untrained eye. When police learned that the Sankeys and their two children lived in Minneapolis from June to September 1932, they focused on them. Bohn soon confirmed that the Sankeys' Minneapolis residence was where he had been held. Police assumed-incorrectly — that Alcorn had joined Sankey in that snatch as well.

The case broke open when Denver police Captain Armstrong came across a reference to one Ray Robinson at Sankey's ranch, that implicated Robinson in the Bohn abduction. Following that lead, authorities learned that Robinson, a Canadian railroad friend of both Sankey and Alcorn had deposited ten thousand dollars in his own name in a Winnipeg bank account a week after the Bohn abduction.

The Canadian Mounted Police caught up with Robinson on the last day of March, two hundred miles north of Winnipeg in an isolated, thinly populated hamlet called Rorketon, where he purported to represent a radical organization known as the Farmers Unity League. When arrested, Robinson not only admitted his complicity in the Bohn abduction but also implicated both Sankeys, claiming Fern aided her husband in the planning and prepared several meals for the unwilling guest. Robinson told police that when he and Sankey abducted Bohn, they were drunk. When Robinson had finally sobered up, he and Fern both tried to convince Sankey to set Bohn free but Sankey was adamant: he promised to hold Bohn until they collected the loot, even if it took six months.

Ray Robinson's statement sealed Ramsey County's decision to indict Fern for Bohn's abduction. When she had been interviewed in mid-March, Fern had steadfastly denied knowing anything about Haskell Bohn's kidnapping, but authorities planned to bring Bohn to Denver to see if he could identify Fern's facial features or her voice.

Two days before Ray Robinson's Canadian arrest for the Bohn abduction, a federal grand jury in Denver indicted the Sankeys, Alcorn, Youngberg, Pearce, and Kohler in a fifty-nine count indictment for violations of the Lindbergh kidnapping law. By the end of March, the facade the Sankeys had maintained was crumbling along with the family itself: Fern Sankey sat listlessly in jail, facing possible life imprisonment, with another charge pending in Minnesota; her children remained in the care of relatives in Denver; meanwhile, Verne Sankey and Gordon Alcorn continued to elude the patchwork of law enforcement agencies that pursued them.

In mid-March, the Denver police packed up their submachine guns, abandoned their vigil at the Sankey ranch, and returned to Colorado. Sankey and Alcorn had now become the most hunted fugitives in all of America.

7

Desperadoes Waiting for a Train

The Lindbergh kidnapping remained unsolved in the spring of 1933. In its wake, Congress authorized Hoover's bureau to investigate such crimes when evidence suggested that the victim had been transported across state lines. There was, ironically, no such evidence in the case of the Lindbergh child, and so the bureau had no actual authority to work it. Moreover, New Jersey authorities jealously guarded their jurisdictional turf. These factors limited the bureau's role in the case through early 1933. The lack of cooperation and duplication of effort made solving the case more difficult, further adding to the growing body of evidence that the system for fighting crime needed a massive overhaul.

The extensive manhunt for Charlie Boettcher's abductors had produced similarly paltry results in the long weeks following Roosevelt's inauguration. Now with the nationwide search for Sankey and Alcorn focused on St. Paul, Chicago, and Denver, the government began bearing down on Arthur Youngberg, confident he knew where at least some of the ransom had been stockpiled.

Youngberg, however, was not cooperating. He realized the only face card he held was the ability to locate some of the ransom, and so, in the absence of a deal, he remained reticent. "I might know where some of the money is and I might not," Youngberg told them. "What good would it do to tell if I did know?"

In April, Gordon Alcorn — as Walter B. Thomas — fell in love with a young divorcée, Angeline "Birdie" Christopherson Paul, and the pair was married in May. Although living in Chicago, Birdie hailed from tiny Corson, in southeastern South Dakota, on Sioux Falls' outskirts, and still had two young sons back in South Dakota.

Although it seemed that Verne Sankey had vanished, like Alcorn he hovered around Chicago, blending into the city's nameless masses as William E. Clark, maintaining a low profile, portraying himself as a successful entrepreneur, little different from the false fronts he had successfully employed elsewhere. Sankey could live such a life because he clung to no real gangster connections that exposed him, and had been in no serious criminal trouble.

This is not to say that Sankey had no gang affiliations. His circumstantial links to Denver's bootlegger underworld manifested themselves when Fern was arrested in Denver and quickly contacted Ben Laska. That Fern was able to do so without speaking to Verne, who did not learn of her arrest for days — and though she and Verne had arrived in Denver only two months before — was particularly remarkable unless she already knew of Laska. Similarly, when Carl Pearce had earlier been arrested on an insufficient funds check charge, Denver bootlegger king Joe Roma's beautiful young wife, Nettie, posted his bail bond. Sankey, well-connected to Twin Cities bootleggers, had similar connections in Denver, including William Ellsworth. More evidence of Verne Sankey's bootlegger affiliations would unfold in the succeeding months.

Sankey's gangster relationships provided little solace to him on the run. He chose not to seek harbor in St. Paul — perhaps because he had committed the Bohn kidnapping in nearby Minneapolis and had spent time there, making him recognizable to more people. Nor could he safely return to Denver in light of the intense manhunt for him. His rural bootlegging haunts in the northern United States and Canada could not provide the anonymity he required. In Chicago, though, he blended into the fabric of any neighborhood in which he dwelled. As he easily dropped a twenty-dollar bill on the drugstore counter or at the racetrack and took back clean money in change or winnings, his cherubic, pleasant countenance and short, squat stature attracted no unwanted attention. All this allowed him to function in the city under the nose of the bureau.

Sankey did not remain *entirely* "crime free." One day, he boldly executed a daylight armed robbery on a Chicago street. The victim failed to report the crime, however. It happened this way: Alcorn still smoldered over being shortchanged on the ransom distribution. When the pair arrived in Chicago, they agreed that it would be wise to bury a portion of the money in a common locale, rather than keep the bills in their apartments. They found an isolated spot north of the city and plunked their cash into a hole. Sometime after they did so, Alcorn returned, dug up the loot, and moved out of his apartment with his new bride. When Sankey discovered the money was gone, he searched for Alcorn and caught up with him outside Alcorn's new apartment. Gun drawn, Sankey greeted him with the words, "Stick 'em up!"

As Birdie was about to become hysterical, Alcorn told her, "Don't scream," then turned to Sankey. "Put that gun in your pocket. I'll talk to you." Sankey declined the invitation to set aside his gun, keeping it trained on his former partner. Alcorn led the way into the bathroom of his apartment, where he opened his club bag that held the money. He told Sankey he had moved the money out of fear that someone else might take it and was merely holding it for safekeeping. Unimpressed, Sankey demanded that Alcorn cough up the cash. Alcorn complied and took fifteen thousand dollars out of the club bag. "That's the money," Alcorn told him. Sankey was not satisfied. He grabbed the money with his gun still trained on Alcorn, took what he estimated to be his twelve-thousand-dollar share, and left the rest for Alcorn. With that, he shook Alcorn's hand, wished him luck, and left. It was the last time the pair spoke.

In April, the government and Claude Boettcher's attorneys finally prevailed on Arthur Youngberg to cooperate in the ransom money search. It was an odd arrangement: Claude Boettcher agreed to pay Youngberg a finder's fee for any recovered funds. On April 24, bureau agent J. F. O'Connell, working with Buffalo County sheriff Lars Rasmussen, dug up $9,360 that Youngberg had buried in a can at the foot of a fencepost. It was all Youngberg claimed to have left. Claude Boettcher quietly paid Youngberg the agreed sum of nine hundred dollars for his help.

Later the same month, Sankey again traversed back roads to the ranch. He had not learned of the recovery of Youngberg's funds, since it was not reported for several days, and he figured Youngberg's stash was of no use to him in prison. This time it was Sankey who was disappointed, finding only an empty hole where Youngberg's share had rested. He later read in a Chicago newspaper that law enforcement had uncovered the loot only a few short days before his return to the ranch.

Youngberg gave authorities another map on which he identified where Sankey and Alcorn's shares were supposedly buried, but later admitted to fabricating it while he held out for a deal on sentencing. Finally, with no plea agreement in sight, Youngberg caved, hoping for leniency. He gave the government what it wanted—a detailed map of where the rest of the money had been buried. What neither he nor the authorities could know was that Sankey had already retrieved his own share and Alcorn's as well.

Youngberg reckoned that Sankey and Alcorn's shares, together with his own recovered portion, would account for all but a few thousand dollars of the ransom. Encouraged by the Youngberg find, Claude's attorneys sought Attorney General Cummings's approval to take Youngberg to the ranch. Cummings, immersed in FDR's furious first hundred days of legislation, did not immediately act on their request. As Boettcher's men waited, they hired private detective Dan Gleason — at five dollars a day — to guard the ranch until Youngberg could reach the scene.

In mid-May Cummings finally authorized Youngberg to travel with federal authorities to the ranch to identify where the rest of the ransom lay. The search was, of course, fruitless. Youngberg also told authorities a gun and about four thousand dollars was hidden in a stove pipe in the grain bin of a barn. The press learned of—and published—Youngberg's story. Neither the money nor the gun was recovered. Youngberg took bureau agents through at least one cemetery near the ranch, which prompted the press to suspect they were searching for murder victims, speculation which the government emphatically denied.

The ransom search developed into something of a cottage industry. Boettcher detectives Gleason and Ray Barger stayed at the ranch, which was cared for by Mike and Andrew Chopskie and Andrew's wife. The men supervised the digging of a hole fifty feet square and three feet deep. They found nothing, but trudged on undeterred, staying on the ranch for weeks while the Chopskies provided their room and board—all reimbursed by Claude Boettcher.

Investigators met American Legion members from Pukwana who were Sankey drinking friends, Gann Valley ranchers who were Sankey pals, and Kimball farmers with whom Sankey had partied. From them they learned almost nothing. Bureau agent Werner Hanni received word that a local real estate man, Paul Lenz, had reliable information that Sankey was hiding out on an island ten miles southeast of Chamberlain, a hangout and rendezvous for bootleggers. Hanni assembled U.S. marshals, deputies, prohibition agents, and Boettcher investigators and headed for the island. Their thorough search produced no sign of human occupancy.

The Gann Valley and Kimball communities hummed with each sensational report about their now famous neighbor. Reactions alternated between shock and amazement that one of their own—a man they knew personally—had become such a notorious national figure. Even so, Sankey was not the only area resident of that era to stride across the national stage.

In 1920, young Verne Miller, born in Kimball and raised in the area, and a decorated veteran of the World War, won a tight three-way race for Beadle County sheriff. The new sheriff hit the ground running—or, more aptly, spinning around in his Stutz Bearcat. Brassy and belligerent with criminals, he enforced the newly enacted Prohibition Amendment so aggressively that the county began using confiscated moonshine as antifreeze in its vehicles.

Miller was nominated for a second term in 1922 but then disappeared in early August. Shocking news unfolded: the state sheriff reported that Miller was wanted for embezzlement of county funds. He had slipped to St. Paul, utilizing contacts within its corrupt police department to his benefit. A St. Paul hotel manager called local police to report Miller was staying in his establishment. When told that Miller was no longer wanted, the doubting proprietor called South Dakota authorities directly, who rushed a detective to St. Paul and placed the unresisting Miller under arrest.

Miller eventually pled guilty to embezzling twenty-six hundred dollars and served two years in the South Dakota State Penitentiary in Sioux Falls. Soon after his parole discharge, he became a player in the St. Paul bootleg market where he developed contacts he would carry into the next decade.

Because it was a haven for gangsters, St. Paul had become a crossroads for nearly every major midwestern outlaw by 1930. Sankey frequented the city, did bootlegging business there, and had lived in nearby Minneapolis during the summer of 1932, when he executed the Haskell Bohn kidnapping. The *Denver Post*'s Charlie O'Brien reported that Denver police believed that Sankey and Miller were working together in the summer of 1933 to "bring together a band of sinister criminals with no regard for human life" to execute kidnappings.

The story went that Miller brought together George "Machine Gun" Kelly and remnants of the Roger Touhy and Harvey Bailey gangs, but it was pure fabrication. Whether the two men with Kimball ties ever crossed paths in St. Paul or elsewhere is unclear. What *is* known is that Miller was at the hub of St. Paul's gangland and fraternized with many of the outlaws who drifted in and out of town. It was there that he met the man whose name would forever be linked with his own, a man who would become one of his closest friends — Frank Nash.

The lives of Miller, Nash, and other midwestern crime figures provide helpful context to the crime wave that culminated in 1933 and how it impacted the hunt for Verne Sankey. Frank Nash was from Oklahoma, the product — in spirit at least — of a long line of robber-bandits, dating to before the Civil War: William Quantrill and his raiders, the Jameses, the Youngers, the Daltons, the Doolins, Belle Starr, and others. Each successive outfit was populated by one or more members of a previous gang. The Jameses were cousins of the Youngers, whose cousins the Daltons eventually formed their own gang. The Youngers intermarried with the Starr family; the Doolins rode with the Daltons; and so it went. Nash teamed with Al Spencer, who had ridden with Henry Starr.

Nash and Spencer executed a spree of robberies, including their 1923 train heist in northeast Oklahoma's Osage Hills — the last U.S. train robbery executed on horseback. Nash was caught and sentenced to life at Leavenworth Prison. In 1931, by then a trustee, he walked away from the institution and resumed his trade with new associates Tommy Holden, Francis Keating, and Harvey Bailey — perhaps the most successful bank robber of them all.

In some ways, Bailey's career paralleled Verne Sankey's. He was a railroader turned bootlegger, transporting liquor from Canada across the border into Minot, North Dakota, and other locales. In time Bailey drifted into stealing from banks, launching a career that extended over thirteen years, during which he was responsible for some of the largest bank heists in America — the theft of $265,000 from a Cincinnati bank; $200,000 from the Denver Mint; and from Lincoln National Bank and Trust Company of Lincoln, Nebraska, a whopping $2.8 million in cash and bonds, reportedly the largest bank heist ever to that time.

Despite Bailey's extensive career, he remained unknown to America and, more important, to law enforcement. He moved confidently, dressed gentlemanly; nothing in his life or habits aroused suspicion. Bailey left crime for a time and operated gas stations and car washes but lost most of his wealth in the crash of 1929. So he hooked up with old acquaintance Holden and began robbing banks again. Holden and Keating knew George Kelly from Leavenworth, and when Kelly was released from prison, he sought out and worked with Bailey on several jobs — it was more a favor to Kelly; Bailey considered him second-rate.

In 1930 Bailey went to St. Paul, where he met Verne Miller. In September, the pair struck in Iowa, robbing the Ottumwa Savings Bank, the first of several jobs they worked together. Soon after connecting with Miller, Bailey met Freddy Barker, a 135-pound dynamo, who had also done time in Leavenworth for robbery. Miller, Keating, Holden, Barker, Barker's brother Dock, Alvin "Creepy" Karpis, and a handful of others formed a gang of sorts; actually it was more like a loose confederacy that worked on an ad hoc basis in different groupings. Together, these men were, more than any other group, responsible for the crime spree that swept the Midwest in 1933 and 1934; yet the federal government hardly knew they existed. Time and again authorities apprehended — and often convicted — innocent men for crimes this group committed.

The beginning of the end of Bailey's criminal life came in June 1932 at Fort Scott, Kansas, where he and others methodically robbed the Citizen's National Bank, escaping with their usual fluidity. Then in July, Keating and Holden were apprehended on a green at Kansas City's Mission Hills Golf Club when authorities searched Bailey, who was golfing with them, and found stolen bonds. Bailey was convicted and sentenced to a term of from ten to fifty years in Lansing, Kansas. On Memorial Day 1933, he led a massive breakout — joined by two men wrongly convicted of the Fort Scott robbery. The bureau correctly suspected that Frank Nash had supplied weapons to the escapees.

The bureau had sought Nash at least as far back as December 1931, after his own prison break, but in the wake of the Memorial Day Lansing breakout, its search intensified. The bureau dogged Nash to the bitter and controversial end.

By now the bureau had taken control of the Sankey manhunt. But even as it intensified its search for Frank Nash, it remained clueless as to Verne Sankey's whereabouts. Its search extended from coast to coast and from the Canadian border to Mexico; Canadian authorities aggressively pursued their own investigations. The bureau had inklings that Sankey might be in Chicago, Detroit, or St. Paul, and concentrated efforts there, but with no real leads.

Then in late May, a Chicago policeman spotted Sankey at a soccer game. Chicago authorities had been warned Sankey liked to hang out at sporting events — and bet on them — so they monitored such venues. When the officer saw Sankey, he gave chase, but Sankey vanished into the crowd.

The bureau's ire at being left out of the raid on the Sankey ranch in early March had resulted in a fissure with Denver police. Once federal charges were filed, the bureau simply froze Denver police out of their case. When the Justice Department took Youngberg to the Sankey ranch to search for the ransom, for instance, it failed even to notify Chief Clark. All this was more evidence of the bureau's distrust of, perhaps contempt for, local law enforcement.

The Boettcher kidnapping defendants' trial was set for May 23 in Denver, just after Youngberg's return from South Dakota. Before Youngberg was taken to South Dakota, however, he had been given assurances of leniency, so he pled guilty to kidnapping, conspiracy, and using the mails to extort. That left only Pearce and the two women to go to trial. Pearce held out for a deal that would set the women free and thought he got it, but was mistaken: when Pearce pled guilty shortly before the scheduled trial, the Justice Department authorized the women's release on their own personal recognizance — their promise to appear at future hearings. Naively, Pearce thought it meant that charges against them would be dismissed, but the government was not about to do so.

On May 27, Youngberg and Pearce appeared before Federal judge Symes in Denver for sentencing. Claude, Charlie, and Anna Lou Boettcher, as well as Fern Sankey and Ruth Kohler were in the courtroom. Pearce was characteristically nervous, constantly twitching his head and picking at his clothing. In contrast, Youngberg calmly faced the judge.

Prosecutor Carr called the men Sankey's "hirelings." "As far as we have determined, neither Pearce nor Youngberg has profited financially from the kidnapping," Carr told the Court. "Youngberg revealed the hiding place of the major part of his share and he claims he spent the rest."

Carr told the judge that Youngberg's reputation back home in Canada had been excellent. He also spoke well of Pearce, saying that he was a World War veteran and had been a good stenographer. Carr said, "The two principals in this case, Sankey and Alcorn. . . . used these men with weaker mentalities to put over the deal." Youngberg's lawyer, Joel Stone, told the judge that Youngberg had protested to Sankey and Alcorn at the ranch that they should return Charlie Boettcher to his home — a claim that, although true, was only part of the story.

Judge Symes considered Youngberg's clean record and his cooperation and sentenced him to two concurrent sixteen-year terms — meaning they would be served simultaneously — and fined him a thousand dollars.

Desperadoes Waiting for a Train • *91*

That made Youngberg parole-eligible in five years and four months. Symes was harsher with Pearce, sentencing him to twenty-six years — based, the judge said, on Pearce's prior record, which consisted only of two minor bad-check convictions. There was little doubt that Pearce's failure to cooperate with the government hurt him the most. On his arrest, he had acknowledged that Ruth Kohler was in the car with him when he delivered the final ransom notes and confirmed for Sankey and Alcorn that the ransom would be paid. Pearce refused, however, to sign a statement. The troubled but loyal Pearce had been defiant with the government.

"I will rot in jail before I'll do anything to implicate Mrs. Kohler," Pearce had told officers. "She did not know what she was doing when she went with me. She is innocent and I am going to do everything I can to prevent her from going to trial."

As they led Pearce into a cab for his ride to prison, a jailer told him, "You'll be all right if you behave yourself." Pearce's only reply was, "I'm countin' on nothin'. . . . They say I can't last very long in prison. Well, we shall see."

Youngberg also was visibly glum after sentencing. When he returned to his cell, his cell mates asked how it went. He told them, "Not so good. . . . The judge threw the book at me. I'll certainly be an old man when I get out. They gave me sixty years." He remained morose all afternoon until his lawyer, Stone, came to see him. "Why so down-hearted?" Stone inquired. "It could have been worse."

"Not much worse," Youngberg replied. "It was virtually a life sentence. I'll never live to serve it out." Stone then explained that the sentence had been *sixteen* years, not *sixty*, as Youngberg had understood.

The *Post*'s Charlie O'Brien interviewed the "overgrown, gawky, Canadian woodsman" before the U.S. marshal took him to Leavenworth. Youngberg was his usual overly candid self as he recalled his role in Charlie Boettcher's kidnapping.

"I was out of work and dead broke in Canada when I met Sankey and Alcorn in Winnipeg in early November," he related. Youngberg called Verne Sankey "a kindly employer. . . . Boettcher was nice thru it all. We often talked about his wife and about his folks. Gee, I felt awful sorry for him, but there wasn't anything I could do then, excepting to go thru with the deal."

In his naiveté, Youngberg told the reporter something he had clearly not mentioned to the Justice Department. "I've still got about $2,000 buried in cans on the Sankey farm," Youngberg said. "When I get out of prison I'll give half of it to pay my $1,000 fine and try to get a new start on the other half. I returned all the remainder of my share."

Fern and Ruth wept throughout the sentencing hearing. When Judge Symes pronounced Pearce's sentence, Ruth verged on hysteria, so much so that Ben Laska had to quiet her. These tearful courtroom outbursts would become routine under Laska's representation of the women.

Fern actually had a great deal to cry over. Days before, Ramsey County authorities had charged her as an accomplice in the kidnapping of Haskell Bohn, based in part on the claim of admitted conspirator Ray Robinson that Fern had participated. When the federal government released the women on their personal recognizance, Ruth was free to go but Minnesota authorities detained Fern and took her to St. Paul, where she was scheduled to face trial in three weeks. Laska arranged a good-bye with Echo and Orville at the family's Denver home, where the kids were staying with Fern's sister, Evelyn Moore. Fern hugged and kissed Orville and Echo and stroked their hair when it was time to part. She again lost her composure, screaming inconsolably as she clung tightly to her precious children. Authorities led her out of the home as the two bid their mother another farewell. "And don't forget to study hard," she tearfully urged. "And you always be a good girl, won't you, Echo." Fern gave Evelyn $290 in cash and a diamond ring for their care. It was all she had left.

Ramsey County's case against Fern Sankey was straightforward: Haskell Bohn drove into his St. Paul garage late one summer night in 1932 and was greeted by two armed men who loaded him in a car and taped his eyes. They drove Bohn to a house and led him to a basement. Bohn was treated humanely; he ate cooked meals served by a woman. The kidnappers had demanded a ransom of thirty-five thousand dollars, but lowered it to twelve thousand dollars. When the lesser sum was finally paid a week later, the men again loaded Bohn into the car, drove to Medicine Lake, near Minneapolis, and released him.

A few days before the St. Paul trial was to begin, Ben Laska commented that he had received a letter from Verne Sankey asking him to represent Fern against the Minnesota charges. When the remark hit the press, it created an uproar, forcing Laska to repeatedly deny that he knew the hunted man's whereabouts.

In his opening statement in St. Paul's Ramsey County courtroom, Laska told the Bohn jury of eight men and four women that Verne Sankey had "left his wife in the lurch" to face the Bohn charges and that he sought no advice from her — he just gave orders. Jurors heard Bohn testify to his limited knowledge of the two men who held him and the female who served some of the meals. The state then called convicted conspirator Ray Robinson. Robinson acknowledged to Laska that Fern had not participated in the actual kidnapping. He said Fern had gone into the basement where Bohn was held on one occasion. Laska asked him, "'Didn't she protest about keeping that man there and beg Sankey to turn him loose?'" Robinson admitted that she had urged her husband to release Bohn on about the third day of captivity.

Laska decided that the jury needed to hear Fern Sankey tell them she had not helped kidnap Haskell Bohn. It was a questionable call. In the witness box she spoke softly, haltingly; it was evident that she was extremely nervous. In answer to Laska's questions, she characterized herself as a dutiful wife who was unaware of her husband's actions. It was the same story she had given Denver police, The *Denver Post*, and Ramsey County authorities when they questioned her. As Fern spoke, she twisted a handkerchief with her hands.

Laska asked if she had ever heard from her husband since her Denver arrest. She answered "Only through you." This last statement brought Ramsey County district attorney Mike Kinkead, to his feet as he began his cross-examination. "Oh, so Laska told you where Sankey was." "No, sir," Fern replied. She allowed only that Laska told her he had heard indirectly from Sankey before her trial. The questioning on the subject went no further.

Fern admitted that Verne Sankey traveled widely and often took her along to places like Juarez, Mexico, and to various parts of Canada. When Kinkead prodded her to tell the jury what business took him to those venues, she quietly replied, "He's a gambler." Pressed further, she admitted that he also hauled liquor, "but never when I was along."

Kinkead bore down on Fern. She had stayed in Minneapolis that summer of 1932 with Verne and the children in the house they rented. How could she not know her husband was holding a hostage in their own basement? Finally she crumbled. Screaming hysterically, she admitted she knew Haskell Bohn was being held for ransom in the family home. The AP captured the scene: "After testifying she had prepared breakfast for young Bohn in the home, Mrs. Sankey nearly collapsed in the witness chair. Ben B. Laska of Denver, her counsel, and relatives rushed to her side and helped her arise as court recessed at noon."

Mrs. Sankey told jurors,

[I] begged and pleaded with my husband to release the boy. I told him I had two brothers and how I would feel if one of them were in such a position. But he told me to mind my own business. I pleaded with him again the following day, July 2, but with no results. The next day, July 3, I was so heartbroken and sick that I went to a hotel. I returned home July 4, but only to get some clothing for my children.

She told jurors that Verne Sankey never confided in her and that she was not with him when any negotiations were made.

The jury got the case in the late afternoon, deliberated for five hours, and found Fern Sankey not guilty of conspiring to kidnap Haskell Bohn. She smiled limply and slumped in her chair, able only to respond with a faint "I am so glad."

As Fern Sankey endured Kinkead's withering cross-examination in St. Paul's Ramsey County Courthouse, another major kidnapping was unfolding only blocks away. Hamm Brewing Company's thirty-eight-year-old president, William Hamm, emerged from the brewery's stately St. Paul headquarters during the noon hour. A well-dressed gentleman on the sidewalk reached out to greet him, placing his left hand on Hamm's right elbow. At that point, the greeter was joined by another man who approached from Hamm's rear and ushered him into a car that sped away. Inside the car, Hamm was presented with a ransom note for his signature and politely asked to bend down low so that he could not be viewed by passing motorists.

Like Charlie Boettcher and Haskell Bohn, William Hamm was the son of great privilege. With Fern Sankey on trial in the same city only a short distance away, it was difficult not to suspect her notorious husband. Purported evidence of Verne Sankey's involvement quickly surfaced. A taxi driver identified the man who gave him two dollars to deliver a ransom note as Sankey; the timing of Hamm's abduction drew attention back to Fern's trial testimony that Laska had heard indirectly from her husband. A tempest now brewed over *that* statement. The day after the trial, Fern steadfastly denied it. "That absolutely is not true. . . . I have had no word from my husband, have not seen him, and do not know where he is."

Ben Laska professed his belief that Sankey had nothing to do with the Hamm abduction, telling reporters, "I heard from him thru his 13-year-old daughter the day before I left Denver for St. Paul. . . . She came to my office and said: 'Bring back my mamma to me.'" That moment Laska decided to go to St. Paul to defend Fern Sankey, he said. But he had not answered the question—what did the girl say to you? he was asked. "I cannot tell you," Laska blurted. "Do you want me to get my throat cut?"

Nonetheless, Laska claimed not to know Verne Sankey's whereabouts. It was classic Laska; he was never shorthanded with quips. When word leaked during the Bohn trial that William Hamm had just been kidnapped, reporters asked Laska about a report that he himself was having Hamm held as a hostage until authorities released Fern Sankey. Laska replied, "Boys, I am a Jew. . . . Whoever heard of a Sheeney stealing a Hamm?"

The bureau's suspicions of Verne Sankey's involvement in the Hamm kidnapping were hardly allayed when they noticed Sankey's bullet-riddled Ford outside the Ramsey County Courthouse shortly after Fern's acquittal. It turned out that Denver police had released the souped-up sedan to Fern's two sisters, Evelyn Moore and Ruth Kohler, who drove it to the Minnesota trial, no doubt drawing more than a little attention.

In reality, Verne Sankey had nothing to do with William Hamm's kidnapping, but it would take months for the authorities to figure that out. The real culprits were the Barker-Karpis gang. Although the bureau knew about several of its members, it was still not yet aware of the extent of their affiliations with one another. The Barker-Karpis gang was audacious and possessed intimate connections both with St. Paul's underworld and its police department.

Several Barker-Karpis gang members were ex-bootleggers and knew that few businesses produced as much beer as St. Paul's Hamm Brewery, now that hops were again legal in cities across America. The gang had until then focused on robberies and saw Hamm as an obvious choice for their first kidnapping. After they abducted Hamm they demanded a contact person. Hamm offered the name of the company's vice-president of sales, William Dunn. It was too easy: Dunn was gang member Harry Sawyer's pal and also had close St. Paul mob connections. The gang presented Dunn with a $100,000 ransom demand. When Dunn delivered the bad news to the captive's family, Hamm's mother insisted that the police be informed — and the gang members got still another break: the St. Paul police force had been recently shuffled and Chief Tom Brown, long suspected — and correctly so — of mob affiliations had been demoted, although he remained within the department. Brown leaked crucial information to the gang.

Hamm's kidnapping stunned the nation as had Charlie Boettcher's four months earlier. It did not monopolize the front pages for long, though; two short days later, an even bolder event roused America from its late spring slumber.

As the bureau searched for Frank Nash, it closely monitored his known hangouts in Chicago, Kansas City, St. Paul, and especially Hot Springs, Arkansas, a favorite underworld recreation spot. The city's police chief and its chief of detectives allowed gangland figures to lounge in the health resort environment so long as they did not ply their trade in town.

As a result, the underworld mixed freely with the respectably rich and well-heeled.

On the same June 15 afternoon that jurors in St. Paul deliberated Fern Sankey's fate and William Hamm was kidnapped blocks away, bureau agents, accompanied by a couple other law enforcers, arrested Nash in Hot Springs, at the White Front cigar store owned by a man named Galatas, a Hot Springs underworld lord. Despite the agents' efforts to keep their travel route a secret, Nash's associates learned that the agents and Nash would arrive at Union Station on Saturday morning, June 16. They informed Nash's best friend, Verne Miller.

Miller contacted Johnny Lazia, the Capone organization's point man in the Kansas City racket. Lazia's influence was so pervasive that when a federal agent investigating Lazia's activities called Kansas City's police headquarters one day, Lazia answered the phone. Miller asked Lazia for local machine-gunner help, but Lazia declined. "You know the rules," Lazia replied. "No local boys."

At this point, the stories diverge. The official version is that Lazia suggested Arthur "Pretty Boy" Floyd and Adam "Eddie" Richetti, a couple of regional bank robbers who happened to be in town. What is known for certain is that the train arrived on time at Kansas City's Union Station at seven on that June Saturday morning. At about a quarter past seven, Miller and his accomplices were in the train station's parking lot, alongside one of the police cars. A few minutes later, the officers, with Nash in tow, left the building and walked toward the waiting vehicles. They led Nash to the front seat on the driver's side. Suddenly, a member of the group — likely Miller — shouted, "Put 'em up! Up! Up!" Each of the three gunmen, spread apart by several yards, stood with weapons raised. Miller was on the far end, submachine gun in hand, poised to fire. Immediately after the command rang out, Kansas City detective W. J. "Red" Grooms drew his gun and fired two shots.

Miller shouted, "Let 'em have it!" Nash cried out, "For God's sake! Don't shoot *me*."

The crackle of gunfire shattered the bright June calm. When it was over, five men lay dead: Kansas City police detectives Grooms and Frank Hermanson; bureau agent Ray Caffrey; and McAlester, Oklahoma, police chief Otto Reed, who had gone to Hot Springs only to identify Nash. Dead too was Nash himself. The gunmen leapt into their vehicle and fled. Several eyewitnesses collectively documented the path of the fleeing car as it burned through the city at high speeds, turning corners at times on two wheels. Eventually, it disappeared.

Addressing the nation in the aftermath of the slaughter, J. Edgar Hoover pledged: "No time, money or labor will be spared toward bringing about the apprehension of the individuals responsible for this cowardly and despicable act. . . . They must be exterminated by us, and to this end we are dedicating ourselves." Hoover's boss, Attorney General Cummings, ordered "the entire Justice Department on the trail of the killers." He used the killings as a platform, urging "better coordination of State and Federal activities." Cummings assured Americans that the government would "wipe out" the racketeers and gunmen.

In a few minutes' time, Verne Miller achieved what Cummings and Hoover had been unable to accomplish on their own. The brutality of the killings had galvanized the nation's outrage for the outlaw gangs. This, in turn, provided the crucial impetus for the passage of laws that would facilitate the bureau's rise as a national crime fighting force. The Justice Department's chief priority immediately became the capture of those responsible for what quickly became known as "the Union Station Massacre." Within days, the shooting became a symbol of crime in America.

It did not bode well for Verne Sankey's freedom.

Kidnapper, bootlegger, gangster — and family man — Verne Sankey is photographed during a family outing ca. 1932 with wife, Fern; son, Orville (left); and daughter, Echo. Courtesy Stephen H. Hart Library, Colorado Historical Society.

Charles Boettcher, Sr. Courtesy
Stephen H. Hart Library,
Colorado Historical Society.

Mrs. Charles Boettcher, Sr.
Courtesy Stephen H. Hart
Library, Colorado Historical
Society.

Claude K. Boettcher. Courtesy
Stephen H. Hart Library,
Colorado Historical Society.

Mrs. Anna Lou Boettcher, ca. 1928.
Courtesy Stephen H. Hart Library,
Colorado Historical Society.

Verne Sankey in custody, February 1934.
Courtesy Stephen H. Hart Library,
Colorado Historical Society.

Charles Boettcher II, on the morning following his return to Denver after being freed. Courtesy Stephen H. Hart Library, Colorado Historical Society.

Les Trois Tours, Charles and Anna Lou's home in Denver's fashionable Capitol Hill district. Charles was abducted at gunpoint from the car Anna Lou was driving as she prepared to park it in the garage. Courtesy Stephen H. Hart Library, Colorado Historical Society.

Colorado manager of safety Carl S. Milliken (right) and Denver police chief Albert T. Clark investigate Boettcher's kidnapping at the scene of the crime, the Boettcher home. Courtesy Stephen H. Hart Library, Colorado Historical Society.

Above. The Sankey Farm in Buffalo County, South Dakota. The muddy dirt road in the left foreground was the only vehicle approach. Anyone traveling this road could be seen from the windows, and the only door was on the far side of the house. Courtesy Stephen H. Hart Library, Colorado Historical Society.

At left. Arthur Youngberg. Courtesy Stephen H. Hart Library, Colorado Historical Society.

The kitchen inside the Sankey farmhouse. Behind the black-paneled door to the left of the stove was a stairway leading to the basement, where Boettcher was held. Courtesy Stephen H. Hart Library, Colorado Historical Society.

Sankey (center) is led by U.S. marshals into the South Dakota State Penitentiary at Sioux Falls. Courtesy Stephen H. Hart Library, Colorado Historical Society.

Mrs. Gordon Alcorn, Alcorn (center), and Deputy U.S. Marshal Art Anderson outside the Pierre, South Dakota, city jail following Alcorn's testimony for the federal government against Fern Sankey. Courtesy Stephen H. Hart Library, Colorado Historical Society.

Attorney Ben Laska prepares his clients, Fern Sankey and Ruth Kohler, for trial, May 1934. Courtesy Stephen H. Hart Library, Colorado Historical Society.

Carl W. Pearce. Courtesy Stephen H. Hart Library, Colorado Historical Society.

The Charlie Boettcher family ca. 1934. Charles and Anna Lou with daughters Ann (left) and Claudia. Courtesy Claudia Boettcher Merthan.

Claudia Boettcher Merthan in 2003 with sons Thurn (left) and Charles Boettcher Hoffman. Courtesy Claudia Boettcher Merthan.

Orville Sankey, Verne's son, in 2007.
Courtesy Nicole Shanks.

8

Enemies of the Public

The Union Station Massacre was only the beginning of a summer of crime run amok. In 1933 alone, midwestern gangs ransacked more than sixty of the banks that had been sufficiently solvent to reopen. Will Rogers posed a solution:

> We don't seem to be able to even check crime. Why not legalize it and put a heavy tax on it? Make the tax for robbery so high that a bandit couldn't afford to rob anyone unless he knew he had a lot of dough. We have taxed other industries out of business, it might work here.

To upper-class Americans' psyche, the more disturbing trend was the spate of kidnappings. Six ransom kidnappings quickly followed Charlie Boettcher's over a five-week span that summer. With each new abduction, Sankey rematerialized — at least in witnesses' imaginations. Authorities pointedly implicated him in no fewer than four more abductions over the next several months.

The day after St. Paul Police chief Thomas Dahill and County Attorney M. F. Kinkead concluded their unsuccessful prosecution of Fern Sankey, they and Minneapolis bureau agent Werner Hanni focused on Sankey's suspected role in William Hamm's abduction. They promised Fern that if she spoke candidly, she could go home to her family. Fern answered their questions — an enormous mistake that would in time haunt her.

The spate of kidnappings intensified the fervor across America for stronger laws. Thoughtful people referred to kidnapping as the most heinous of offenses. Said Edmund Pearson, then America's foremost writer on true crime, it will "be a very fortunate and comfortable day for the people of this country when some kidnapper sits down in the electric chair.... The crime of kidnapping ... is a piece of carefully thought out and calculated devilishness. ... The men who plan kidnappings ought never to be allowed outside a prison again."

Now with three major unsolved crimes on its hands — the Lindbergh and Hamm kidnappings and the Union Station Massacre — and with Sankey and Alcorn still on the loose, pressure increased on J. Edgar Hoover to produce results. The heat focused not just on the bureau director but radiated up the chain of command to Cummings and down to bureau outposts and special agents-in-charge, known as SACs. The times called for leaders to step forward and produce results and within the bureau in the summer of 1933, Hoover valued none of his agents more than Chicago's Melvin Purvis.

The twenty-nine-year-old Purvis was a graduate of University of South Carolina's School of Law. After practicing for a time in his home-town, he joined the bureau in 1927, just as Hoover was transforming the agency. Slightly built and a little more than five feet tall, Purvis was the sort of agent Hoover sought: the perfect southern gentleman — articulate, earnest, and law-trained. He soon caught Hoover's eye.

Purvis had recently transferred to Chicago from the bureau's Birmingham, Alabama, office. Although courtly, his persona bore a confidence that at times translated as cockiness. He wore double-breasted suits and straw boat hats. Unlike the other bachelor agents who roomed together in groups, Purvis lived in South Chicago with a single room-mate. He kept a horse in a stable on the city's outskirts and a chauffeur drove him to the Chicago bureau's nineteenth-floor offices in a Pierce Arrow. While he was ambitious and well-trained in the law, Purvis was unsophisticated about the ways of the underworld. That naiveté would repeatedly reveal itself over the next year.

In early July, a month after William Hamm's kidnapping, came news that notorious Chicago swindler John Factor had been abducted by men who demanded seventy thousand dollars in ransom. Chicago authorities suspected "some of the Sankey gang" but ex-Chicago policeman, Dan "Tubbo" Gilbert, then working as chief investigator for the Illinois attorney general, identified Chicago gangster Roger Touhy as the likely culprit in both abductions. Based on Gilbert's lead, Purvis sent his agents to accompany Gilbert to Elkhorn, Wisconsin, where Touhy gang members were being held following a car wreck. The agents placed the gang members in federal custody and took them to Purvis's Chicago headquarters.

Purvis himself interviewed a brash, ridiculing Roger Touhy about the Hamm kidnapping: "What do you mean a ham, Mr. Purvis? A ham sandwich? Or did I kidnap a ham steak?" The next day, William Hamm and several other witnesses viewed the suspects through a one-way mirror. Hamm was not at all confident the men were his abductors. In fact, he had told police shortly after his release a month earlier that his kidnapper resembled Verne Sankey. But a witness claimed he was confident Hamm's kidnappers were the Touhy gang. On July 25, armed with that single eyewitness account, Purvis announced that the bureau had established "an ironclad case against Touhy. . . . We have positive identification of all four of the prisoners. The government men worked carefully and thoroughly on this case, and we are sure of ourselves."

Back in Washington, a jubilant Hoover wrote to Purvis: "This is a splendid piece of work, which was consummated only by the untiring and resourceful efforts of the entire Chicago staff." The Justice Department charged the Touhy gang with the kidnappings of both William Hamm and Jake Factor. What the authorities did *not* know was that during Gilbert's tenure not a single mob-affiliated individual was charged with a crime. More important, neither the government nor the juries that eventually tried the Touhy gang for the Factor and Hamm kidnappings knew that at the time Gilbert fingered the Touhy gang, he himself was in league with the Capone syndicate to eliminate Touhy from competition.

Nonetheless, Purvis's announcement that he had conclusively solved both the Touhy and the Hamm cases provided Hoover an invaluable endorsement. Purvis had come through for Hoover when most needed.

Five days later—July 30, 1933—Attorney General Cummings named tough former Ohio prosecutor Joseph B. Keenan as his special assistant to head the Justice Department's Criminal Division and director of the administration's War on Crime. Cummings also appointed Hoover director of the "new Division of Investigation," an entity that combined the old Bureau of Investigation with the then obsolete Prohibition Bureau. These men, Cummings announced, would "conduct the nation-wide warfare against racketeers, kidnappers and other criminals." Hoover's agency would henceforth be known as the Division of Investigation.

Most of America still had never heard of Hoover but his political detractors of a decade earlier lurked. *Newsweek*, then in its inaugural year, noted the astonishment of some Washington observers at Hoover's appointment to the newly created post in light of his role in the Red Scare raids. *Collier's* Ray Tucker ridiculed Hoover's bureau, calling his men "immature gumshoes" whom criminals could too easily shake. There remained, in the summer of 1933, some truth in Tucker's assessment.

Two days after Purvis bought Gilbert's false leads, Sankey's kidnappings inspired another one, this time in the Southwest, where gunmen snatched wealthy oilman Charles Urschel from his Oklahoma City estate. A Tennessee-bred college dropout named George Barnes, a bootlegger who had on occasion hung out with Harvey Bailey and the Barker-Karpis gang, executed this abduction. Barnes used the name George Kelly. His second wife, Kathryn ("Kit"), whom he married in 1932, played a vital role in developing the myth of "Machine Gun" Kelly. Shrewd and persuasive, easily able to control her pliable spouse, Kit one day returned home with a gift for her beloved: a Thompson submachine gun. "Now we'll call you 'Machine Gun Kelly,' George. That should scare the hell out of bank presidents." Despite the hair-raising moniker, Kelly never posted a single documented killing. In fact, he shot a man only once—in the arm—during a bank robbery.

Kit brainstormed for ways to make lots of money, and quickly. The Lindbergh child kidnapping repulsed her, but Verne Sankey's kidnapping of the adult Charlie Boettcher intrigued her. She followed the Boettcher kidnapping story as it unfolded in the nation's newspapers and began formulating a plan of her own to kidnap a wealthy adult male.

Those plans culminated on the July 22, 1933, when her husband and Albert Bates abducted Urschel and held him for $200,000 ransom. Kelly and Bates held their prey for nine days, releasing him unharmed at Norman, Oklahoma, after elaborate negotiations finally produced the ransom outside a Kansas City hotel.

A few days later, President Roosevelt pledged from his Hyde Park home that he would marshal the full force of the federal government against what he called society's greatest foes — kidnappers and the racketeers. Roosevelt called them "enemies of the public," a phrase already coined in a similar form, but one which would gain renewed currency over the months to follow.

After Charles Urschel was released, San Antonio SAC Gus Jones, the gritty Texan gunslinger Hoover brought into the bureau to give it some practical lawman experience, interviewed Urschel. The victim recalled hearing a remark at a gas station about "broom corn," and the twice-daily sound of an airplane overhead. Jones searched airline flight schedules to pinpoint the location where Urschel had been held.

Jones used that information and some other facts pointing to the Kellys' involvement, and led agents in a raid of a ranch owned by Kitty Kelly's mother and stepfather, Ora and Boss Shannon. There he found Harvey Bailey asleep on a cot, a machine gun nearby. Bailey vigorously denied involvement in the Urschel kidnapping, but he was implicated by eight hundred dollars in marked ransom money police found in his possession. In reality, Bailey had *not* been involved: Kelly had given him the ransom money to repay a debt.

It was irony of the highest order: This bank robber par excellence, never caught robbing a bank, was now implicated in a crime in which he had no involvement. But as a prison escapee and a suspect in the Union Station Massacre, Bailey was still one of America's most wanted gunmen.

A federal grand jury in Oklahoma City indicted Bailey, the Kellys, the Shannons, their son Armon, and several others. Joseph B. Keenan led the prosecution, announcing that he would seek life terms for each of the suspects. The press portrayed Bailey as "the worst criminal unhung — the close associate of Al Capone . . . leader in the Denver Mint and the world's biggest bank robberies; the brains and chief trigger man in the Union Station Massacre." The possibility that Bailey might be innocent of the particular crime with which he was charged appeared lost on a press, which seemed ready to assume his guilt.

Within hours of the bureau arrests at the Shannon farm, Denver police arrested Kelly's partner, multistate robber Albert Bates. Bates's arrest created quite a stir in Denver. Shortly after his capture, Bates sat in the Denver jail, singing the blues. "Sittin' in the jailhouse, looking at the wall, and a redheaded woman was the cause of it all." He claimed an old acquaintance had informed on him. "The dirty rat beat it to the police and told them I was 'hot.' That guy never was good." Then Bates heard a reporter nearby and covered his face under the jail's mattress. "Will youse guys beat it? I hate reporters, all reporters." He was asked if he knew Harvey Bailey. No reply. Verne Sankey? Again, no reply.

As reports circulated that witnesses' lives were being threatened through letters and phone calls, Keenan stated that Bailey and Bates would be transported to Oklahoma City "without specific desire for secrecy, and if any of their confederates want to meet the cavalcade along the road, any desire they may have will not be denied them." Keenan's words were unambiguous: the government would not be intimidated by what had happened in Kansas City.

Denver buzzed with a report that "Machine Gun Kelly" had been seen in North Platte, Nebraska, headed toward Denver, presumably to free Bates. A city motorist later claimed Kelly had stolen his license plates. Denver's police captain Armstrong insisted that Bates remain in Colorado to stand trial for a bank robbery. Armstrong was beginning to sound like Joseph Keenan: "Let Kelly and his gang come on," he blared. "We are ready." But the feds insisted that by prosecuting Bates federally, they could do more to stem the tide of kidnappings sweeping the nation. Two days later, Denver surrendered Bates to the Justice Department and moved him out of the police jail into the county jail, in part due to concerns about a Kelly-led escape attempt.

The Bates-Kelly episode grew even stranger. On the night of August 17, a chauffeur waiting for his employer outside Denver's Brown Palace Hotel saw a man who looked strangely familiar, then realized he was gazing into the face of "Machine Gun Kelly," whose image had appeared in the *Denver Post* that day. When the bull-necked man saw the driver stare at him he quickly covered his face. Just then the woman for whom the driver awaited exited the hotel and her chauffeur drew her attention to the man.

"Oh, what a terrible looking man—Isn't he terrible, George?" she asked, and then suffered the same revelation as her driver: "Why, that is the man whose picture was in the *Post*—the man in the kidnapping." The woman was Anna Lou Boettcher, still recovering from the emotional strain of the events six months earlier. The man that Anna Lou and her driver (and others) saw may actually have been Kelly. He had been in St. Paul in early August to exchange some of the ransom, then headed for West Texas. He was reportedly spotted in North Platte on the day before his Denver sightings, a fact broadcast by Denver police, and was later at the ranch house of a West Texas relative.

The Kellys had assumed near mythical status in the minds of police and the press. Their auto, supposedly sixteen-cylindered and armored, created the aura of invincibility. One Denver detective expressed this view: "Like Bates and the other Bailey men, [Kelly] does not know the meaning of fear."

Bates, however, was learning it. Assistant Attorney General Keenan's announcement following Bates's capture contained these well-chosen words: "I am not attempting to be melodramatic, but I want to say that the government desires to see [Bates, Bailey, and Kelly] not behind prison bars, but hanged or electrocuted. The government will have no hesitation in delivering them to state authorities to answer state charges where the death penalty is provided by law."

Bates, who had hired Ben Laska to defend him, somberly looked at Laska and asked, "What does he mean?"

The public's reactions to bank robbery were noticeably less vociferous than its reactions to kidnapping. There existed among ordinary people a belief that the country's financial institutions had failed them. They had lost trust in one of society's hallowed institutions. The sentiment, clearly discernible among much of the country's middle and lower classes, was that bank robberies held a certain poetic justice. Bank robber Harry

Pierpont gave expression to the sentiment: "I'm not like some bank robbers—I didn't get myself elected president of the bank first." But by the summer of 1933, it was becoming increasingly clear even to jaded Americans that things were getting out of hand.

While all the commotion caused by the Hamm and Urschel kidnappings and the ongoing spate of bank robberies distracted government agents, Verne Sankey moved about quietly, vigilantly in Chicago, exchanging his ransom money, and monitoring events around him.

9

Summer of Discontent

South Dakotans found themselves clutched in the grip of a long hot summer in 1933. Because little snow had fallen the previous winter, there was little runoff in the spring. Already by May, Sankey's neighbors had looked out on parched soil and braced for another dry season. The first week of June at Gann Valley produced nary a day with a high below 96; the thermometer flared as high as 103. Later in the month it got even hotter.

Still, as bad as things were on the ranch that summer, they were even worse where Fern Sankey was residing. Just before her St. Paul trial in June, Charlie Boettcher had flown to Deadwood to provide testimony to a federal grand jury that indicted the Sankeys, Alcorn, and Kohler for his abduction. The same night the Bohn jury acquitted Fern Sankey, a U.S. marshal rearrested her on the South Dakota arrest warrant. She remained jailed in St. Paul until late June, when federal authorities delivered her into the hands of the marshal in Sioux Falls.

Fern Sankey's South Dakota return drew attention from a local press curious about the demurely attractive Dakota native and mother of two. Fern Mae Sankey had come to the Wilmot area with her homesteader parents when she was two, in about 1896. Her family took land about a mile south of the Sankeys. There she met and fell in love with the

Sankeys' youngest son, three years her senior. Now the thirty-nine-year-old brunette dressed stylishly — not pretentiously, but in a way that complimented her features and cloaked her with an unmistakable dignity. She possessed a polite, courteous, and soft-spoken demeanor.

The *Argus Leader* pursued the story of the once-tried-and-acquitted mother with zest. The undisputed king of South Dakota newspapers was published in the state's largest city. Its editor, Charles M. Day, was born during the Civil War to an Iowa Supreme Court chief justice. Day transformed the Sioux Falls *Argus Leader* from a small daily with local competition and a circulation of around seven hundred into the state's most influential and widely read publication. In 1933, the *Argus Leader* rarely restrained itself from printing a story that appealed to the prurient or sensational. Day's successor, Fred C. Christopherson, praised Day for his "sharp eye for news and [noted that] nobody could keep anything out of the *Argus Leader*."

The *Argus Leader* could not resist the story of the jailed mother's brief visit with her daughter:

> A child's love for her mother, whetted and enhanced by long days of absence, bloomed tearfully in the Minnehaha county jail. . . .
>
> "Hello, Mama," the little girl cried through her tears, "I am so glad to see you again." Mother and daughter then embraced. It was the first time Echo had seen her mother since she had been brought here from St. Paul.

Fern and her family had friends back in Buffalo County, and on July 19 her Gann Valley benefactors secured five thousand dollars for her bail by pledging assets. Finally, after seven and one-half months, Fern returned to the ranch and to Echo and Orville. The loyal Chopskie brothers, the Sankeys' closest neighbors and friends, had tended to the farm during much of their long absence. It was Mike Chopskie who had brought Echo to visit her mother and who became a surrogate parent for the Sankey kids. But the burden to care for the Sankey farm wore on the Chopskies. While Fern was jailed in St. Paul, Mike wrote telling her they could not continue much longer. "The turkeys have been laying eggs faster than cold and rain make hailstones," he wrote. "Get somebody down here as soon as possible because you know how hard it is to raise turkeys." To solve this problem, after her release from Colorado custody, Ruth Kohler took the kids to the ranch and cared for them there, tending to the farm as well. On Fern's return to the ranch and her kids, Ruth stayed on.

Mike Chopskie hung around, too, despite his earlier pleas. Claude Boettcher had hired Laramie, Wyoming's county sheriff, George Carroll, to lead his investigation. Carroll shadowed Sankey family members and in August trekked to the ranch seeking clues. He obtained little help but found the Sankeys, Ruth Kohler, and some other family members there, including Fern's father. He also noticed that Mike Chopskie seemed to be in charge of the farm's management, "putting in nearly all of his time." What, Carroll wondered, was his interest there?

As Fern again settled into farm life, the Denver woman whose tip broke the Boettcher kidnap case encountered terror. Frances Ellsworth's husband was a Denver bootlegger and a friend of both Sankey and Pearce. It was her fellow dress shop employee, Lucille Fletcher, who had gone to police after she overheard Frances Ellsworth repeat Pearce's incriminating comment. Shortly after going to police with Pearce's remarks that same day, Ellsworth left her dress shop job. Now the Ellsworths, Fletcher, and their former employer, J. C. Feinberg—who had also gone to the police—each claimed a portion of Claude Boettcher's twenty-five-thousand-dollar reward.

Shortly after the claimants' names became public, the Ellsworths began receiving threats. On July 29, four shots from a machine gun shattered a front window in the Ellsworth's home and pierced the divan on which Frances had been seated moments earlier. Police initially suspected Sankey, but as time passed they began to suspect others.

In early September a car with three occupants attempted to run William Ellsworth's car off a Denver street. Ellsworth averted a crash by steering onto the sidewalk, but two weeks later he was not so fortunate. This time, a car overtook Ellsworth's, forcing it into a curb. Three men leapt out and fractured Ellsworth's skull. Chief Clark said one of the assailants resembled Verne Sankey. Was it retaliation for his role in fingering Sankey? Had the competition for the reward taken a churlish turn? Or had Ellsworth simply suffered the consequences of a bad boot-legging transaction? The mystery and violence surrounding the Boettcher reward claimants was far from over.

It was a summer of upheaval across America. While Roosevelt's first one hundred days had created a surge of optimism, most Americans noticed little improvement in their lives as the summer wore on. Some escaped by suicide. While it is a myth that Wall Street businessmen jumped to their deaths when the stock market crashed in October, 1929, the truth was worse. As the Depression wore on, suicides spiked dramatically, far exceeding those that had occurred just after the crash. The worst years were 1932 and 1933. The Sankeys, the Boettchers, and others whose lives they impacted would each, in time, contribute to those dreary numbers.

Suicides among men surpassed those committed by women. Parents were especially vulnerable to the impulse, often daily encountering the fear of not knowing whence food for the next meal would come. Although relatively few acted on their impulse, legions contemplated it. The *Argus Leader* reported stories of druggists, government officials, bankers, and farmers all purposefully ending their lives.

Sometimes the suicides took on an air of maudlin humor. An AP story told of a hapless soul: "John Holman failed in his attempt to commit suicide but the coroner says he died trying. Holman, who was 63, was found dead of a fractured skull in the cellar of his home with a noose of insulated wire clutched in his hands and a box at his feet. Coroner L. U. Zech said last night he believed Holman fell and struck his head while groping in the dark for a place to tie the loop." A Sioux Falls woman placed a long-barreled pistol to her chest, pulled the trigger, but suffered only flesh wounds from which she quickly recovered. A week later she left home on the pretext of going to the store, but instead slipped into her neighbor's home. Knowing no one was there, she found a .410 shotgun and turned it on herself, this time succeeding. She left behind a bewildered husband of fourteen years to bury her body at Mt. Pleasant Cemetery and ponder for a lifetime the note she left him.

Bleak as circumstances had become in the summer of 1933, life still offered small compensations. Sports and entertainment temporarily distracted. Ruth eventually signed another Yankee contract. Even the Bambino, however, could not draw destitute fans through the turnstiles. Major League attendance fell to its lowest numbers in years. The Depression affected the box office too.

America's best entertainment that summer was not sports nor movies but the real life crime dramas to which the country was treated almost daily. The Oklahoma City trial, *U.S. v. Albert Bates, Harvey Bailey et al.*, in September, amused some, appalled others, but generally fascinated the nation. Bates, Bailey, the Shannons, their son Armon, and several others — a total of nineteen defendants in all — stood trial for kidnapping Charles Urschel, the first trial to be held under the new Lindberg Law.

Ben Laska represented Bates at trial, having accepted a ten-thousand-dollar retainer he would one day regret. In September 1933, however, Laska reveled in the attention the case generated, some of which centered on his budding national reputation as a skilled kidnap defense attorney. The little magician wearing a pince-nez, seldom sat still, darting up to the bench to argue the smallest points, hands fluttering in the air. "When not arguing with the court or fellow attorneys, Laska engages in apparently violent whispered arguments with his hulking blond client, Albert Bates. In Bates's hearing, Laska makes derogatory remarks about his client during recesses.

"I've got the hardest job of anybody on the defense side, taking care of this lug."

At one point in the trial, Keenan threatened to prosecute any defense lawyer who accepted ransom money as a fee. Laska became indignant. "Can you imagine anyone making a statement like that?" he asked. He pulled a roll of bills from his pocket. "Look, this bill is Boettcher money; this one is Bohn, and here is Hamm money." When someone suggested he should have been a showman, he replied, "Hell, I am one."

For all the circus atmosphere that had descended on Oklahoma City, the Justice Department had not yet reeled in the biggest Urschel fish — the Kellys. When Hoover's second-in-command, Harold Nathan learned that the Kellys would appear at a Chicago tavern at an appointed time on September 21, he alerted Melvin Purvis, who was to arrange the

Kellys' arrest. There was just one little hitch: Purvis somehow forgot. The bureau lost the Kelly scent once again.

The bureau again picked up their trail in Memphis, where agents tracked them to a house where the Kellys were staying. Inside, agents found empty bottles of Old Log Cabin whiskey strewn about and "Machine Gun Kelly" and Kit passed out in separate rooms. While the men canvassed the house, Kelly, apparently awakened by the noise, entered the room where agents worked, clad only in his underwear. A .45-caliber in hand, Kelly stared down the end of a double-barreled shotgun. When the agents told him to drop his gun, the legendary outlaw's only response was, "I've been waiting all night for you." It hardly seemed so to the officers, strung out as he appeared. Nonetheless, the bureau had its biggest ever catch.

On September 30, 1933, four days after the Kellys' capture, the jury deliberated briefly over the fates of Bailey, Bates, and the others. The evidence against Bailey was circumstantial but jurors deemed it sufficient. The trial was over a mere month after the defendants' arrests. Bailey, Bates, Boss and Ora Shannon, and several others received life sentences. Within *sixteen days* of their capture, the Kellys were tried, convicted, and sentenced to life in prison.

The Urschel convictions marked the government's first demonstrable success in the war on crime: the defendants had been brought to trial speedily and with resounding success. The message was intended not only for criminals but also for the weary nation — kidnappers and other law breakers would be caught and the government would deal with them summarily and severely.

It was clear, too, that the general public was becoming fully engaged in the war with the criminals, the ultimate of whom, in the minds of many, was the kidnapper. A few months earlier, a Kansas City jury sentenced Walter McGee, who had been inspired by Sankey's kidnapping of Charlie Boettcher, to death for the ransom kidnapping of a young woman, even though he returned the victim unharmed and confessed his role. There the prosecutor argued: " The nation is watching this courtroom today. . . . As soon as a message is sent out from this room that a jury has said a man shall hang by the neck until he is dead for this kidnapping, you will have taken a big step to stop this wave." It was the national crusade's first death sentence in a kidnapping case.

The public's exasperation with government's failure to stop crime turned to vigilante action frequently that autumn. Although the extra-judicial practice enjoyed an ignoble history in America long before the 1930s, the summer and fall of 1933 produced a rush of vigilante fever. Often, it had more to do with intimidating blacks than enforcing law. In Opelousas, Louisiana, in September, vigilantes wrested from a sheriff's deputy African American John White, suspected of attacking a white farmwoman, and riddled him with bullets.

In November, an angry San Jose, California, mob broke into the county jail after a two-hour struggle with authorities and seized two confessed kidnapper-murderers. A "whooping, cheering crowd" of six thousand watched as a throng dragged the men, partially stripped and beat them, then strung them on a tree. California's governor James Rolph lauded the lynchings, calling them a lesson to the nation's kidnappers. The governor expressed a desire to place all kidnappers into the custody of "those fine, patriotic San Jose citizens who know how to handle such a situation," and promised pardons to any participants.

Two days later, in St. Joseph, Missouri, forty national guardsmen and police were unable to prevent a mob from entering the jail where muscular but terror-stricken Lloyd Warner, a nineteen-year-old black man, was being held for attacking two women. When the mob reached the county jail's third floor, they met the sheriff, who guarded the cell where Warner cowered. As the mob approached, the sheriff unlocked the cell, allowing the crowd to descend on the man. The mob stripped Warner to the waist, then kicked and beat him, cheered by an estimated seven thousand onlookers. Once outside, it rushed Warner to an elm tree, threw a rope over a high branch, and slipped a noose around his neck. He tried to speak but shouts of "string him up" drowned out his pleas.

In photos preserved from such scenes, vigilantes and their audiences routinely posed for the camera. They are chilling images, laden with countenances of satisfied white men, often women and children, too, energized by the excitement of forced death, grinning for the photographer.

By the end of September, only Verne Sankey and Gordon Alcorn remained at large from the year's major kidnappings. The bureau continued to monitor Sankey's family for indications where he might be hiding, but their efforts achieved paltry results. In Chicago Sankey laid low with one exception: he ventured out to feed his gambling addiction. He convinced himself that racetrack betting and the futures market were effective ways to exchange his hot funds for clean money but it got the best of him in Chicago as it had elsewhere. Commodities futures were his worst nemesis—the ultimate pitfall for a farmer drawn to the fascinating enterprise of casting educated guesses about whether prices will rise or fall at a given point in the future.

If not for his gambling addiction, Sankey might have maintained a genteel existence indefinitely, but his nature simply overcame him. He ploughed money into wheat futures during the depths of the worst depression and drought the nation had ever witnessed. Once he got down, he could not extricate himself. Eventually, Sankey dropped at least ten thousand dollars on commodities futures alone.

Other than this single toxic vice, Sankey lived simply and quietly, exhibiting that pleasant, cheerful demeanor in his low-key rural way. He drew to himself no undue attention. He did not, however, forsake female companionship. Sankey—or William Clark as he was there known—met an attractive twenty-eight-year-old waitress, Angeline Sindzenski, who also used the name, Helen Mattern. He hired her as his cook/housekeeper; eventually the pair shared an apartment. Sankey even met Mattern's father, who considered them a well-matched couple. Yet, Sankey also remained in contact with Fern and the children, usually by telephone. In September, Fern visited the Windy City, and the couple attended the 1933 Chicago World's Fair. She came again in December, this time meeting Mattern. Verne introduced her to Mattern, as his sister, Mrs. Moore.

In addition to laundering his cut of the ransom by investing in commodities futures and by betting at the horse track, Sankey changed money in a more piecemeal way. He took a twenty-dollar bill, or sent Mattern with one, to the neighborhood drugstore to purchase a toiletry — talcum powder, shaving cream, perhaps razor blades. The cashier returned the clean change. It was far cheaper than a fence. In the process, Sankey accumulated massive quantities of items, so much so that the products filled several suitcases that somehow found their way to the basement of the Sankey ranch, stacked one on another.

At the ranch, the Sankeys' lender sued to foreclose on his mortgage. The family faced loss of the land and their home if the principal of $2,480 together with unpaid interest was not paid in full. The press reported that the unsatisfied mortgage was the catalyst that had driven desperate farmer, Verne Sankey, into the kidnapping racket. It made wonderful print but bore little truth. It is almost certainly true, though, that Verne Sankey planned to pay off the mortgage with some of the Boettcher ransom proceeds. He had most likely used some of his other ill-got gains to build the ranch house in the first place and to pay the two thousand dollars toward the land's purchase price. After Sankey was implicated in Charlie Boettcher's kidnapping, however, there was simply no practical way for him to satisfy the mortgage. After all, any money he gave Fern could only further embroil her in the kidnapping.

Of course, while much about the Sankeys made them unique in Buffalo County, their foreclosure problems did not. The entire county consisted of only a few thousand residents but they had witnessed dozens of mortgage foreclosure proceedings and sheriff's sales in 1932 and 1933. It is difficult to overstate the effects the drought and poor farm prices had on the state, particularly its central region. Only one in three Buffalo County farmers had tractors; almost no farm home had electricity. Although in 1930 about half of Buffalo County's farms had telephones, as the Depression wore on, many surrendered them, so that by the end of the decade, only one in three had them. Land values, too, reflected the slide. Land worth more than seventy dollars an acre in 1920 had, by 1933, diminished in value to around twenty dollars per acre.

The devastating drought, coupled with years of depressed farm conditions, forced proud, independent South Dakotans onto the welfare rolls at rates higher than those anywhere else in America — fully 39 percent by the end of 1934. Among farmers, it was worse; more than half received emergency relief—as many as four of five in some counties.

The short grass area of central and western South Dakota became some of the most distressed areas in the country. Conditions got so bad the New Deal government enacted a series of emergency programs, which provided seed and feed loans, cattle purchases and subsistence grants, together with public works projects. It all did little to stem the losses.

It is not surprising that by 1933, South Dakota was well into the throes of an exodus that exceeded that of Oklahoma, Texas, Kansas, and every other state in the nation, save North Dakota. During the 1930s, South Dakota's net out-migration totaled almost one-fifth of its population, mostly from its farm and ranch population.

The depth of the crisis is shown by the number of sheriff's deeds— issued to the buyer at the conclusion of a foreclosure proceeding. No such deeds were issued in Buffalo County from 1920 through 1922, but over the next five years such deeds became common, averaging seventeen a year. The issuance of sheriff's deeds spiked in 1929, but the worst year was 1933, in which thirty such deeds were issued.

The Sankeys were not alone. There were plenty of others whose land was being auctioned off at foreclosure sales, and many more who owned no land at all. Statistics, though, were of little comfort to Fern Sankey as her farm was readied for the auction block.

10

Harvest of Wind and Dust

In October, Purvis obtained information linking Verne Sankey to the Lindbergh baby's kidnapping and death. Purvis refused to disclose either the nature of the information or its source, but it came from St. Paul prosecutor Kinkead, who, based on a string of circumstantial evidence, had been theorizing since spring that Sankey might be the Lindbergh kidnapper.

Early the same month, Denver police supplied Purvis with a tip that Sankey was in Chicago, frequenting the Windy City's race tracks and the Chicago Grain Exchange. The bureau and Chicago's chief of detectives posted policemen at the exchange and at all tracks throughout the city and searched all "known criminal haunts," but Sankey did not surface. It was, they thought, as if he intuitively sensed he had been sighted and moved further underground. The truth was far less arcane: what the unrelenting bureau agents did not know is that Sankey's sizeable commodities futures losses had left him with little cash.

In Denver the escalating violence surrounding the Boettcher reward claimants placed Mayor Begole in a quandary. He preferred to wait until authorities captured Sankey and Alcorn before distributing the reward funds, knowing those responsible for their arrest would assert a claim. But if the men were never arrested, he would be criticized for not paying it out. Finally, after conferring with Claude Boettcher, Begole formed a committee comprised of Claude's personal attorney and close friend, James "Bruce" Grant, City Attorney James Parriot, and former district attorney and ex-Klan fighter Philip Van Cise. The committee's charge was to recommend apportionment of the reward among the current claimants and set aside an amount for those who would aid in the capture of Sankey and Alcorn.

In October, the committee recommended that $10,000 be set aside for Sankey and Alcorn's arrest and that the other $15,000 be immediately distributed. It then convened a hearing at which the claimants argued their cases for a reward share. In an atmosphere charged with excitement, petitioners lined the walls of Parriot's office, each with their own pitches. This was serious money. The average laborer, after all, earned about $450 a year. The committee recommended that the largest shares go to Frances Ellsworth ($3,400), her husband ($400), and Lucille Fletcher ($2,200). The other $4,000 was to be divided among law enforcement officers who participated in the investigation. Claude issued the check and the mayor distributed the $15,000. A calm ensued among the reward disputants, but it proved only temporary.

Claude Boettcher's own investigation proceeded quite separate from and in many ways superior to the ongoing efforts of the bureau and Denver police. The day after Charlie's kidnapping, Claude had engaged Denver investigator Walter Byron and his team of gumshoes — ten different operatives in all — to pursue leads in Charlie's abduction. The investigators remained on the job after Charlie's release. Throughout the spring, summer, and fall, Claude hired others who roamed the States and Canada pursuing leads, including Wyoming sheriff George Carroll, who journeyed as far and wide as any investigator. Carroll also shadowed Sankey family members, seeking clues. It was for Claude an expensive undertaking, but the man was true to his word: he was going to do whatever it took to recover what he could and capture the fugitives.

Bruce Grant represented Claude in Denver with help from Robert Stearns. Grant supervised much of the investigation while the Sioux Falls law firm of Boyce, Warren, and Fairbanks handled legal matters in

South Dakota. The investigators hired other investigators to assist them, drivers and pilots to transport them, and paid informants who yielded tips. Bills flooded into Claude Boettcher's office from every direction and Claude paid them all. Even Lars Rasmussen, Buffalo County's sheriff, wrote Claude, seeking pay for his efforts — while on the county payroll — to uncover the $9,360 ransom share buried at the ranch. "I was positive that it was your money, and I did all that I possibly could do to save it for you. Do you think that I'm entitled to any reward of that money? If not, say so. I have been treated pretty rotten over the Boettcher kidnapping case, ever since last spring."

All investigators and attorneys on Claude's well-coordinated team reported ultimately to him. When requested to do so, Claude shared his information with the bureau. Strikingly, the federal government's internal coordination was so poor that the bureau actually asked Claude to provide information he obtained from the U.S. Postal Inspector's investigation. Claude also sent Agent Hanni a copy of the Canadian National Railway's investigation into the case.

The investigations, both private and governmental, uncovered interesting facts and stories about the fascinating kidnapper, bootlegger, and turkey farmer, Verne Sankey, and generated no lack of theories concerning his whereabouts, but no hard leads.

In October, Fern Sankey got more help at the ranch. This time, it came from within her family. Calista Gibbs — Ruth Kohler's daughter — and her husband, Roy, lived in Denver, where he worked as a power lineman. Shortly after Charlie Boettcher's release, authorities arrested Roy Gibbs as part of the kidnapping investigation but Gibbs convinced bureau agents that he knew little and had played no role in Charlie Boettcher's abduction, so authorities released him. Unable to find employment in Denver, Gibbs moved west to the village of Algona, Washington, where he cut timber and picked peas for area farmers while Calista worked at a roadhouse. That fall, Gibbs offered his services and Calista's at the Sankey ranch, since Fern and Ruth had no man on the place to help with chores. When the Gibbs arrived in late October, Roy performed odd jobs around the place for Fern. In exchange, Fern provided the Gibbs food and shelter. The arrangement seemed mutually beneficial. Fern and the kids, together with their new housemates, reestablished some of the routine that had existed in their lives before they left South Dakota for Denver the previous December. Echo, back in school, was a member of Gann Valley High's ninth-grade class.

The miserably hot, dry summer was now a memory; the grasshoppers that had infested the ground had died off. But Gann Valley's main street suffered a major setback when fire destroyed several buildings.

In late October 1933, with the Kellys, Bates, and Bailey safely behind bars, Verne Sankey, Gordon Alcorn, and Verne Miller were the bureau's key fugitives.

J. Edgar Hoover had meant what he said in the days after the Kansas City Massacre: It was not enough that Miller be "exterminated"; the bureau must be the exterminator. The bureau finally caught up with Miller and his mate, Vi Mathias, at the apartment of the Millers' good friend, Bobbie Moore. Despite an extensive stakeout and the aid of Purvis's twenty-four-year-old secretary, Doris Rogers, who grew up in the Huron, South Dakota, area and knew Miller by sight, Miller escaped in his Auburn, a hail of gunfire pelting the sleek automobile.

In the aftermath, everyone pointed fingers — some with both hands and in different directions. There was plenty of blame to go around. Agents' cars were out of position, unable to give quick chase; men left their posts at crucial times. The chief blunder, though, had been Hoover's instruction to take Miller only once he had left the apartment. Hoover feared a shootout with Miller because children had been in the apartment. Miller almost certainly would have shot it out, but after the children left for the night that danger no longer existed.

On November 29, a citizen reported a suspicious-looking bundle in a vacant lot near a culvert. It was Verne Miller's nude body, his legs drawn tightly against his torso, his body wrapped with clothesline, skull crushed, the victim of the sort of gangland execution he himself had often flawlessly executed. The national manhunt for Verne Miller was ended not by the bureau, but by the gangland itself. Pastor F. E. Lochridge, conducting Miller's funeral in Huron's First Methodist Episcopal Church, spoke from Galatians 4:7: "Be not deceived; God is not mocked: for whatsoever a man sows, so also shall he reap." It had worked that way in Verne Miller's life.

Nothing the state had experienced that year — not drought, nor extreme heat, nor Depression, nor even the shocking notoriety of Verne Sankey and Verne Miller — prepared South Dakotans for what they were about to experience that fall — a storm unlike any in history. It unleashed itself on the state and across the Middle West on Armistice Day 1933. The *Argus Leader* recounted it the next day:

> A raging dust storm . . . plunged Sioux Falls into darkness
> Sunday. . . . Gathering menacing momentum at 9 o'clock Sunday
> morning, a 40 to 60 mile wind howled throughout the day, snapping
> off telephone poles and trees, smashing windows, grounding fences
> and picking up so much dust that motorists drove with lights ablaze,
> and Sunday merchants and housekeepers spent the day under artificial
> light.

The winds swept topsoil across the plains and cast a surreal pall of darkness, surpassing even the darkest night. Inside homes and businesses the eerie glow of lamps illuminated the fine dust that silted into every crevice, through window cracks and into drawers, cupboards, even iceboxes. In a few hours it ended but the land had been permanently changed. Roads had disappeared beneath drifts of dirt; ditches were full; farmyard lawns could no longer be seen, supplanted by the dirt dunes. Machinery lay buried in piles of topsoil.

It was the first of some sixty dust storms to strike the state through the following May. The loss of nutrient-rich topsoil would have long-term adverse effects on the land, but the harrowing images of uncontrollable winds piling dirt into ditches and driving it inside buildings and homes left psychological scars that lasted lifetimes.

In the midst of drought and dust, Buffalo County residents experienced still another strange calamity that fall — a cloudburst that caused massive flooding along the Missouri River at Fort Thompson, killing eight people. "Where would it all end?" the people wondered.

Ten days after the Armistice Day dust storm, Sheriff Lars Rasmussen auctioned off the Sankey ranch from the front steps of the Buffalo County courthouse. Rasmussen presented the high bidder with a certificate that entitled him to a sheriff's deed one year from that date unless the Sankeys redeemed by paying the full amount owed. During that year, the Sankeys could remain on the property.

Through it all, Fern and the children struggled to survive on the ranch. The Chopskies helped care for the turkeys and livestock and the family grew some wheat, but grasshoppers licked off what little emerged. It was a subsistence lifestyle; at times, the family went without enough food.

Gann Valley native Dureene Petersen knew Fern and Echo in those years. In 1932, Mrs. Petersen, then Miss Appleby, earned her teaching degree from South Dakota State College and returned home to launch a teaching career that would span thirty-six years. It was during the darkest days after the kidnapping, Petersen recalled, that the Gann Valley community again rallied around Fern and her children, providing as they could to help the family survive.

And while the Sankey foreclosure sale transpired without violence, many others that fall were not so peaceful. Farmers and ranchers — sober men, Baptists, Presbyterians, Catholics, Democrats, Republicans — saw the equity they once held in their land vanish as they became unable to pay even the interest on their mortgages. The Farm Holiday movement sprang up in 1932 as a result, its aim to raise farm prices by stopping the shipment of food to cities. Serious men spoke of revolution. In May 1933 Congress passed the Agricultural Adjustment Act (AAA), a program designed to provide cash to impoverished farmers and ranchers in an effort to avert threatened violence. Unfortunately, it became effective too late to benefit farmers for the 1933 crop year. Among those joining the chorus for farm price supports was South Dakota's governor, Tom Berry, a Democrat from West River — that vast expanse of grassland west of the Missouri River. Berry operated a thirty-thousand-acre ranch, wore a white cowboy hat, and walked as though he still had on his chaps and boots. His looks and expressions reminded people of Will Rogers.

In the spring of 1933, Congress also established the Federal Emergency Relief Administration [FERA], which represented the largest organized effort ever undertaken in the United States to relieve nationwide distress. By fall, however, the program had not yet had sufficient time to implement programs that could meaningfully impact rural life. Harry Hopkins, appointed by Roosevelt to head the agency, sent investigators into the countryside to report actual conditions across America. His first investigator, Lorena A. Hickok, was a veteran news woman and Eleanor Roosevelt's intimate friend. Over the next year and a half Hickok visited the most devastated areas of the nation, frankly reporting to Hopkins what she saw and heard.

Hickok came to Aberdeen, South Dakota, near her hometown of Bowdle, in early November 1933 to observe conditions. From there she wrote to Hopkins:

> If the President ever becomes dictator, I've got a grand idea for him. He can label this country out here "Siberia" and send all his exiles here. . . . A more hopeless place I never saw. Half the people — farmers particularly — are scared to death.

Hickok's portrait of South Dakota life was bleak.

> Such dreary little towns. Traveling across the Northern part of the state, I visited three towns where I lived as a child — Milbank, Summit and Bowdle. . . . Real estate in those towns is nothing but a liability. . . . West of the Missouri — out where governor Tom Berry used to be a cow puncher — things are even worse. Somebody today made the remark that that country should never have been opened up. I think he was right.
>
> Miles and miles and miles of flat brown country. Snow drifts here and there. Russian thistles rolling across the roads. Unpainted buildings. . . . Now and then a shabby little town spread out around two or three gaunt, ugly green elevators. What a country — to keep out of!

Hickok also witnessed unrest flare at farmer's meetings, saw normally docile men seething with discontent. She reported to Hopkins that in the first week of November a Farm Holiday group attacked a sheriff, ripped off his clothes, and beat him.

Traveling the state from north to south, she saw farmyards without so much as a spear of prairie grass and horses and cattle more often than not listless and emaciated. She wrote of women afraid to hang their wash out because the "hoppers" ate the clothes off the line. Hickok's meeting with Governor Berry left her impressed and buoyed by Berry's inexplicable optimism. "There's two crops out here that never fail," he told her, "Russian thistles and kids." But optimism was a rare and precious commodity.

Hickok was stunned by the severity of conditions she saw in the region, which exceeded those in any other area to which she traveled. She concluded that South Dakotans' most dominant emotion was fright — of low prices, dust, grasshoppers, and wind. "The thing that is behind whatever unrest there is in the state, is sheer terror. Those people are afraid of the future. Some of them are almost hysterical. . . . The whole darned state apparently is drying up and blowing away."

By late December, far away from the desperate conditions on the dry, dusty prairie, bureau agents searching for Verne Sankey found only a cold trail. Despite later claims by the bureau and Denver authorities that they closely monitored the activities of Fern and her family, in December, Echo became at least the second Sankey family member to journey to Chicago. At her father's request, she spent Christmas with him. The bond between the two was strong, and she had grown extremely lonesome for him. Until her dad kidnapped Charlie Boettcher in February 1933, Echo had rarely been apart from him for more than a few days at a time, so when Verne called to ask her to come to the city for Christmas, she eagerly accepted.

She traveled by car to St. Paul and from there by train to Chicago, the modes of travel chosen for her so she could more easily slip past bureau agents and others monitoring the family's activities.

Echo was just shy of fifteen. There was in her sugary eyes and soft demeanor the hint of a child who had been exposed to much that was not good for her, and whose life had experienced moments of piercing emotional pain. She was growing into a talented young woman, both a musician and a tap dancer. Echo had begun her education in Melville, Saskatchewan, but had bounced among several schools before joining the kids at the Victory School in the country south of Gann Valley.

Seventy years later her lifelong friend, Carol Stephens, remembered the day in 1932 that Echo first came to the brown prairies around Gann Valley. Carol herself had arrived there only two years earlier. When Echo joined the group at Victory School she and Carol comprised the entire sixth-grade class and quickly became soul mates. The girls' homes were separated only by gentle hills and occasionally they would serenade one another, Echo playing her saxophone and Carol the accordion.

Stephens's memories of Echo's father were also fond. She recalled an affable, seemingly carefree man who loved his family and would do most anything for them. Before the Boettcher kidnapping, Verne Sankey seemed like the ideal father. He provided well for his wife and children, took them on family trips, attended his daughter's school programs, even performed with her. Like his daughter, Verne Sankey was nimble on his feet and loved to dance and entertain. Stephens vividly recollected the 1932 Congregational Church Christmas program, at which Sankey and Echo performed their saxophone duet.

When Echo returned from Chicago, Fern began to develop suspicions about Roy Gibbs. Perhaps it was his demeanor or something he said; it could have been the sort of questions he asked Echo about her father. The suspicion may even have been raised by Verne himself after learning that Gibbs was living at the ranch. Whatever prompted her concerns, Fern began to suspect that Gibbs was passing information to bureau agents. When she confronted him, Ruth defended Gibbs. The sisters became embroiled in a heated argument, during which Ruth voiced hostile feelings she harbored toward Verne. The argument escalated to the point that Fern ordered Ruth and the Gibbs off the ranch. The sisters' relationship had been seriously, perhaps irreconcilably damaged. The Gibbses returned to Denver. Ruth drifted to Minneapolis.

11

America's Original Public Enemy No. 1

The concept of a "public enemy" entered the American lexicon in the mid-1920s when Chicago's leaders realized they needed to act forcefully and adeptly to combat the city's leading Prohibition mobsters, who had already acquired a celebrity rivaling that of movie stars. The problem was how to do it. The job fell largely to the city's Crime Commission, formed by the Chicago Association of Commerce years earlier. The commission — a hundred lawyers and other businessmen, armed with their own investigative staff — had as its sole function helping police identify the city's most heinous criminals. As a part of its efforts, the commission conceived the "public enemies list."

The inaugural list, released in February 1930, contained the names of twenty-eight men prominent in Chicago organized crime. The list, headed by Al "Scarface" Capone, quickly captured the public's interest, and other jurisdictions soon followed Chicago's lead, identifying and ranking their own public enemies.

It has been frequently written that on the national scale, the concept of a "Public Enemy No. 1" was the product of the press rather than the government. One author attributes the origin of the term's use by the Justice Department to the 1935 movie, *G-Men*, after the film adopted the term from the Chicago Crime Commission. Others record that the

Justice Department at least informally assigned the moniker to John Dillinger in June 1934, suggesting he was the first.

However, the historical record and the Justice Department's own public statements in early 1934 point to a different conclusion. As glamorous and popular as the Chicago list and others like it became, Justice had no equivalent by late 1933. In light of the events of the previous summer, in October Chicago Crime Commission president Frank Loesch invited the Justice Department to appropriate its "public enemy" model on a national scale. Hoover resisted identifying a "No. 1 public enemy" as it seemed to him a title that any ego-driven criminal would strive after. Thus, the bureau refrained from ranking criminals until the 1950s when it issued its "Ten Most Wanted" list.

Even while Hoover took no action to identify a chief public enemy, his superiors at Justice — Homer Cummings and Joseph B. Keenan — could not resist its appeal. As 1934 dawned, "Machine Gun Kelly," Bates, and Bailey had been stowed away serving life terms, and Verne Miller had been found dead the previous fall. Double-kidnapper Verne Sankey — and the still unidentified Lindbergh baby's murderer — loomed largest on the bureau's watch list. Events would soon also entwine Sankey with the Lindbergh abduction in the bureau's mind.

John Dillinger and members of his gang were captured later that month in Arizona and returned to Indiana to stand trial for bank robbery and murder. The day agents delivered Dillinger to the custody of Indiana's Crown Point jail in late January, Keenan — Cummings's second-in-command at Justice and prosecutor of the War on Crime — announced the capture of "America's Public Enemy No. 1." His words echoed in newspapers throughout the nation.

Keenan was not speaking of Dillinger, however.

Dillinger had only recently emerged in the national media. The *New York Times* first mentioned him on Christmas Eve 1933. Charlie "Pretty Boy" Floyd, although wanted as one of several suspects in the Union Station Massacre, was still a little-known commodity outside the Southwest, except to the bureau. Lester Gillis ("Baby Face Nelson"), the Barkers, and Alvin "Creepy" Karpis would all become well-known to the bureau and to America in the months that followed, but in the winter of

1934 the bureau's knowledge of them was sketchy. None of these men were on Keenan's mind that wintry day. The man Keenan referred to was Verne Sankey. It developed like this.

As the bureau's pursuit of Sankey and Alcorn wilted in the hot, dry 1933 summer sun, agents tracked down Roy Gibbs in Washington and made him a proposition. They knew that Sankey, always intimate with his family, would not stop communicating with them. Figuring that Gibbs, as Ruth Kohler's son-in-law, might be its best bet for locating Sankey, bureau agents asked him to go undercover to learn Sankey's whereabouts. Reminded of Claude Boettcher's hefty reward, Gibbs agreed to cooperate.

Gibbs's disingenuous offer in the fall of 1933 to help at the ranch was the main component of that undercover effort. After he and Calista arrived there on October 21, Gibbs watched and listened carefully, at first arousing little suspicion. Fern occasionally spoke by telephone with her husband and in time, Gibbs learned Verne Sankey was somewhere in the Chicago area. Gibbs also discovered — and passed onto bureau authorities — that Sankey had twice ventured back to the ranch for visits. Gibbs left the ranch only once, for a secret St. Paul debriefing by bureau agents.

After Fern ordered Gibbs, Calista, and Ruth off the ranch, Gibbs returned to Denver with the lead that Sankey was living at 4823 North Damen Avenue in Chicago. At this same time, the Gibbs's marriage was failing. After Fern ordered the couple to leave the ranch, Calista, who had not known of Gibb's treachery, left him.

Still, Gibbs did not immediately take his case-breaking information to the bureau, perhaps hoping for a reconciliation with Calista. Whatever the cause, he did not contact the bureau until January 22 — several weeks after leaving the Sankey ranch — when he placed a telephone call to Denver bureau agent Val Zimmer. Zimmer, however, was away in Salt Lake City on other business. So Gibbs went directly to the top: he telephoned J. Edgar Hoover in Washington and told him he had important news about Sankey. Hoover ordered Gibbs to leave immediately for St. Paul to meet with bureau agents. When he arrived in St. Paul on January 27, Gibbs delivered the information the agency had fervently sought for nearly a year. Purvis's men stormed the Damen Avenue apartment on the city's north side but Sankey had moved. Still, the lead held incalculable value: agents learned from interviews that Sankey used the alias, W. E. Clark and had been living at the apartment in the company of Helen Mattern.

As Purvis and his Chicago agents closed in on Sankey, evidence of more nefarious Sankey plans surfaced back in South Dakota. Ramsey County, Minnesota, prosecutor M. F. Kinkead, while investigating Sankey's role in St. Paul's Haskell Bohn abduction, searched the Sankey ranch basement and uncovered evidence that incriminated Sankey in two other planned kidnappings, each involving American sports stars. Prosecutors found this information in a letter file that contained financial data about Babe Ruth and boxing great Jack Dempsey. One paper contained Ruth's photograph with the notation, "will present this."

When the Bambino learned that he had been the subject of Sankey's kidnapping plans, he was first incredulous then slightly perturbed: "I never got any letters from him or anything, but I don't want him coming my way unless I can get my hands on a bat," the slugger quipped.

Kinkead made another, more ominous discovery at the ranch: newspaper accounts of the Lindbergh kidnapping case. Even before his find, Kinkead had suspected that Sankey was involved in the Lindbergh child's abduction and now his suspicions gained traction in circumstantial evidence. After all, the Lindbergh, Bohn, and Boettcher kidnappings occurred within a year of one another, well spaced, to allow ample time for planning each. They were among the earliest and most significant of the recent spate of ransom kidnappings. A cursory examination of the handwriting used in the Boettcher ransom notes added to Kinkead's suspicions: the Boettcher notes in Sankey's handwriting bore a resemblance to those sent to the Lindbergh family. The authorities had also learned that Sankey had placed telephone calls to New Jersey in the weeks leading up to the Lindbergh abduction. The fact that Boettcher and Charles Lindbergh were said to be close friends heightened speculation about Sankey's involvement in both abductions.

Kinkead relayed his suspicions to St. Paul Bureau chief Werner Hanni, with whom he was working on the Bohn case. The evidence also drew the attention of Colonel Norman Schwarzkopf, who, as head of New Jersey's state police, was the man in charge of the Lindbergh investigation. With fresh leads and new suspicions, the bureau pressed its search for Sankey, now its chief at-large outlaw.

By January 1934, the government's resolve to crush the kidnapping racket was reaching its zenith. In his annual report to Congress, Attorney General Cummings urged legislators to strengthen the federal government's authority to fight kidnappings and other major crimes by adopting his twelve-point plan to combat crime. Bureau director Hoover, in his segment of the report, conceded that the nation had experienced more kidnappings in the year since the Lindbergh Law's enactment than at any other time in history, but insisted the effort to combat kidnapping had increased dramatically.

Even President Roosevelt devoted a segment of his 1934 State of the Union Address to the subject of kidnapping and rampant crime, framing crime as a threat to national security. He, too, urged Congress to adopt Cummings's twelve-point plan.

In the midst of increased national attention, kidnappers in January 1934 claimed another St. Paul victim: banker Edward G. Bremer disappeared as he dropped his daughter off at a local school. The son of Adolf Bremer — a close Roosevelt friend who owned the controlling interest in Jacob Schmidt Brewing Company — Bremer, like Charles Urschel, was a prominent Democrat. His captors held him for $200,000, twice the sum paid only seven months earlier for William Hamm, Jr.'s, release. Predictably, Verne Sankey immediately again became the chief suspect.

But Sankey had nothing to do with Bremer's abduction either. The day Bremer was snatched, Sankey was in Chicago on a bus bound for Detroit. Financially, Sankey was sinking fast, having gambled away nearly all his money in less than a year. Now, the hustler who relished the feel of a wad of greenbacks, who had nonchalantly surrendered his railroad job while millions searched for work, was himself forced to do the same. That day Sankey hoped to check out a Detroit delicatessen he heard was for sale.

As Sankey sat on the bus that afternoon, there was a buzz on the street that a bank robber named Dillinger had just withdrawn twenty thousand dollars from East Chicago, Indiana's, First National Bank. The robbery's significance to Sankey at the time had nothing to do with who had perpetrated it. Sankey's concern was that, with the robbery so near north Chicago, police would likely stop and search buses leaving the city. He contemplated hopping off the bus and abandoning the trip but he was so low on funds he did not want to forfeit his return ticket. So he remained on the bus and, as it turned out, police did not search it. He returned to Chicago soon after.

Authorities would eventually learn that the Bremer kidnappers were the same men who had nabbed Hamm: the Barker-Karpis gang. The gang was confident, even cocky, in planning and executing Bremer's taking, and they had good reason. They had seen others tried, sometimes even convicted, for crimes they themselves had committed. Most important, the gang had a shameless inside contact. After Hamm's kidnapping, St. Paul police established a squad to protect other wealthy businessmen from abduction but incredibly, the department appointed its Hamm case informant and former chief, Thomas Brown, to head the squad. Brown leaked crucial information to the gang about Bremer's habits that enabled them to find and abduct him.

In light of January's events — the discovery of the planned Ruth and Dempsey abductions, the suspected Lindbergh connection, and finally, Bremer's kidnapping — Hoover ordered his agents to intensify the Sankey search. Agents and police were already hot on his trail.

In canvassing Chicago's north side in search of Mr. Clark's new home, bureau agents did not need to look far. He and Helen Mattern had taken a modest apartment two miles away, just north of the Chicago Cubs' Wrigley Field. What's more, Sankey continued to frequent his old Damen Avenue barbershop. It was a two-chair affair, operated by John Mueller, with whom Sankey had developed a friendly relationship. Sankey had his mail delivered to Mueller's shop, and routinely stopped for a shave, haircut, a massage or other tonsorial treatment.

Sankey had seen newspaper descriptions that referred to three prominent moles on his face, and decided to have them removed. So, on a mid-

January day, Sankey had a physician remove them with an electric needle. While the incisions healed, Sankey let his beard grow, but Mueller continued to cut his hair. He appeared again at the barbershop on Friday, January 26, a day before Gibbs reached St. Paul. Sankey received his mail, but his face was still too tender for a shave.

Days before Sankey's moles were removed, Purvis got another crucial tip. Like so many others before it, this tip fell into his lap. A north-side Chicago resident, Mrs. Carrie Fischer, had noticed a picture of Sankey in a Chicago newspaper and recognized him as a man whom she had seen in the North Damen neighborhood and who frequented Mueller's barbershop. The net was closing more tightly around Sankey.

Then days after the Gibbs lead, Purvis located Sankey's new home — an apartment at 4062 Kenmore Avenue, across from Chicago's Graceland Cemetery and north of Wrigley Field. Purvis decided not to try to take Sankey at his apartment, recalling reports that Verne Sankey vowed he would never be taken alive. So, instead of storming Sankey's home, Purvis waited for Sankey to place himself in a vulnerable position. Because bureau agents still had no authority to make arrests or carry firearms, local law enforcement was a necessary component of any plan to take Sankey, and Purvis handpicked several Chicago policemen to assist his agents. They monitored John Mueller's barber shop, waiting for Sankey to show.

The bureau's failure to capture Verne Miller in Chicago three months earlier was still fresh in agents' minds; the decision not to strike immediately while Verne Miller remained in Bobbie Moore's apartment had cost the bureau dearly — it left them unable to fulfill Hoover's vow that Miller would be exterminated by the bureau's hand. Purvis's plan now was that police and bureau agents would wait at the barber shop until Sankey came in for a shave or haircut. Once he was seated in Mueller's chair, reclined and draped with the barber's sheet, the agents and Chicago policemen would take him.

If this sounded more like the strategy of lawyers than G-Men, Purvis and his agents *were* young lawyers, after all — often with more aptitude and appetite for the law itself than for its enforcement. A shoot-out was not their idea of a good day on the job. They had not gotten law degrees, as Doris Rogers recalled a lifetime later, to be shot by some crazed outlaw. The reality was far different than the image the bureau and its writers were creating for its agents. And in fact, in a matter of months, shoot-outs involving agents would become much more common. But not in January 1934.

Purvis's plan had a vulnerability, though: what if Sankey sensed the bureau was closing in and stopped coming to Mueller's shop? Worse yet, what if he bolted his apartment and fled Chicago?

Purvis went to Mueller's barbershop on Saturday, January 27, and showed Mueller a photograph of Sankey. Mueller acknowledged it was his customer, W. E. Clark. Purvis and his men staked Mueller's barbershop, inside and out, but Sankey did not show. They returned on Monday when Mueller opened his shop and they set up their posts. Again Sankey was a no-show. The vigil continued throughout Tuesday and resumed on Wednesday, the last day of January. At times, agents slept in caskets at the undertaking business next door. By then, Sankey had developed some serious facial growth which left him looking like a bum — not a bad disguise but Sankey was vain to a fault and unwilling to surrender his appearance even when his freedom depended on it. So it was that on a chilly Wednesday afternoon, January 31, 1934, Verne Sankey returned to Barber Mueller's shop to restore his clean-shaven charm.

Chicago police sergeant Thomas Curtain recounted what followed.

> We knew [Sankey] had sworn never to be taken alive and we took plenty of precautions. We let him get all set in the barber's chair, with the big sheet wrapped around him.
>
> Then we stepped in with guns in our hands while the barber's back was turned. [Chicago policeman] Donovan laid back, with two pistols, ready for any kind of a break. [Policeman] Lynch and I walked up, one on either side, and pushed the muzzles of our guns against Sankey's bald head.
>
> I said: "Don't move, Verne. We're police officers. You're under arrest."
>
> With that, he started up and we grabbed him and flung him back on

the chair. We gave him a quick frisk and he didn't have a gun. Then we made him stand up. I warned him again about giving us any argument.

"That ain't what I was going to do when I started to get up," he said. "I didn't know if I should give up or not. I was thinking of running to make you shoot. You might as well kill me, anyway." . . .

He had no weapons, but in the hem of his overcoat we found a half dozen pills. He said they were poison and he intended to commit suicide, but he didn't get a chance to take them. . . . We knew he was plenty tough, and we figured we would have to shoot it out with him when we got him, but it didn't break that way.

Purvis watched the arrest from a distance. It was an enormous morale boost for him and his beleaguered men after the demoralizing escape of Verne Miller months earlier.

At the time of his arrest, Sankey was the chief suspect in nearly every major unsolved kidnapping in America — Haskell Bohn's, Charles Boettcher's, Edward Bremer's, the Lindbergh child's. His arrest seized headlines across the country: "America's Public Enemy No. 1 Captured as He Lies in Chicago Barber Chair."

Purvis released no information until calling Hoover. Hoover's superior, Keenan, the Justice Department's gritty general of the War on Crime, made the announcement to the nation. "This means the end of the man who is really America's Public Enemy No. 1. We have him now and you can be sure that we'll keep him. He's much too important a man to be allowed any chance to escape and we'll find a safe jail for him."

Keenan's statement set off a buzz; it was the first time the U.S. Department of Justice publicly identified an individual as the nation's chief public enemy. Many in and out of government suspected the Justice Department had proof linking Sankey to the Lindbergh child's abduction; reporters queried Purvis about a Lindbergh connection.

"We will question him about that crime," Purvis replied, "and all others of importance until we are thoroly [*sic*] convinced he had nothing to do with them."

When reporters reached J. Edgar Hoover about Sankey's failure to get to the poison pills he carried, Hoover replied, "He had no chance."

As police drove Sankey away in handcuffs, barber John Mueller reveled in the attention he garnered but also lamented the fact that for six months he had given Sankey shaves and haircuts, oblivious to the bounty on his head. "And to think of all the times I had that man in my chair," Mueller sighed. "I never dreamed he was Sankey."

After agents delivered Sankey to Purvis, they raided Sankey's Kenmore Avenue apartment, where they found a small cache of weapons, a large supply of ammunition, and $3,450 cash in a tin box. They also found the attractive twenty-eight-year-old Helen Mattern, the woman who had once been Sankey's maid, and who had been living with him for two months. Mattern spent the remainder of the day in custody shedding tears, appearing convincingly bewildered by the events. She professed that she had never heard of the desperado Verne Sankey and knew nothing of the presence of any weapons in the couple's home. "Mr. Clark never spent much on me," she told agents. Their life together had always been quiet and orderly, she said. Most of all, she pleaded, she had no idea that her "Mr. Clark" was a kidnapper.

The manager of the apartment building validated her claim. "They looked like the nicest sort of people," the stunned manager said. "I thought they were a country couple who came to the city for the winter. They were really model tenants, never made any fuss and nobody saw much of them. The woman looked like a nice girl. She never used makeup. When the federal agents came, I almost fainted, I was so shocked."

Sankey had that effect on people.

Police also came across a letter addressed to Claude Boettcher. It was written in Sankey's pen shortly after Charlie Boettcher's release, but never delivered. In the letter, Sankey, full of invective, explained that he had *again* kidnapped Charlie Boettcher, this time for revenge.

When — [obvious reference to Charlie Boettcher] was taken in
February you were told not to notify police, but you disregarded those
instructions. Now that I have him safely hidden you can do as you
please, but I will tell you here that my life does not mean a thing to me
and if I am caught and if anyone gets near our hideout — will be the
first one to die. . . . You and him have made plenty of innocent people

suffer on that deal and we will see that you and yours suffer. . . . There is to be no perfumed money or no new bills as they were last time. . . . I am doing this more for revenge than money this time as life means nothing to me. Now . . . [t]here will be no letters back and forth. . . . . No more gun battles by taking your word. You are dealing with the same person in flesh, but not the same person in heart and mind.

I got out at Greeley . . . to shoot it out with those bulls. I was ready to die then, but I wanted to crack down some of them before they got me even more determined to do so, especially to get even with you and — .

Sankey concluded the letter, "I will keep my word even to the killing. If you are in doubt ask any of my friends whom I sold liquor to in D. [Denver] They will tell you if my word is good."

It was a window into Sankey's soul. He was obviously bitter; yet it was the acrimony of the irrational. By Sankey's reckoning, Claude and even Charlie Boettcher had wronged him. The shootout in Greeley had obviously frightened him. More than anything, though, Sankey's anger seemed to well from the knowledge that he had ultimately failed to outwit law enforcement and, far worse, that his hidden identity had been exposed to his children's shame. He had been forced to lead the life of a fugitive, a life that could lead to no more than an anonymous freedom, knowing he could never again live among his loved ones and friends.

As Sankey passed the long Chicago hours, it burned him that Claude Boettcher had outwitted him. What's more, it showed Sankey's warped self-image as an honorable man who kept his word, unlike the vile Claude Boettcher. Honorable — at least, for the business he was in.

If Sankey had ever been serious about kidnapping Charlie Boettcher a second time, he quickly abandoned the notion. He apparently had not even settled on a ransom amount, since the letter contained none. Perhaps he gave up on the idea after his falling out with Alcorn. The most likely explanation is that he wrote the rambling epistle in a fit of rage and frustration, then set it aside.

In the wake of Sankey's capture, the Justice Department announced it had solved twenty kidnappings since instituting its campaign in March

1933 following Charlie Boettcher's abduction. Edward G. Bremer remained a hostage two weeks after his nabbing, but Sankey's arrest lifted Bremer family spirits because authorities and the press suspected his involvement. Thomas F. Cullen, the former SAC of the New York bureau office, then an International News Service correspondent, found similarities in what he termed the "daring manner" in which Bohn, Boettcher, and Bremer all had been seized, the locale from which they were taken, and as Cullen put it, the "cool calculation" employed in each case.

Sankey's capture also reinvigorated the languishing Lindbergh investigation. Investigators who examined the Charlie Boettcher abduction remained impressed that its careful planning resembled the Lindbergh crime. The Justice Department dispatched Sankey's handwritten Bohn and Boettcher ransom notes to its newly created crime laboratory for comparison with notes sent to Colonel Lindbergh. When police found poison pills in Sankey's possession, they recalled that the Lindbergh family watchdog had become ill several days before the kidnapping and speculated that it had been poisoned by the child's kidnappers to disable it. Investigators also found similarities in the mode of operation Sankey and the Lindbergh abductor employed. They believed the Lindbergh kidnapper had operated alone or, at most, with a single accomplice and knew Sankey was a "lone wolf" of sorts. He had used others to assist in his crime but they were lackeys more than gangsters.

These and other circumstantial bits of evidence made New Jersey and bureau authorities — desperate for a solution to the Lindbergh baby's murder — anxious to hear what Verne Sankey had to say for himself.

Armed with extradition papers and eager to interrogate Sankey about his role in the Bohn case and his suspected role in the Bremer case, Ramsey County, Minnesota, prosecutor M. F. Kinkead and St. Paul police chief Thomas Dahill hustled to Chicago when they learned of Sankey's capture.

After police captured Sankey, they took him to the bureau's downtown Chicago offices on the nineteenth floor of the Bankers Building. Purvis and his agents interrogated him in a marathon session lasting some thirty hours. Purvis's personal secretary that day was young Doris

Rogers. Sankey's face lacked color, and he was trembling as he passed her desk. Seventy years later, Rogers recalled Sankey's capture and the interrogation techniques Purvis and his agents employed. Sankey and other suspects were questioned, Rogers remembers, without stenographers present. "We had two competent stenographers [who] could take dictation for weeks and still transcribe it." But the agents preferred their own notes and their interrogation sessions were generally closed. The youthful Rogers served as a receptionist at her front-desk post. "That doesn't mean that I was receiving anyone," she said. "I was usually stopping them."

Rogers rarely sat in on interrogations but she knew nearly all the agents professionally and socially. From her desk she caught the flavor of the agents' interrogation methods. Rogers paints a picture of the 1934 Chicago bureau's questioning procedures that varies from some portraits of the day.

"These [agents] were all lawyers—well-educated men. They would have asked questions until they bored the suspects," she recalled. Rogers witnessed none of the abusive interrogation techniques allegedly practiced by the bureau in that era. "There were no heavy-handed tactics, no shouting. The interviews were decorous things. I don't think that any abuse or strong-arming was involved [in the Chicago office at that time]."

Purvis normally delegated the questioning to subordinates and seldom sat in on the interrogations for any length of time, instead stepping in and out. Sankey's case was different. Purvis led much of the questioning as a dozen bureau agents stood guard about the room. This was long before the U.S. Supreme Court interpreted the Constitution to afford an accused the right to be represented by an attorney during custodial questioning. Sankey was on his own. He did not remain silent under Purvis's grilling nor did he seek a lawyer. Instead, he forthrightly admitted his involvement in the Bohn and Boettcher cases but denied any role in Bremer's abduction.

Purvis came away from the Verne Sankey interrogation intrigued. He found Sankey oddly pleasant, disarming, even engaging. It was obvious to him Sankey was bright enough to have masterminded two or more major kidnappings, yet no trace of such a character emerged from their hours together. Sankey was sad; at times during questioning he wept. In fact, he was so low, bureau agents feared he might leap to his death from one of the room's windows. But he was also a storyteller with Purvis, candidly recounting episode on episode about the days after he and Alcorn released Charlie Boettcher. Photographs taken of him during the questioning show him at times laughing heartily, often grinning. In fact, he was so frank with his interrogators about his crimes that they suspected he might be trying to distract them from others to which he was not confessing.

The closest Sankey came to revealing what drew him to the life he had chosen slipped out when he discussed his love of true crime magazines. He could read them for hours, he recalled, yet was contemptuous of the approach employed by the criminals who inevitably got caught. "I decided that I could improve upon the methods," he recalled, "and I proceeded to try it." The only time during the long hours of questioning that Sankey exhibited anger was when Purvis suggested he had been involved in the Lindbergh child's abduction. Sankey then turned curt. "I am a man. I would kidnap a man," he told Purvis indignantly. "I would never kidnap a child."

By the time Purvis finished his interview of Verne Sankey, he doubted Sankey had anything to do with the Lindbergh child's disappearance. Beyond his own credible denial, Sankey had a reputable alibi witness: his old Gann Valley friend and lawyer, Harold Brown, Buffalo County's states attorney. Brown informed South Dakota authorities that, on the day that kidnappers abducted the Lindbergh child, he had been with Verne Sankey at Gann Valley. Later that same day, Brown reported, Sankey left for Minneapolis. After the Purvis interrogation and with Brown's alibi, suspicions concerning Sankey's alleged involvement in the Lindbergh abduction gradually subsided. The Chicago Crime Commission's Frank Loesch hailed the capture of Sankey and others in the city as a courageous overthrow of gun government.

Even if he had not been the Lindbergh kidnapper, Sankey was a big fish the Justice Department had reeled in. Keenan made it clear he would lead the Sankey prosecution and viewed a speedy trial as vital to the war on crime. The only remaining question, where would Sankey be prosecuted? Once authorities satisfied themselves that Sankey had not been involved in the Lindbergh child's killing, which under New Jersey law subjected the violator to the death penalty, three other states presented themselves as candidates. Because the kidnapping statutes in Minnesota — where Sankey had abducted Bohn — and those of Colorado and South Dakota each provided for a maximum sentences less than life, it was likely that Sankey would be tried in federal court in either Colorado or South Dakota-where the maximum sentence was life — since Boettcher had been taken across state lines.

To many, including the *Denver Post*, it was beyond question that he should be tried in Denver; virtually all the witnesses resided there and the crime arose there against a prominent Colorado resident.

While Justice department agents interrogated Verne Sankey and charted their next move, Indiana authorities less than a hundred miles away, in Crown Point, Indiana, welcomed back John Dillinger, the state's favorite son — in the criminal sense, anyway — and locked him up under enhanced security to await trial. The *Chicago Tribune* described his demeanor as meek and resigned.

Dillinger, then thirty-one, had shown promise as a smooth shortstop on his local baseball team but other voices beckoned. In 1924, when he was barely twenty, a judge sent him to prison for robbing a grocery store. Not released until May 1933, and having missed much of the Roaring Twenties and early thirties, Dillinger did his utmost to make up for lost time. His résumé of major crimes — probably fewer than ten bank robberies — was comparatively thin by the standards of men like Bailey, the Barker-Karpis gang, Nash, and Floyd, but he was rapidly developing a reputation among ordinary folk as something of a Robin Hood. A photograph taken shortly after his arrival at the Crown Point jail brought him instant nationwide notoriety.

While Purvis queried Verne Sankey in Chicago, Dillinger posed with Sheriff Lillian Holley and Lake County prosecutor, Robert Estill. It is a fascinating shot — Estill stands, smiling broadly, left arm around the indicted murderer he hoped to send to the electric chair. Dillinger, wearing a supercilious grin, rests his right arm on the prosecutor's shoulder, his posture suggesting contempt for his captors. To their right stands Sheriff Holley, dressed for the occasion and looking pleased to jail such a celebrity.

The *New York Times* carried the photograph next to that of Verne Sankey and alongside the story of Sankey's capture—a story that had been continued from the *front* page. It was fitting. Here were two men, one dubbed that day the nation's chief outlaw, the other his successor-in-waiting. Their lives had intersected for that fleeting moment, if only in the medium of journalism. Dillinger, the ex-convict only recently released from prison, appeared bound for the electric chair. Who could have known that his notoriety was just beginning? As for Holley and Estill, what hint was there then that they would regret the pose for the rest of their lives?

Purvis's marathon interrogation of Verne Sankey, begun a day earlier, finally ended late in the afternoon on the first of February. The Justice Department decided to prosecute Sankey in South Dakota despite the fact that authorities there had made no overtures to prosecute him, as had law enforcement officials in Colorado and Minnesota. The bureau easily factored Minnesota out of the equation but the choice between federal charges in South Dakota and Colorado was a tougher call. Sioux Falls was closer to Chicago than Denver, and Fern Sankey, already in South Dakota, would not require extradition. When Verne Sankey agreed late in the afternoon to waive extradition to South Dakota, the location issue was settled.

United States marshals whisked Sankey into a taxi to the Chicago, Milwaukee, St. Paul, and Pacific train station for delivery by rail to Sioux Falls. He was dressed in an overcoat, hat tipped low over his head. Purvis exercised supreme caution transporting his high-visibility human cargo to South Dakota. In fact, he accompanied the marshals and Sankey for extra measure. Within twenty minutes of his waiver, Sankey was on the train that had been held for his anticipated boarding and bound for South Dakota. The International News Service recorded their departure.

Closely guarded by federal operatives, Verne Sankey, "America's
public enemy No. 1," left Thursday night . . . . in a private car on the
Milwaukee railroad. . . . Department of justice operatives accompanied
the bad man.

Purvis was intent on insuring against mistakes as had occurred with
the delivery of Frank Nash in Kansas City seven months earlier. Purvis
remembered his efforts with Sankey years later.

[Sankey] had a car to himself; he was manacled; and there were six or
seven men loaded down with artillery to make sure that he stayed in
his seat. It did seem a lot of attention for an unarmed prisoner, but I
kept in mind the story of a special agent who brought in a man not
only handcuffed but bound about with a huge and bulky cow chain.

When his colleagues mocked Purvis's extraordinary precaution, his
response was dry. "Well," Purvis replied laconically, "he's here, isn't he?"
One of the U.S. marshal's concerns was that Sankey, as morose as
he appeared, might make an attempt on his life.

And so, Public Enemy No. 1 departed Chicago, the epicenter of
American gangland—home to the Capones, the Touhys, and at times
Harvey Bailey, Frank Nash, and a host of others. It had been the city to
which "Machine Gun Kelly" had fled four months earlier before his
capture, and where Verne Miller had shot it out with bureau agents only
three months before. Dillinger had robbed and hidden out there even
more recently. Yet among these and other criminals all across the nation,
the U.S. Justice Department had identified this affable bootlegger-
farmer who had, as he told bureau agents, never before been "in real
trouble," as America's chief public enemy.

Jack Lait reported the disbelief many expressed when they heard
Verne Sankey's life story.

It seemed incredible to the local experts on America's criminal mobs
that [Sankey] had started from scratch, an obscure South Dakota
farmer, leaping abruptly into the most high-powered and desperate
type of organized felony from the placid, sluggish estate of a South
Dakota farmer to "public enemy No. 1" of the nation, because he
needed money to pay off the mortgage on his humble homestead.

That was a sanitized version of his life's story, but their surprise struck a chord.

According to Lait, Purvis's agents actually brought four of Chicago's leading racketeers to bureau headquarters. Agents presented the men to Sankey as officers, to see if the thugs could identify Sankey as an affiliate of any Chicago gang. They could not.

> They not only sneered after they had seen him, but seemed honestly resentful of the page one prominence of this unfamiliar rube, who is hogging the spotlight, whereas to them he is a callow amateur. They protested with some indignation against this presumptuous outsider having picked Chicago, of all places, to hide in and be captured, and thus hold up their fair city unjustly as the habitat of criminals.

Irony indeed.

12

Most Often a Gentleman

The Associated Press covered "notorious kidnapper" Verne Sankey's return to Sioux Falls:

> Shaved and apparently refreshed by a night's rest on the journey from Chicago, where he was arrested Wednesday, the outlaw seemed almost jaunty as he stepped from the train preceded by two guards who carried a shotgun and a sub-machine gun. . . .
>
> A crowd of several hundred persons jammed the railroad station platform for a glimpse of the man who is accused of at least two kidnappings. . . .
>
> Shielded by a triangle of automobiles, drawn up at the point of disembarkation, Sankey, wearing a dark overcoat and a soft hat pulled down on one side of his head, was quickly shoved into a taxicab."

There would be no repeat of the Union Station Massacre. The *Argus Leader*'s P. O. Gorder watched the event:

> It is doubtful if Sioux Falls has seen so much excitement since the visit of Col. Charles A. Lindbergh, as accompanied the arrival of the notorious kidnaper when he was returned to South Dakota today. . . .
>
> As the cars [carrying heavily armed officers with Sankey] sped away,

the crowd milled and broke, rushing pell-mell after the cars in a hope of obtaining a view of the notorious desperado, but the federal agents were too fast for them. By the time the crowd reached the jail, Sankey was already inside and behind bars."

Ten U.S. deputy marshals and guards, riot guns in hand, maintained a cordon around Sankey. They scrutinized his most minute movements and those of everyone around him. After they took Sankey to his cell in the Minnehaha County jail, newsman Gorder crept up and spoke briefly with him. The next day he wrote,

> Verne Sankey is a congenial sort of chap. He has a warm hand-clasp and a pleasant smile. And there is nothing about him which would lead one to believe that he is the deep-dyed criminal he is charged with being. . . . I asked him how he felt. . . . He was just being locked in a cell, and as I spoke to him he pushed his hand through the bars and with a firm clasp that indicated he wanted to be friendly, he replied: "I feel fine."

Sankey politely begged off when asked to say a few words about his case. "I can't talk right now, but perhaps a little later I will have some-thing to say." After a few moments of conversation, a federal agent brusquely chased Gorder away. Gorder avenged the slight the next day with his article's headline: "'Public Enemy No. 1' Seems Pleasant Fel-low" and the line below it: "He's Much More Polite than the Cops."

Sankey did not remain in the county jail very long. Less than two hours after his arrival, the marshals whisked him away to the state peni-tentiary, an imposing granite structure high on a hill above the city.

Sankey had long dreaded the thought of prison. The idea of life be-hind bars appalled him. Most of all, he hated the thought that his chil-dren would one day see him in prison garb, deemed unfit to move freely in society. Until his Chicago arrest, for all his bootlegging, robbing, and kidnapping, Sankey had spent no more than a single day in jail in his entire life. The lack of consequences for his conduct had fueled a sense of invulnerability. Now had come the time of recompense. He had told his associates to "bump" themselves off rather than give police the satisfaction of capture, but the manner of his own apprehension had foiled his plan to kill himself.

For awhile, however, the attention distracted him, as reporters nudged closely for an interview and people lined the streets to catch a glimpse of the newly crowned "Public Enemy No. 1." The rest of his life had not yet fully dawned on Verne Sankey. His caravan arrived at the penitentiary gates and, like a movie star arriving on location, he smiled and exchanged light banter with the press and the deputy marshals guarding him. When a photographer asked him to pose with his guards, Sankey consented on the condition that his handcuffs not be shown. The deputy to whom Sankey was cuffed, graciously faced the camera and turned in toward Sankey at his right, hiding the restraints. As the photographer was about to snap the shot, a dynamite blast rung out from a nearby rock quarry, startling the entire group. Sankey smiled and quipped, "They are shooting at us, already."

Assistant Attorney General Keenan told South Dakota prosecutors that Sankey would be given preference over all other federal cases. Federal judge A. Lee Wyman set Verne Sankey's bond at $100,000 but U.S. attorney Olaf Eidem announced that if there was any possibility Sankey could meet that bail amount he would seek to have it increased to $500,000, a number he was confident Judge Wyman would approve. "We're not going to take any chances on him getting away," Eidem added.

Melvin Purvis's presence in Sioux Falls went unnoticed or at least unmentioned in the *Argus Leader*'s coverage. The omission was hardly surprising. Purvis was not yet known to most of America, including, no doubt, the Sioux Falls press corps. Purvis's reputation as the nation's top G-Man would elevate him to near mythical status in a matter of months but at the time he was a relatively anonymous, short, and courtly federal agent. As it turned out, his stay in Sioux Falls lasted longer than planned. After he delivered Sankey to the state penitentiary, Purvis collapsed from fatigue and influenza, which kept him bedridden for a week.

When federal officials had marched Verne Sankey into the Minnehaha County jail that first day of February, his wife could actually catch a glimpse of him from her own perch in the facility. Shortly after South Dakota authorities received word of Verne Sankey's capture, they had rearrested Fern. Deputy marshals had arrived at the ranch about four-thirty on the morning after Verne's Chicago arrest. Fern awoke startled, but remained stoic, quietly packing her belongings. Determined not to awaken her small children, she sadly parted from them as they slept. "Uncle" Mike Chopskie reprised his earlier role, staying with Echo and Orville and tending to chores. So as deputy marshals escorted her husband into the Minnehaha County jail, Fern Sankey sat near a small window in her own cell that afforded her a glimpse of her manacled husband. Did he see her, too? If so, it would be for the last time.

Judge Wyman increased Fern's bond from the five thousand dollars that her Buffalo County friends had posted to twenty-five thousand dollars. Her rearrest and the increased bail prompted a swift reaction from Laska. "Mrs. Sankey has not attempted to leave the jurisdiction of South Dakota Court," Laska railed, "and raising the bond in this case is an outrage." Laska added that he would attempt to raise the additional money from the Buffalo County friends who pledged assets to satisfy her first bond.

Fern fascinated the press. On her arrival at the jail, she smiled at reporters and, like her husband, graciously consented to pose for a photograph. The *Argus Leader*'s Nettie B. Cardin offered her observations of this wife of the country's chief domestic enemy.

> Mrs. Sankey, who looks no more than 30 years of age, is said to be 39 years old. She is slight, about five feet tall and weighs less than 100 pounds. She was dressed smartly yet in simple good taste, no powder nor paint. Her wrap was a black wool boucle trim with a silver fox collar. Her shoes were black satin and her hose of sheer gunmetal. Under her soft, black turban trimmed with a wisp of a veil edged in silver thread, her curly black hair fell softly to one side. She smiled graciously as she was thanked - an [*sic*] as the jail door closed after her one wondered and wondered.

> Somehow, Fern summoned a smile for the photographer, too.

Only Gordon Alcorn remained on the loose. Back in Chicago, as bureau agents grilled Helen Mattern on the night of her mate's arrest, she commented in passing that Alcorn, known to her as Walter Thomas, had bought an inexpensive secondhand car in the city back in March or April of the previous year. Purvis took that nugget of information and directed his agents to canvass the city's automobile dealers. Within a day, they located the dealer that had sold the car to a Walter Thomas, who gave his address as 3125 Addison Street. The day after Sankey's capture, bureau agents placed a telephone call to the Addison Street address. A woman who identified herself as Mrs. Thomas told the caller her husband was out of town and would not return for several weeks.

Agents and police raced to the Addison Street home, arriving there at about eleven o'clock that night. When "Mrs. Thomas" answered the door they burst inside, arrested her, and searched for Alcorn. He was in bed, unarmed, and offered no resistance. The only weapon police found in the apartment of this reputedly dangerous desperado was a .25-caliber pistol — one agent called it a pea shooter — hidden under a parlor sofa cushion. Alcorn readily admitted his true identity and his complicity in Charlie Boettcher's kidnapping, both to police and to his flummoxed wife, who — or so he claimed — was ignorant of his crime and his true identity.

Agents had gotten to Alcorn just in time. He was down to his last eleven bucks. Had he eluded the law much longer, he would have had to search seriously for work. Like Sankey, agents took Alcorn to Chicago's bureau headquarters where they interrogated him, then placed him in solitary confinement. The next day, Purvis's men boarded him onto a Milwaukee westbound for Sioux Falls to unite him with his erstwhile partner. As the train was about to leave the station, Alcorn bid a sorrowful farewell to Birdie. He hugged her and begged forgiveness. "I'm awfully sorry I got you into this mess," he lamented. "I regret deceiving you."

"Don't feel bad," Mrs. Alcorn replied. "I love you and I'll wait for you until you get out."

The statement may have been contrived, inasmuch as it was made within earshot of reporters. After all, Birdie had been present when Sankey had put a gun to Alcorn and demanded the ransom. This fact, coupled with her deceptive response when bureau agents called the apartment shortly before raiding it, raises doubt about her professed ignorance of her husband's true identity.

News that first Sankey and then Alcorn had been captured elated Charlie Boettcher. "That's great," he replied when informed. "Now they've got 'em all." When told that Sankey had drafted another kidnap letter, Charlie remarked, "I wouldn't put anything past him. My observation of him has been that when he gets an idea he carries it out."

The city of Sioux Falls — or at least, its leading newspaper — savored the national attention. "Sioux Falls had the eyes of the nation turned on it today as the notorious Sankey was brought here. And this city and the state will continue to bask in the sunshine of publicity surrounding the case until it is finally disposed of, either by Sankey's imprisonment, or his acquittal."

Authorities parked Alcorn a few cells down from Sankey and, as they did, a Chicago deputy marshal entertained the press by drawing from his pocket the pair of handcuffs used on Alcorn, which, said he, were the same pair that had cuffed Capone during his long ride to prison two years earlier.

Alcorn's subdued demeanor starkly contrasted with Sankey's from a day earlier, but then by late morning, his somber mood shifted to loquacious. "I had a swell time with my share of the ransom," Alcorn wistfully recalled. "I bet I made all the night clubs in Chicago. The money's all gone now, every cent of it, and I'm ready to take the consequences. I never was cut out for this kidnapping racket anyhow."

Alcorn's arrest and his true identity understandably stunned Birdie's father, who had just returned to his Corson, South Dakota, home after visiting the pair in Chicago. "This is the funniest experience I've ever had," he said. "I don't know what to think about it."

Ten deputy U.S. marshals rotated in pairs, guarding Verne Sankey around the clock. When one of them, Walter Goetz, was asked if the desperado the government had labeled America's Public Enemy No. 1 was tough, Goetz brushed him off. "Not so tough. We have tougher horse thieves in the state." Sankey's cheerful mood when he arrived at the Minnehaha County jail discernibly flattened after he arrived at his cell in the state penitentiary. Perhaps it was the dreary quartzite prison's imposing walls, or fatigue from the stress of capture, the intense grilling, and the long train ride. More likely though, Sankey's depressed mood stemmed from the slow dawning of grim reality. His problems were not limited to the bleak circumstances his incarceration posed. He told a reporter that, in light of his dalliance with Helen Mattern, his greatest fear was facing Fern. She had tried to speak with him at the county jail, but authorities would not allow it. Their decision was a relief to him.

Sankey's trepidation concerning Fern was well-founded. When after her rearrest she learned that Verne had been living with another woman, she was beside herself and hinted that she was capable of retribution. "If I find that my husband was really living with that woman and spending his money on her when I was hungry, freezing and praying for him, I not only will leave him flat, but I will tell all I know."

Angry though Fern was, she clung to the faint hope that her husband had simply used Mattern as a maid or perhaps even a front. "Verne is pretty smart. He may have been using that woman for some purpose to aid him in evading the law." Fern also dispelled suggestions that Verne altered his looks to avoid capture. "Nobody knows Verne as I do. He is one of the vainest men in the world. Women fall for him like flies," she said. "If he has had his moles removed it is more likely he did it to be better looking, rather than to get rid of any marks which would identify him."

One question loomed above all others in the press for a few days: Would Fern turn on her husband in light of the Helen Mattern affair? Fern put that to rest. "I'm still for Verne," she told reporters, lips quivering. "I know he has done wrong and that he may have to spend the rest of his life in prison, but I'm still for him."

Nonetheless, stories circulated about a fissure in the couple's relationship. The *Denver Post* and other newspapers reported that Fern had instituted, but had not proceeded with, a divorce action against her husband. The report was false. Rumors also spread in Mitchell and Denver that months earlier Sankey had kidnapped Echo while she visited Minnesota with her mother. Again, untrue.

A dispirited Verne Sankey faced more grilling at the penitentiary. The agents who questioned Sankey there saw a much different man than the one they had delivered forty-eight hours earlier. Gone was the lighthearted banter, the broad smile, the salesman's warmth; now Sankey wore a brooding demeanor. Those around him attributed Sankey's morose mood in part to regret over the predicament into which he had led his little band of friends. "Alcorn is a swell fellow," Sankey told them. "He used to fire for me up in Canada when I was a railroad engineer. He was never in trouble before in his life."

The Justice Department pressed Sankey to decide whether he would plead guilty. He wavered but appeared to lean toward admitting his guilt. He had already done as much at the bureau offices. There appeared to be little reason for a trial, except to perhaps delay the trip to Leavenworth, the prison to which it seemed inevitable he would be consigned for life. That was a long time to spend in Kansas. What was the rush to get there? Or did Verne Sankey have something else on his mind?

Harold Brown met with Sankey on February 4 and 5. Alcorn joined them. Brown made it clear his role was merely advisory. He had sought and secured the Justice Department's permission in advance.

The real legal battle brewing concerned Fern Sankey's role in the abduction. Laska and local counsel Holton Davenport proposed to federal prosecutors that they dismiss charges against Fern in exchange for her husband's guilty plea, but Justice was not interested. After all, it already had Sankey's Chicago confession. The Justice Department desired nothing more than another highly visible kidnapping trial, especially a slam dunk case against Public Enemy No. 1. You can't buy that kind of publicity. No doubt mindful of its success the previous fall in prosecuting a husband and wife kidnap duo — George "Machine Gun" Kelly and his wife, Kit — the government made it plain to Fern's attorneys that, regardless of how her husband pled, it would try her case too.

Keenan therefore dispatched instructions to South Dakota's U.S. attorney Eidem that the case against the Sankeys and Alcorn proceed speedily to trial. Keenan promised the case would be granted preference over every other criminal trial in the country.

Keenan was intent on sending a message to the nation that kidnappers would be swiftly prosecuted. He had already demonstrated that resolve by prosecuting the Kellys, obtaining convictions at trial and securing life sentences, all within sixteen days of their arrest. Laska flew to Sioux Falls on February 5 to confer with Davenport and later with Fern to develop a defense strategy. Their first move was to publicly separate the issue of Fern's guilt or innocence from that of her husband and Alcorn, even as Fern continued to express emotional support for Verne. Laska and Davenport then decided to seek a separate trial. A better scenario still, from Fern's perspective, they thought, was for Verne Sankey and Gordon Alcorn to simply plead guilty, automatically separating Fern from them.

On February 6, Laska met with Verne Sankey — apparently at Fern's request — and then announced that he would also represent Verne Sankey and that Sankey would not fight the charge against him. "There is no doubt whatever that Sankey will plead guilty," Laska announced. "Sankey wants to do everything he can to aid his wife and the mother of his children in this thing." He would begin, Laska said, by admitting his own guilt. This maneuver granted Fern the separate trial Laska and Davenport knew she needed if she stood any chance of acquittal. It also provided her a most persuasive witness — her husband.

With the Sankeys' defense team in place and a strategy settled, Harold Brown packed his suitcase and returned to Gann Valley. "I have not been interested in preparing any defense for Mrs. Sankey," he told the inquisitive press. "My business in the case has been largely a discussion of the arrangements of personal affairs between Mr. and Mrs. Sankey." His immediate goal was to get Fern back home with her kids. Raising the twenty-five-thousand-dollar bail seemed to him an insurmountable assignment. It was, after all, roughly the equivalent of fifty years of wages for the average waitress or textile worker fortunate enough to still have work.

With Sankey and Alcorn expected to plead guilty that same week, prosecutors decided to move briskly with their case against Fern. Based largely on some new, unspecified information they claimed to have garnered, they planned to convene another grand jury later in February to reindict her.

Then another development unfolded in the ongoing kidnap saga: on February 8, after twenty-three days in captivity, his abductors tossed Edward G. Bremer out of a car on a highway near Rochester, Minnesota, south of the Twin Cities, on payment of the $200,000 ransom. The

Roosevelt administration rejoiced with the Bremer family at his release. It was becoming difficult for anyone to assume that Verne Sankey played any role in Bremer's abduction.

As the days of Verne Sankey's solitary confinement passed, he fell deeper into depression. His normally relaxed, almost convivial deportment had entirely disappeared. Some ascribed it to the fact that Public Enemy No. 1 had never experienced jail. It was more than that, though. When Laska met with Sankey for a second time, on Wednesday morning, February 7, in his cell, the despondent farmer-outlaw had Echo and Orville on his mind. He learned they were planning a visit soon, and he told Laska that he dreaded the thought of his precious kids seeing him behind bars. He wanted them to remember him as a "kind father," he told Laska, "rather than as a convict with an ugly prison uniform." He gave Laska instructions for the care of Fern and the kids "in case anything happened," as Laska phrased it. "Just see that they get everything that belongs to them."

"Don't worry—I'll never do a day for this rap," Sankey told him. "I wouldn't give the cops and members of the Boettcher family the satisfaction of seeing me go to the pen. I would rather die first." Then he looked at Laska and motioned with his hands around his neck. Laska knew what was about to happen.

Thursday, February 8, was Orville's fifth birthday. At around nine-thirty that morning, Sankey's guards, A. B. Neely and Frank Gilmore, both U.S. deputy marshals, prepared to take Sankey and Alcorn out to the prison yard for their daily exercise, but Sankey declined. They noticed that his mood had improved, though; he seemed almost jovial again. Another development had occurred: the Justice Department had granted Sankey's request to meet with Fern briefly, after he entered his guilty plea and received his sentence. Sankey told one of his guards he was anxious to see Fern: "I haven't seen her for months and months," he told the guard. "It'll seem good, although it will be short and be the last time." He knew that Fern desperately longed to see him, too.

Around four that afternoon, Birdie came to visit Alcorn, who was two cells down from Sankey. When the visit ended, she passed Sankey's cell weeping. In her periphery, she saw Sankey shake his head in sympathy. Moments later, Harold Alcorn, who had journeyed from Melville, Saskatchewan, arrived to see his errant younger brother. Harold was the eldest of the Alcorn children and a World War I veteran. He was also a longtime railroader out of Melville who had worked with and known Verne Sankey for years. When Harold's visit with Gordon ended, he stopped to chat with Sankey on his way out of the solitary confinement area. As the two parted, Sankey asked Harold to "tell my gambling friends up there I have been paid 20 years in advance and am now working it out." The two shook hands and Harold left, thinking Sankey was preparing himself mentally for life in prison. Harold Alcorn was the last man to shake Verne Sankey's hand.

Guard Frank Gilmore described what followed.

> The cell Sankey occupied is about twenty feet from the door of the deputy warden's office. It was our habit to walk past the cell every five minutes or oftener.
>
> At a few minutes before six . . . Alcorn asked for an aspirin tablet as he had been taking the medicine for a toothache, and. . . . Neely went to a cabinet in the clerk's office across from the deputy warden's office and got the medicine. During this time I was standing in the corridor about 8 feet from the door of Sankey's cell. . . .
>
> Neely thereupon started to Alcorn's cell which is the second down the corridor [the cell between the two was vacant].
>
> As he reached Sankey's cell he noticed Sankey hanging to the bars of the cell and he immediately called for me to hurry.
>
> We opened the door of the cell and Neely took a handkerchief gag from Sankey's mouth, cut the necktie with which he hanged himself and laid him on his bunk.
>
> [Night Captain] Borcherding . . . felt his pulse and said: "The man is dead."

Holton Davenport and Harold Brown, who had rushed back from Gann Valley when he heard the news, bore it to Fern a couple of hours later. She became hysterical, shrieking, "Why couldn't I have spoken to him? Why couldn't I have spoken to him?" Much that she said was unintelligible. Her attorneys asked the prison's physician, Dr. Keller, who had just attended her husband, to provide Fern medical care. When asked if she wished to have her children with her, Fern cried: "I must, I must." Did she want them to start for the city that night? "No, no," she responded. "Not the little baby. Not tonight."

Dr. Keller administered sedatives but still she wept through much of the night, sleeping only intermittently, an hour or two, at most. A nurse, to whom she said nothing, watched over her. The next morning Fern remained in what Dr. Keller described as severe shock. She was still garbed in "a brilliant green gown, reclined on her simple prison cot with its gray blanket," a cold pack resting across her forehead.

Mike Chopskie broke the news to a stunned Echo at the ranch that morning. At first speechless, Echo, too, then wept bitterly, but Orville was still too young and callow to appreciate how his life had forever changed; he was more occupied with the fact that he was now five. He had missed school that day, down with the croup, but his schoolmates had not forgotten him. Someone had baked him a birthday cake and brought it to school, so when he failed to come, one of the kids brought a piece of it to him after school. Chopskie brought the well-mannered children to Sioux Falls to be with their mother, but first the *Argus Leader* invited them to pose at the studio of a local photographer. The *Leader* reported:

> The two children of Mrs. Fern Mae Sankey . . . marched bravely into the Minnehaha county jail at 5:30 o'clock. Echo underwent a search. A box of chocolates, a small gift to her mother was searched.
> And then, in the presence of Mrs. Sankey's nurse, they were permitted to enter the women's ward and visit. The mother was flat on her steel cot, still weak from the shock of Verne Sankey's suicide. . . . She caressed her children and they left.

In the wake of Sankey's suicide, government officials had little to say. Melvin Purvis, still in Sioux Falls recuperating from his influenza bout, said only that the next step in the affair would have to come from Justice prosecutors. State penitentiary warden Eugene Reiley absolved his staff of any wrongdoing in Sankey's hanging, reasoning that Verne Sankey had been a federal prisoner, under federal guard. J. Edgar Hoover exonerated the bureau of any responsibility, curtly noting that since Sankey had not been "in the custody of my men at the time . . . no responsibility attaches to them in his death."

When asked, Hoover refused to comment on the evidence against Sankey in the Lindbergh case, saying only, "That closes the case against [Sankey]. The one against Gordon Alcorn, his ally, will be pressed to a satisfactory finish." Hoover was satisfied at least, that his agents could claim credit for Sankey's capture, even though Sankey had deprived the Justice Department of the honor of convicting him and sending him to Leavenworth for life.

Sankey had implemented his suicide flawlessly. Two cells down, in close proximity to Sankey when he hung himself, Alcorn had not heard a sound. When the guards scurried to help Sankey and the coroner arrived, Alcorn was visibly shaken. As a precaution, the deputy marshals removed from his cell anything that might be used to aid in suicide.

Late that night, Charlie Boettcher heard a rumor that Verne Sankey had hung himself. He and officials from the Denver U.S. attorney's office placed a call to Assistant U.S. Attorney E. D. Barron, who confirmed Sankey's suicide.

"Justice has been served." Charlie told a *Denver Post* reporter that night. "Sankey told me during the time I was held prisoner that he would never be taken alive." Still, Charlie wanted to fly to Sioux Falls. "Just as a matter of curiosity, I would like to see these men, dead or alive."

Chief Albert Clark called Verne Sankey's suicide a blessing. "I have no sympathy at all for kidnappers," he told the press. "They are the most despicable of all criminals."

The press was scathing, filled with a sense that Verne Sankey had cheated justice. Charlie O'Brien, who had followed the case for the *Denver Post* from the beginning, wrote:

> Verne Sankey "couldn't take it." While this notorious outlaw and
> kidnapper was running loose with a gun preying upon unarmed
> victims, he obtained the undeserved title of being a "desperado with
> nerve and bravery."

But when the law finally caught up with him after an eleven-month search and he saw nothing in prospect but a life prison sentence, he cringed, like all other so-called "desperadoes" of his type.

Sankey took the easiest way out — suicide — leaving his widow and two children, Echo, 15, and Orville, 5, to make their way thru life alone.

Beneath the caption, "Crime Never Pays," that appeared between headline and story of all its crime articles of the day, the *Denver Post* stated: "Verne Sankey has kept his word to 'beat the law.' . . . Out of all the blustering company of gang chiefs and 'public enemies,' Verne Sankey, called 'America's public enemy No. 1,' is the only one of national notoriety to die by his own hand."

Ben Laska saw something more than fear in Sankey's motives. Verne Sankey's abiding desire was that his children remember the loving father rather than the convict. Beyond that, Laska thought Sankey to be genuinely depressed that he had not been able to outwit the law. In the end, his fate became that of those many losers about which he had read in the true crime magazines, whose stupidity he scorned.

Columnist Arthur Brisbane wrote that America's Public Enemy No. 1 could not have accomplished his suicidal feat in a French prison. Their rule, he had learned, was "Pour eviter toute possibilite qu'ils ne se pendent," meaning that an inmate was not allowed to possess anything with which he might hang himself.

How *had* it happened, in solitary confinement, with two officers standing guard? That was a question many were asking. Because he had not yet pled guilty, Sankey was not a convicted prisoner; thus, he had been permitted to keep his own clothes. He stuffed his handkerchief deep into his mouth to mute any guttural sounds that might alert his guards, then stepped off his cot into eternity. No more than ten minutes had elapsed from the time he exchanged his last words with a guard.

Even by 1934 standards, the Justice Department's custodial care of Sankey had been abysmal. Here was a man whom the bureau knew had wanted to kill himself on arrest and who possessed poison pills to perform the act. It was not malicious — just incompetent.

The skeptical did not believe that Sankey took his own life. Some among his friends and neighbors in Gann Valley thought the government had killed him because they had not received the Lindbergh confession they sought. Others suspected that Charlie Boettcher was himself in on the kidnapping and had split the proceeds with Sankey and his friends to cover gambling debts. These stories had circulated from the beginning. There was nothing to substantiate them but there was in comments made by Hoover and the state penitentiary warden, a collective washing of the governments' hands in the matter.

The next day, as Sankey's body lay on a slab in the morgue of Banton-Peterson Funeral Home, Gordon Alcorn stood before the Honorable Alfred Wyman, decked out in a blue dress suit, black hair neatly slicked back. He appeared pale standing before this judge empowered to sentence him to life in prison. When the judge asked how he pled to the charge of kidnapping Charlie Boettcher of Denver, Alcorn's only word was "guilty." The judge next asked if Alcorn had any reason why sentence should not then be pronounced. When Alcorn softly responded that there was none, burly Judge Wyman gazed intently at him, and told him he had just pleaded guilty to "one of the most dastardly, most heinous crimes known." Wyman then laid it on Gordon Alcorn. "The facts and circumstances in your case are such that you must be severely punished, and justice would not be done unless the maximum penalty is imposed." The sentence Wyman pronounced was life in prison for twenty-nine-year-old Gordon Alcorn. Deputy marshals whisked Alcorn out of Judge Wyman's courtroom and into a holding cell, where he awaited the long train ride to Leavenworth.

Fern Sankey requested a simple service for her husband. She did not want, as she put it, a "gangster funeral." The government would not reveal where he was to be buried. Speculation was that it would be in Gann Valley. It was not. They buried Verne Sankey on Monday, February 12 — Lincoln's birthday — precisely one year after his abduction of Charlie Boettcher.

Slip back to that dreary 1934 winter day and see the Banton-Peterson Funeral Home on the corner of Eleventh Street and Minnesota Avenue in Sioux Falls. It informs potential clients "Our Service is Within the Means of All," promising quiet, private, and dignified services.

The strains of "In the Garden" waft out of the chapel into the quiet neighborhood. Look inside and see Verne Sankey's body lie in a grey, plush-covered casket, laden with flowers amid friends and family. We cannot view Fern well unless we turn and strain our necks, because she is seated in a small room in the rear of the chapel, the doors of which remain open so she can see and hear what transpires. She listens as Norman Mathers sings of the songwriter's encounter, alone in the garden with the risen Lord. Those present later hear Mathers bellow the powerful lyrics of "The Old Rugged Cross" which, as the lyricist wrote, serves as the emblem of "suffering and shame," concepts Fern Sankey has come to understand well. She hears the gospel through the voice of First Presbyterian Church's pastor, Hugh Jones, who graciously gives up his day off to lead the service. Federal marshals stand guard inside and outside the chapel.

Echo, one with her mother in abject grief, and Orville sit beside Fern. The only other family there to grieve is Ruth Kohler and uncle Frank Sankey, who drives from Clark to be there to help bury his wayward brother. They are all gathered in the rear room. Perhaps three dozen other mourners are present, which is noteworthy since this is a funeral restricted to family and close friends, and because the people who mourn this dead man live more than 140 miles of often jarring roads away from where they are now gathered.

These friends are sturdy people of the prairie — mostly farmers, ranchers, a businessman or two, a professional, all townspeople from in and around Gann Valley. Six pallbearers crowd into the front pew, their hands calloused, hair unruly, garbed in boots and western-cut clothing. That cherubic faced-fellow is Dan Hathaway, the broadly-built veteran who came to the Gann Valley area from Nebraska after the war with his wife and young family. He bought a farm northwest of town and before long was an integral part of the community's fabric. In time, crop failures, poor prices, and grasshoppers will force him from the land but for now, at age forty, he is a sod buster trying to hang on through the drought.

That older, well-dressed man of bearing is Clarence "C. C." Swartout. Son of a minister, Swartout came to Gann Valley at nineteen with his parents and siblings back in 1896, when his father was called to lead the Congregational Church. C. C. is nearly sixty now, an implement dealer in Gann Valley and a good one. Back in the wet year of '28, he sold more than one hundred Farmall tractors, more than anyone else in the state. He has served in the legislature and as justice of the peace.

The fellow with the dark hair combed wildly, bearing the rough look of the land is Herman Viereck. He is about forty-two now, Verne Sankey's age. He and his wife, Anna, like many of their friends and neighbors, are the children of immigrant pioneers drawn to the prairie by promise and hope. Even though it is the Depression, even though it is bone dry, they and their six children are surviving — better than most. It is Herman who helped raise bail for Fern and it is in his barn, just a few miles from the Sankey ranch, that the community still dances and drinks and laughs during these dreary days.

J. R. Dyson, who owns the mercantile store and "Uncle Mike" Chopskie, who has done so much for Fern and the kids already, are among the six, as is Otto Nelson. Early fifties, Norwegian-born, Nelson had come to the county just after the century's turn. He married a Buffalo County pioneer's daughter, worked as a blacksmith and a carpenter. Left the area once and returned. In 1928, Otto sat where Fern now sits, next to a box bearing the lifeless body of his wife, whose Christmas Eve death left him alone to raise five sons and a daughter. These bearers of the pall are each survivors of a decade of low prices and Depression, seasons of drought, grasshoppers, dust storms. New hardships, yet unknown, await them, but the troubles at hand suffice for now.

As the final hymn is sung, these men bear the casket down the aisle and load it into the hearse while hundreds of curious onlookers stand waiting for a glimpse of the casket, the woman, the children. The family, the friends, and the law again gather at Mount Pleasant Cemetery, where the undertaker lowers the body of Public Enemy No. 1 into a cold grave.

13

Gladiators of the Courtroom

By early May the prairie's short grasses had emerged and wild flowers had begun to bloom, but the unseasonably warm sun bore down on the new starts of wheat, and the water holes shrank with each passing day. Farmers planted corn in the thin topsoil that remained, prayed, and wondered if rains would come to coax the reluctant seedlings out of the earth. Had the farmers been able to see into the future, they would not have bothered: it would be a devastating summer, worse even than the one before it.

A dispirited Gordon Alcorn slumped in a tiny holding cell at the U.S. marshal's office on the second floor of the federal courthouse, awaiting the southbound train that would take him, under guard, to Leavenworth. Birdie was on his mind.

"I really feel more sorry for her than I do for myself," he told the *Argus Leader*'s P. O. Gorder. "She has been a wonderful wife, we have been very happy the past 10 months, and I know that if I had met her before this thing happened, I would not be where I am today." Alcorn had a warning for America's youth. "Look into the future first," he told them. "Try to see the terrible consequences and then [you can avoid] what I am facing."

As Alcorn and his guards boarded the Milwaukee train for Leavenworth, Birdie boarded an Illinois Central train car bound for Chicago.

Verne Sankey's suicide had not quenched the government's thirst for justice. Hoover's announcement that Sankey's death ended the case against him did not extend to Fern. Determined to exact punishment, the Justice Department pressed on against her.

Judge Wyman reduced Fern Sankey's bond from the twenty-five thousand dollars he had set on her husband's rearrest, to ten thousand dollars. Again, her Gann Valley friends, led by Herman Viereck and with help from Mike Chopskie and Harold Brown, met the bond and she returned to the ranch.

Within a week of Sankey's death, Claude Boettcher, through his Sioux Falls attorneys at Boyce, Warren & Fairbanks, instituted legal proceedings against Sankey's estate to recover the $3,491.05 found in his Chicago apartment. Holton Davenport filed letters of administration, seeking the appointment of Irvin Knight, Buffalo County's register of deeds, to serve as the estate's administrator. The petition listed as estate assets a one-third interest in Sankey's parents' Roberts County, South Dakota, home; articles of personal property worth about $100.00; and the $3,491.05 found on Sankey at his arrest. Part-time prosecutor Harold Brown served as the attorney for the estate of Public Enemy No. 1, and Irvin Knight filed the required administrator's bond.

Claude sued the estate for $50,000.00. Sankey's estate did not contest the lawsuit, and a judgment against it was entered, but Harold Brown's legal maneuvers held the Boettchers at bay. Brown asked the court on Fern's behalf to set aside the statutorily appointed sum of $750.00 for the Sankey family's care, and the additional sum of $125.00 a month as a family allowance during each month the estate remained open. Claude Boettcher doggedly pursued the ransom money for several more years, finally recovering just under $2,500.00 after legal fees in 1937.

Mike Chopskie had paid for the undertaker's and grave diggers' services and for the cemetery plot. Neither Brown nor Irvin Knight nor Chopskie submitted a bill for their efforts on behalf of Fern and her kids. Buffalo County had taken care of its own. This assistance allowed Fern

to at least meet ongoing monthly expenses. Still, with the farm in foreclosure, a sheriff's deed would issue and she would lose the farm on
December 13, 1934, unless the remaining principal and interest were
paid by then.

The Justice Department had a new source of information — Gordon
Alcorn. After Sankey's suicide, Alcorn again met with prosecutors, hoping for leniency from his life sentence and feeling some bitterness toward
his dead confederate, whom he still believed had betrayed him. In late
March, a federal grand jury reindicted Fern and Ruth. The new indictment alleged that the pair had conspired with the men to write and deliver
the ransom notes. On March 28, federal officers once again swooped
down on the Sankey farm and hauled Fern into custody. Five days later,
when Judge Wyman reduced Fern Sankey's bond from twenty-five thousand dollars to ten thousand dollars, her Gann Valley friends, for a third
time, met the bond, and she once again returned to the ranch to raise her
kids and await trial. Judge Wyman ordered the two women to stand trial
on May 7, in Pierre, eighteen days later.

As the winter of 1934 dragged on, John Dillinger faded from the news.
Sheriff Lillian Holley expected no trouble from the convict. After all, as
she put it, "I warned him the first thing that we would stand for no
monkey business." Dillinger whiled away his hours bragging to whoever would listen that no cell could hold him. It was an audacious claim
considering Indiana's prison had done just that for nine years. So when
he told fellow inmates at the jail that he would "shoot [his] way out" of
Crown Point, they roared with laughter. His guards were sufficiently
confident in the jail's security that they permitted Dillinger to pass his
hours whittling wood — with a knife.

On a rainy March Saturday morning Dillinger thrust a whittled "pistol" into the stomach of an elderly janitor and bid farewell to Crown
Point jail, speeding away in the sheriff's car. The next day, Dillinger
joined Lester Gillis, also known as "Baby Face" Nelson — a sociopathic
killer — and Nelson's gang in St. Paul. Two days later, Dillinger and
Nelson's gang reemerged in, of all places, Sioux Falls. On the morning
of Tuesday, March 6, six unshaven men clad in dark overcoats, fedoras

low over their foreheads, relieved the Security National Bank and Trust Company in downtown Sioux Falls of $46,000. During the heist, Nelson shot through the bank's window, murdering a police officer.

In early April, the Denver mayor's committee on ransom apportionment issued its final report. Chicago barber Mueller got $1,750 for his aid to Chicago police. Helen Mattern got $1,500 for the lead that resulted in Alcorn's arrest. Others, including the Ellsworths, each received small amounts. The committee rejected several claims, including that of an individual who claimed that he had "sold the neckties to Sankey with which he hanged himself, and that saved the state more than anyone else." Roy Gibbs was the big winner, though, receiving more than half of the remaining fifteen thousand dollars left to be distributed. Gibbs snatched his reward check and hastily left Denver, destination unknown. Two days later his attorney filed Gibbs's petition for divorce from Calista.

Events turned more bizarre for Gibbs's archnemeses, the Ellsworths. Both Gibbs and the Ellsworths expressed fears of retaliation for their role in helping police solve the Boettcher kidnaping, but Ellsworth had alleged the previous fall that Gibbs had played a role in the kidnaping itself. The charge only heightened police suspicions that the men were feuding among themselves. Ellsworth eventually lost his railroad job; his wife had given up her dress shop job. The couple told police they had received death threats. Then followed the shooting into their home, the attempts to run Ellsworth off the road, and the beating that had fractured his skull. The Ellsworths sought police protection, but in December, Frances Ellsworth sought shelter from her husband, claiming she was not safe in the home with him. Shortly after, they moved south of Denver with their two boys to the mining town of Cripple Creek, where Ellsworth worked in a mine.

Three days after Gibbs left Denver, on April 24, the Ellsworths and their youngest son were on the road from Denver toward Cripple Creek, when Ellsworth wove to the left, sped past another motorist, then swerved back to the right. His car clipped the car he was passing, which sent the Ellsworth vehicle careening out of control. It rolled several times, spewing its passengers in various directions. Ellsworth escaped with minor cuts; the couple's little boy suffered some leg injuries, but Frances Ellsworth's neck was broken and she died almost instantly. Inexplicably, Ellsworth told police he had struck a car traveling in the opposite direction, but all witnesses to the accident, including the driver of the vehicle he struck contradicted him. Ellsworth disappeared from the scene, sought a gun, resurfaced the next day, claiming to have suffered from shock. No inquest was conducted, leaving only questions in the accident's wake.

As the Boettcher kidnapping trial approached, bureau agents pursuing John Dillinger narrowly missed him on several occasions, often through their own failures. Once out of Chicago, Dillinger, Nelson, and the gang found a remote little bar with cabins in northern Wisconsin known as Little Bohemia. The proprietor's wife leaked to a family member who was leaving the lodge that the outlaws were there. On a Sunday afternoon word reached Purvis at his Chicago apartment. He summoned every available man to Rhinelander, a town near the lodge.

As the agents reached the lodge, a car pulled away, radio blasting loudly. The officers commanded it to stop. When the driver failed to comply, agents fired on its occupants. Purvis and his men, certain that several gang members were still inside the lodge, waited outside for them to come out. And they waited-and they waited — for the entire evening. Finally agents lobbed teargas inside to flush out the remaining occupants but only the women were still inside. Dillinger, Nelson, and the others were long gone. In the process of his escape through the woods behind the lodge, Nelson encountered and killed two bureau agents at a neighboring home. Most disastrously, the occupants of the car leaving the scene as agents arrived were innocent lodge guests who had driven to the resort from a nearby work camp. The agents' shooting left one of them dead and two others injured.

The next day, several papers called for Purvis to resign; some suggested Hoover do so also. Will Rogers tried to make sense of the bureau's raid. "Well, they had Dillinger surrounded, and were all ready to shoot him when he came out. But another bunch of folks came out ahead; so they shot them instead. Dillinger is going to get in accidentally with some innocent bystanders some time, then he will get shot."

As the nation's headlines reported each new day's turn in the chase for the man who had become the nation's most notorious criminal, the second kidnapping case to be prosecuted under the Lindbergh Law was about to come to trial. On May 8, Fern Sankey and Ruth Kohler appeared before Judge Wyman and entered not guilty pleas. Jury selection began on May 9.

Ben Laska's defense of Albert Bates in the September 1933 Urschel kidnapping had so bolstered his national reputation that by May 1934 he was America's premier kidnap defense lawyer. The Urschel and Boettcher cases were, after all, the first two kidnapping cases tried by juries under the Lindbergh Law. What Laska couldn't know was that an event from his past would, in a matter of months, change the course of his life and make him the subject of a separate bureau investigation.

Laska's cocounsel, Holton Davenport, was unknown outside Sioux Falls, but soon proved his value to Laska and to their mutual clients. Davenport was a New England native, born in 1892 in the southern Vermont town of Brattleboro. After graduating from law school, he came to Sioux Falls in 1918 at twenty-six, to visit a relative there. He became enchanted by young Dorothy Day, the daughter of the *Argus Leader*'s publisher, and never left.

Davenport possessed a superb command of the language and an impeccably articulate delivery in front of a jury — cool, quiet, respectful, alert. He was a busy practitioner, at both the trial and appellate level. The year before he took up Fern Sankey's cause, South Dakota's Supreme Court decided seventeen cases in which he was counsel for one of the parties.

Ellsworth Evans, one of his law partners, remembered Davenport's defense of a deputy clerk of courts accused of stealing at her job. "She was guilty as hell," Evans recalled. Davenport feared that if he called her to the stand, the prosecution's cross-examination would expose her. Yet he knew the jury would want to hear what his client had to say about the matter and might hold against her a failure to testify.

Davenport resolved the dilemma with a little coaching. He directed his client to approach the stand after the prosecution had rested its case. As she left her chair and began walking toward the witness box, Davenport reached for her arm and pulled her back, saying, just loud enough for the jurors' benefit, "If that's all they've got, you don't have to take it." The jury returned a not guilty verdict.

Davenport provided a home-cooked antidote to Laska's slick, urban, out-of-state presence. More important, Davenport was an adroit trial lawyer, with cross-examination skills Laska lacked and for which Laska attempted to compensate with showmanship. Davenport's quiet dignity balanced Laska's acerbic wit. Perhaps most of all, Davenport held the respect of the trial judge. Former partner and nonagenarian Louis Hurwitz recalled: "I think in all Lee Wyman's years, no one ever faced him who stood above Holton Davenport" in his esteem.

Alfred Lee Wyman was the son of a Civil War veteran who had fought under Grant in some of the war's bloodiest battles — at Shiloh, where twenty-four thousand fell in two days, and at Vicksburg. He was born in December 1874; as a young man he read the law in a local law office and was admitted to the State Bar. He was Republican, Episcopalian, and a leader in Yankton's Masonic Lodge. He also drank too much liquor in those days. Leo Flynn, later one of Wyman's close friends, and a man who served as U.S. attorney during the latter part of Wyman's federal court tenure, recalled a story from Wyman's lodge days. As Flynn told it, the Yankton Lodge arranged for the organization's national Grand Master to come to a local lodge celebration. As the local membership waited for their dignitary to arrive, Wyman and some of the others began to imbibe. Time passed and the high-up still did not show. When the tardy national figure finally reached the Masonic hall, Wyman, by then well-lit, extended a greeting the Grand Master almost certainly had never before experienced. Burly Wyman grabbed him by the crotch with one hand and by the collar with the other, threw him on the floor and sat on him. It was a memorable welcome, but the Grand Master did not receive it well. It took Wyman awhile to live down the episode.

In 1928, Hoover appointed Wyman to the federal district court bench.

Part of the deal that came with Wyman's appointment, according to Flynn, was that the drinking had to end. It did. The new judge moved his family to a house at 1200 South Main, in Sioux Falls, and settled into his new office a few blocks away in the federal court building.

Wyman possessed what one writer described as a stern face and reproachful eyes. His large frame and gruff voice enhanced the intimidating pall he cast; but behind the curmudgeonly exterior hid a kindhearted, even likeable man, revealed only to a few and then only in relaxed settings. A contemporary recalled that Wyman "possessed an innate sense of right and justice . . .and while he was not always right, he was seldom in doubt." He was fond of telling lawyers who argued before him, "Any damn fool can know what the law *should* be. I want to know what it *is*." Despite a reputation as a mediocre but well-connected practitioner, Wyman proved to be an excellent trial judge. Lawyers liked the fact that he kept up on his work, so they were not forced to wait interminably for his ruling once oral arguments or written briefs were submitted to him.

Wyman had the unique habit of doodling, acquired in his childhood. It allowed him to enter into the deeper recesses of his mind, where his thought processes relaxed and intensified. He called it his "subconscious mind at work." Wyman's best doodling earned comparisons with that of commercial artists, but strikingly, he confessed that if he consciously tried to draw, he simply could not do it. The *Argus Leader* in time dubbed Wyman the "Yankee doodler." His doodling drew heavily from Old West and American Indian motifs, liberally sprinkled with nature scenes and the letters "U.S."

Wyman was a noticeably more prolific doodler in jury trials, with their slower pace, than in actions tried to the court. Usually the court's bailiff was assigned the task of equitably distributing Wyman's work product to jurors and parties. Those who knew him best thought Wyman produced his finest artistry during the trial of Fern Sankey and Ruth Kohler that was about to begin.

The Nineteenth Amendment had secured for women the right to vote, but they were not yet welcome on South Dakota's federal juries. In those days, the process for selecting jurors in South Dakota's federal courts began with Clerk Roy Marker writing to county officials, state court jurists, his own friends — any reliable source — asking them to "send names of men who have been good jurors in your courts."

The Sankey-Kohler defense team faced serious problems, not the least of which was the unresolved enmity between the sisters that had lingered over Roy Gibb's role in Verne Sankey's capture and Fern's rearrest. The women's attorneys requested a meeting with both women simultaneously to seek a reconciliation — or at least a truce that would allow the pair to work together — but the government would not permit it. Judge Wyman refused to intervene, stating he lacked jurisdiction to do so.

The government had its own problems. Its star witness, Gordon Alcorn, was experiencing health troubles. Prison dentists had removed all Alcorn's teeth and fit him for a false set because of the damage done in the beating Youngberg administered to him at the ranch a year earlier. Pyorrhea, which caused a puss-filled inflammation in the sockets, aggravated his condition. The problem was the false set never arrived. Alcorn told Justice Department officials that he would testify only if he had his new false teeth, but when guards loaded him at Leavenworth for the trip to South Dakota, Acorn still had not received the false teeth. The now toothless Gordon Alcorn was having a difficult time enunciating, and he remained recalcitrant. Alcorn's resistance forced prosecutors to assuage the lifer. They granted an extensive visit with Birdie that allowed the couple to celebrate their first wedding anniversary together. Government prosecutors also granted Alcorn the liberty of ordering whatever meals he desired and promised him an automobile ride the night before his scheduled testimony.

On the morning of May 10, spring winds whipped up a massive black blizzard more ferocious and widespread than that of the previous fall. Outside the federal building and all across the prairie towns, people shuffled against a wall of dirt, handkerchiefs around faces to slow the dust's entry into the mucus and lungs. Two days later, dust sifted onto President Roosevelt's desk. Farmers who had already planted, were forced to replant. Others simply gave up; the storms were the last blow they would allow the land to inflict on them. The storm heralded the

start of the worst growing season of the Depression. Was it the beginning of Armageddon?

As the trial began, spectators packed the federal courtroom in Pierre's
post office building, with 150 more overflowing into the hall. Many
pressed through the courtroom doors for even a glimpse of the defendants. The rail intended to separate the audience from the participants
was invisible, with chairs in front of it. Only the attorneys' table stopped
the encroachment toward the bench. The spectators—mostly women
—witnessed a striking spectacle. The two diminutive Wilmot sisters sat
at counsel's table next to their two male attorneys; across from them sat
the two male prosecutors, Olaf Eidem and Assistant U.S. Attorney E. D.
Barron. At 9:00 A.M. federal judge A. Lee Wyman stalked into the courtroom. Aside from the defendants, all trial participants, including the jury
that would decide the women's guilt or innocence, were men.

In jury selection, Eidem asked prospective jurors if they would be
swayed by exhibits of "tears or hysteria" or by the fact that the defendants were "comely and clever women." Ben Laska, still basking in the
Urschel kidnapping case's notoriety, quickly drew Judge Wyman's wrath
as he questioned prospective jurors. In framing his questions, Laska
continually referred to his clients as innocent, naive, and timid. His use
of such terms was, Wyman told him, "highly improper." Wyman's ad-
monishments of Laska became so vociferous that Davenport replaced
him and completed jury selection.

Four farmers, five businessmen, a store clerk, a bank clerk, and a
commercial artist constituted the jury. Half were from Sioux Falls or
the small towns just outside it. All but one were from East River. The
jurors listened carefully while Eidem portrayed Fern Sankey as an archconspirator who drove her husband into crime and was intimately involved in all major details of Charlie Boettcher's abduction. It was her
constant demand for money, Eidem asserted, that fueled her husband's
criminal career. Eidem told jurors that the plan to kidnap Boettcher
began in June 1932 when the Sankeys bought their South Dakota ranch
in her name alone to use as a kidnapping base, complete with its cell-like
basement chamber designed to hold victims.

Laska objected repeatedly to Eidem's opening remarks, peppering his objections with comments that generated another stern rebuke from the burly judge. "Now look here, Mr. Laska," Wyman bellowed, "You and I will get along a whole lot better, if when you have anything to say you stand up and say it and not make any speeches.'"

Late in the afternoon on May 10, as the U.S. Senate and House Conference Committee met to consider amending the Lindbergh Law to provide for the death penalty, the federal government called its first witness against the little women on trial for Lindbergh Law violations in South Dakota.

Once Eidem completed his opening statement, he called Charlie Boettcher to the stand followed by a series of brief witnesses. Chief among them was Claude Boettcher, who identified eleven notes the kidnappers sent him. Laska cross-examined each only briefly, the main inquiry being whether the witness had seen Mrs. Sankey or Mrs. Kohler carry out any act in connection with the ransom notes or knew of any such conduct on either woman's part. Each responded no.

The next day, Gordon Alcorn took the stand. As often happens with a nervous witness, his voice projected poorly; the absence of teeth exacerbated the problem. The *Denver Post*'s Charles O'Brien noted an almost palpable tension in the courtroom.

> Sharp hatred flashed between Alcorn, one-time trusted lieutenant of Verne Sankey . . . and Sankey's widow and her sister, Mrs. Alvina Ruth Kohler. . . . They turned bitter glares on him and he returned these with a stare of defiance. . . .
>
> Alcorn unrolled an absorbing tale.

Alcorn portrayed Verne Sankey as a ruthless, resourceful operator, and his widow as an archconspirator, at times directing even her husband.

Alcorn testified that Fern Sankey had been deeply involved in planning the kidnapping and that both women knew of the plan from its outset. He told the jury both women rode with him and Sankey as they drove past the homes of potential victims. Each morning during the week before Charlie Boettcher was abducted, the little group met at Sankeys' Denver home after Echo left for school.

"Mrs. Sankey was in favor of kidnapping a child, because she said it would not be so hard to take care of," Alcorn testified. "Sankey insisted on asking for $100,000. I suggested $25,000, and Mrs. Sankey finally suggested $50,000 or $60,000." According to Alcorn, Mrs. Sankey suggested the ransom be large enough so they "wouldn't have to do it again.

"Mrs. Kohler and Mrs. Sankey rode around with us one night when we were looking over the houses of prospective victims," Alcorn testified. "Sankey remarked: 'We'll have some of their money soon,' and Mrs. Kohler said: 'Be sure and don't forget me.' One night the whole bunch of us went out together to look over the houses of prospective kidnap victims. In the car were Sankey, Mrs. Sankey, Mrs. Kohler, Carl W. Pearce and myself."

The jury was rapt. Laska objected futilely, but it was not likely that even a handkerchief changing hue would have distracted the jury's attention, and Laska did not attempt it.

"During the two weeks we discussed our plans in Sankey's Denver home, Mrs. Kohler was present at least every other day," Alcorn recounted. He said that Fern Sankey had boasted to the others that she had assisted her husband in collecting the Bohn ransom.

Alcorn replayed for jurors the night of the kidnapping, February 12, 1933. Alcorn and Sankey were driving around the city when they noticed Charlie Boettcher and his wife riding in an automobile, so they followed the couple to the Brown Palace. Sankey and Alcorn went back to Sankey's home, got two guns, and told Fern their plans.

"During this conversation, Mrs. Sankey told us that she still had $500 of the Bohn ransom money left, sewed to a pillow on Echo's bed. Sankey said that the rest of the Bohn ransom money had been exchanged."

The men then left again for the Brown Palace Hotel.

O'Brien kept an eye on Fern Sankey and Ruth Kohler throughout Alcorn's testimony and wrote in that day's coverage that as the two mothers "stared at him with hot resentment, they must have felt the shadow of prison drawing about them." Alcorn held his composure and responded with an icy stare.

Eidem asked Alcorn if he had participated in any discussions with Mrs. Sankey about dividing the ransom. Alcorn replied that he had. "Sankey said that Youngberg and I were to get $30,000 and that the other $30,000 would go to him and his wife."

The problem with Alcorn's testimony was that it painted an entirely different picture of the kidnapping plot to jurors than Alcorn had provided to bureau agents shortly after his capture, three months earlier. Back on February 2, 1934, in the Chicago bureau's nineteenth-floor offices, Alcorn gave Purvis and his agents a written confession — eight single-spaced typed pages — that detailed the kidnappers' planning and execution. Alcorn's statement then bore the hallmark of a scared man who knew he had to come clean. He readily admitted his role in Charlie Boettcher's abduction. Incredibly, throughout his lengthy bureau statement, Alcorn had not even mentioned Fern Sankey's name in connection with the kidnapping's planning and execution. He had said nothing about any role Fern played in selecting a victim or establishing the ransom demand. There was no mention of her name regarding events the night the duo abducted Boettcher. Despite all this, the federal attorneys elicited testimony from Alcorn that Fern Sankey had actually been the group's leader, directing her notorious husband's activities. Alcorn would have been cannon fodder on cross-examination, except for one additional fact: Laska and Davenport were not aware that the February bureau statement even existed, because at that time no rule required the government to produce it. If the defense *had* been provided a copy of the statement, it would have served as the centerpiece of their cross, allowing them to neutralize the prosecution's key witness with that document alone.

Alcorn gave jurors a version different than he had provided bureau agents on other key points as well. For example, he told bureau agents that when he and Sankey confronted Charles and Anna Boettcher in their driveway, Sankey, revolver in hand, approached Charlie and directed him to Sankey's car. Boettcher appeared to be drunk. "As soon as Boettcher . . . got over to our car, he reeled as if to fall and I caught him and put him in the back seat of our car on Sankey's orders." After giving Anna Lou instructions, they were off for the ranch. Jurors heard none of this — from Charlie or from Gordon Alcorn.

Davenport's cross-examination of Alcorn focused on the assertion that

Alcorn's testimony was motivated by a desire for a sentence reduction and revenge against Sankey's widow for Sankey's wrongs to him. But Alcorn was unwavering in denying that Verne dominated his wife. "When she said anything, he minded her," Alcorn testified. When Davenport reminded Alcorn about his falling out with Sankey in Chicago, Alcorn admitted that he had dug up money he and Sankey had earlier buried north of Chicago, but denied he intended to steal it from Sankey. Alcorn told jurors that he had dug up the money for safekeeping in his apartment, but that Sankey then approached him at his apartment and took twelve thousand dollars of his share. His testimony on this point also contradicted the earlier statement he had given to bureau agents. He had told them Sankey had taken twelve thousand dollars, which included about two thousand dollars of Alcorn's share. Of course, neither the defense nor the jury was aware of the contradiction.

The government's case concluded with testimony from bureau agent Werner Hanni and St. Paul chief of police Thomas Dahill. Fern's ill-advised statements to them after the Bohn trial were now used against her. Hanni, fresh from his involvement a month earlier in the bureau's disastrous shootout at Little Bohemia, testified that after Mrs. Sankey had been acquitted in Ramsey County Court in the Bohn case, she admitted to him that she had cooked meals in the house where Bohn was being held. A fellow agent corroborated Hanni's account. While the evidence of Fern's alleged role in the Bohn case was admissible only as evidence of "other acts" to show a plan to kidnap for ransom, and not to establish her guilt in the Boettcher case, it was nonetheless damaging.

After the government rested its case, the defense asked the judge to direct a verdict of acquittal, which Wyman denied. Fern Sankey and Ruth Kohler both broke down in tears. The defense then made its opening statement and re-called government witness Ray Robinson. It elicited testimony from him that when he and Sankey were holding Haskell Bohn, Sankey came into the basement and told him, "The old lady wants us to turn Bohn loose," to which Robinson said he replied, "I'm in favor of that."

Davenport and Laska knew jurors needed to hear from Fern Sankey that she was not a criminal. Thus Fern Sankey took the witness seat, swore to tell the whole truth, and answered questions in hushed tones.

Jurors and those in the audience strained to hear her words; even the judge struggled to do so. Even when he admonished her to speak up, she continued to speak in muted tones.

She told jurors she had not gone with Pearce the night the ransom was delivered. "I know this because my baby was sick on that night. Mrs. Kohler and I were at my home." When asked if she had suggested abducting a child, she replied, "That is impossible. I have two children of my own and that would be the last thing I would think of." Fern characterized her dead husband as someone who "gave orders and took no advice." Fern said that when he abducted and held Haskell Bohn for money, Vern ordered her to cook for one more person. She begged her husband to set Bohn loose but was told to mind her own business. Fern said she was heartbroken, took the kids to a motel, and came back only for clothes.

The barely audible tones in which she testified finally caused Wyman to erupt. "If you haven't enough interest in this trial not to speak up so the jury can hear you," he barked, "I can't help it. I'm through trying to hear the evidence myself."

Davenport and Laska then called Ruth Kohler to the stand. On direct examination, she denied any involvement in Charlie Boettcher's heist, as her sister had. Assistant U.S. Attorney Barron cross-examined her relentlessly for nearly two hours and, if anything, Kohler's presentation was worse than Fern's. When Barron asked her if she was to get any of the Boettcher ransom, she lamely replied, "Not that I remember."

Ruth frequently claimed, as Fern had earlier done, that she could not remember facts. Barron finally overplayed his hand, asking, inanely, "Do you believe kidnapping is the most dastardly of all crimes?" Ruth replied with what seems like the obvious response: "I think murder is worse"; but the question revealed the mindset prevalent in 1933 and 1934, that kidnapping was indeed the most heinous of crimes.

Kohler's mannerisms also hurt her credibility. She appeared agitated, constantly picking at imaginary threads on her dress as Barron pressed her. The prosecutor was forced to repeat questions as Ruth "gazed at the ceiling and about the room and at times her answers were so nearly inaudible that she [too] was admonished by the court."

The defense resorted to traipsing Echo to the stand to try to salvage her mother's case. Fern again broke down as her daughter took the witness seat. The defense ended their presentation with Harold Brown, the Buffalo County state's attorney and Sankey family lawyer and friend. Brown testified that when he talked to Alcorn at the penitentiary, Alcorn told Brown that the women had "nothing to do with the Boettcher kidnapping." The defense staggered through to the end of their evidence but it had lost a lot of blood.

In closing arguments, District Attorney Eidem called the women disgraceful mothers. Directing an accusatory finger in their direction, he employed a stream of invectives to characterize them—archconspirators, prime movers, gangster molls, "clever, heartless plotters." He told jurors that a conviction in this case would strike a blow to gangland's use of molls. "To stop kidnapping or racketeering by gangsters," Eidem railed, "we must take away from them their women who act as cover. No major gangster can carry on his trade without having some woman for cover." Eidem ridiculed the defense's suggestions that the women were incapable of helping plan such a bold, audacious crime, portraying Fern Sankey as an exceptionally bright woman.

Holton Davenport presented the defendants' initial closing argument. He played on the jurors' sympathies, asking them to consider the well-being of Echo and Orville. He labeled his clients "stupid women," and "timid as frightened rabbits" in front of the all-male jury, acknowledging that both women either knew or suspected that their men were involved in the kidnapping, but reasoned that it was only out of love and loyalty that Fern Sankey did not leave. It was the best he could muster.

In the government's rebuttal, Barron focused on Alcorn's searing testimony that Fern Sankey had urged the kidnapping of the Boettchers' five-year-old daughter. "[Mrs. Sankey] called herself a mother yet she had no consideration for other mothers." Fern Sankey had wept throughout much of the trial but now wailed. Undeterred, Barron directed jurors' attentions to the nice clothes and the rings Mrs. Sankey wore—all made possible, he told them, by the ransom paid for Charlie Boettcher's freedom. The statement had nothing to do with the evidence, but it was potent. In his segment of the closing, Laska tried to recover from the blunder of allowing Fern to wear jewelry, telling jurors Fern's was of the "tin store variety" and not the real thing. What else could he say?

After the attorneys completed closing arguments, Judge Wyman instructed the jury as to the law — from memory, as was his routine. Wyman explained to jurors that Alcorn was an admitted accomplice to the kidnapping and, as such, they must carefully weigh his testimony and act on it cautiously. Yet, if they were satisfied he was telling the truth, there was no reason Alcorn's testimony should be considered any differently from that of any other witness.

Wyman told the jury they must consider his instructions in whole and not single out any one instruction above the rest, but one instruction loomed largest — and was the bedrock of the defense hopes. Today it seems an archaic, quaint reminder of a not-so-distant past when the law treated relationships between men and women much differently, but Judge Wyman told the jurors that the law imposed a duty on a wife to hold her husband in utmost respect and esteem; in exchange, it cloaked her with the presumption that any acts she performed in his presence were performed under coercion. The presumption covered any conduct Mrs. Sankey carried out in the immediate presence of her husband. He cautioned them that if they were satisfied she was not acting under Verne Sankey's duress or coercion, or if she committed acts aiding the kidnapping effort outside her husband's immediate presence, such evidence could overcome the presumption that she acted under coercion. It was over this point of law that the jurors would most struggle.

At about 6:00 P.M. Judge Wyman placed the fate of Fern Sankey and Ruth Kohler in the jurors' hands. A guilty verdict meant a sentence of up to life behind bars. The jury deliberated into the night without reaching a verdict. They reconvened the following day, May 18, deliberated through the lunch hour, past the supper hour, and into a second night.

Accounts of the deliberations depict a sharply divided jury. Its first vote revealed six favoring conviction for both women and six for acquittal. The ballots that followed ranged from as many as nine for conviction, to as many as eight for acquittal. Late on the second day, the jury submitted questions to the judge that sought additional explanation of three separate aspects of Wyman's instructions: the doctrines of conspiracy, reasonable doubt, and the law that presumed a wife acts under duress in her husband's presence. Wyman clarified those legal points and the jurors deliberated further.

Shortly before 10:00 P.M., they returned to the courtroom, where foreman B. E. Ketcham of Madison stood to tell the judge they were "hopelessly deadlocked." The final tally was the same as the first — six to six.

Fern Sankey remained free on ten-thousand-dollars bond. She vowed to return to the ranch, saying only that she "hoped it would rain." Loquacious Ben Laska sounded sanguine about the outcome. It was, he chortled, "as good as a victory." That was not at all true, of course, but it was clear that the government had oversold its case to the jury by portraying Fern Sankey as not merely a participant but as an "archconspirator" and "prime mover" in the kidnapping. The deadpan Eidem flatly announced that the case would be retried at the next term of federal court in October. He would not be in office to retry it: as a Republican, he was about to be replaced by an FDR appointee.

14

Convicting Dead Cats?

A few days after the trial concluded, police gunned down the young Texas outlaws Bonnie Parker and Clyde Barrow on a dusty Louisiana road. The couple's robberies had often as not brought paltry financial returns but frequently left dead and wounded in their wake.

John Dillinger continued to evade the nationwide effort to nab him, and in late June Attorney General Cummings issued a $10,000 reward for his capture. Cummings refrained from using the terms "public enemy" and "dead or alive" in his statement, but the reward, authorized as part of the twelve-point plan, most of which Congress had recently adopted, was the first ever issued by the Justice Department. The implication was clear that Dillinger was now the nation's most important criminal.

The government's efforts culminated when more than twenty bureau agents — now authorized to carry guns — alerted by Melvin Purvis's pre-arranged signal, closed in on Dillinger as he exited Chicago's Biograph Theatre, where agents shot him to death. Dillinger had held the press-designated title of Public Enemy No. 1 for all of one month. With Dillinger dead, the unofficial moniker of America's chief public enemy fell to Arthur "Pretty Boy" Floyd, who, along with his alcoholic partner

Eddie Richetti, were the chief surviving suspects in the Union Station Massacre.

South Dakota's new U.S. attorney, George Philip, was confirmed by the Senate, replacing Eidem. Born in 1880 and raised in the Scottish Highlands along the southwestern shores of Loch Ness, Philip followed four of his father's brothers to America when he was seventeen, settling on the ranch of an uncle whom he had never met, James "Scotty" Philip. Scotty Philip's ranch outside Fort Pierre was one of the state's largest cattle operations. He also bought one of the last bison herds in captivity and dedicated himself to saving the animal from extinction—a goal he accomplished. Scotty Philip was also the brother-in-law of the famed Sioux Chief Crazy Horse, the men having married part-French, part-Indian sisters.

Scotty treated George like his own son, and George rode the range, cowboying alongside Scotty's ranch hands. But when a con man fleeced him in a transaction that cost him his own growing herd, he left the ranch for the University of Michigan's law school, determined to "learn to draw a contract so I would never fall prey to a hustler again." After he was graduated, in 1906, Philip barely got his law office opened back in Ft. Pierre, when his Uncle Scotty commissioned him and a couple of veteran cowboys to chaperone two bison bulls by train to Juarez for a contest in which an argument would be settled: Was the North American bison or the Mexican fighting bull the fiercest animal? The story George later recounted of the adventure was a hilarious romp by train across the border into Mexico, colored by dealings with corrupt officials and wild escapades.

In 1917, Philip moved his law practice and growing family from Fort Pierre to Rapid City. Philip was a Democrat and a close friend and advisor of "Cowboy Governor" Tom Berry. He served on the Mount Rushmore National Memorial Commission, a group dedicated to raising money to help a dreamer carve the images of four presidents on a granite mountain. When Roosevelt defeated Hoover in 1932, Governor Berry nominated his friend Philip as the state's next U.S. attorney.

When he took office, Philip saw the Sankey retrial on the horizon. It would prove to be one of the most significant and difficult cases he would handle.

The first trial — in Pierre — had brought about a thaw of sorts in the relationship between the two estranged sisters. They were talking again and even appeared cordial with one another. Ruth Kohler and Calista had clearly distanced themselves from Roy Gibbs's betrayal of the Sankey family. The government had not called Gibbs as a witness in the first trial but it subpoenaed him for the retrial, which was to be held in Sioux Falls rather than Pierre — this, at the request of the defense for the convenience of witnesses traveling from out of state.

Gibbs's life had been threatened, reportedly because of his cooperation with federal authorities in the case. A few weeks before the October retrial, Colorado U.S. attorney Tom Morrissey leaked to Denver reporter Charles O'Brien that he was working with South Dakota authorities on new evidence that the government would use against Mrs. Sankey. Presumably, that evidence involved Gibbs.

Then on October 12, just days before the retrial, the twenty-eight-year-old Gibbs was shot to death in the mountains near Estes Park, Colorado. Gibbs, who at the time was working as a bookbinder, was traveling in the company of a friend, John Hammond, a thirty-year-old utility company lineman. According to Hammond, the men were on their way to hunt deer — at one o'clock in the morning — when, as they drove along a mountain road, Gibbs saw a fox cross the road in the headlights' beam. Hammond claimed that Gibbs then yelled, "There's a fox! Shoot him!" and lunged for his revolver. The car careened right then overturned and plunged into a ravine. Hammond said he heard the gun discharge as Gibbs flew out of the car. Gibbs's body came to rest in the ravine, a .32-caliber slug through his head. Hammond remarkably sustained only minor injuries.

He told an inquest panel that he had reached for Gibbs's pistol after opening the passenger door to attempt to fire on the fox, but seemed unsure of what followed. "The car went off the road and overturned,"

Hammond told the panel. "I don't think I got the gun, unless I grabbed it as the car went over. I believe Gibbs snatched it and it went off when the car was wrecked."

The inquest panel concluded Gibbs's death was accidental. Gibbs carried with him to the grave the story of how he learned of Sankey's whereabouts.

Gibbs's estranged but not-yet-divorced wife Calista sought the re-maining fruits of his estate, pitted against Gibbs' parents. It raised the specter of Claude Boettcher's reward being used by faithful daughter Calista to finance her mother's kidnapping defense.

In August, Gordon Alcorn, Capone, "Machine Gun Kelly," Albert Bates, and a host of other notorious federal prisoners were transferred to the government's new island prison at Alcatraz, a converted army bar-racks off the San Francisco coast. When authorities returned Alcorn to Sioux Falls for the October trial, he bragged that he had become good friends with Capone who was, Alcorn said, the "life of the party." Alcorn also claimed that he had befriended Kelly there.

While jurors gathered in Sioux Falls on October 22 for the retrial of the wife of the country's first Public Enemy No. 1, Melvin Purvis and his agents gunned down America's then unofficial Public Enemy No. 1, Arthur "Pretty Boy" Floyd, in a rural Ohio field. Floyd's partner, Rich-etti, was captured near Wellsville, Ohio, that same day. Floyd's reign had lasted three months. That same day the AP reported that an unidentified Justice Department source announced that "Baby Face" Nelson was the nation's new chief enemy. It also reported that New Jersey officials had announced a solution to the two-and-one-half-year-old Lindbergh case with the arrest of Bruno Richard Hauptmann, who reportedly sought Ben Laska's counsel.

The tempo of the second Sankey trial would be far different than the first. The attorneys for both parties had access to the court reporter's transcript of the first trial to aid them in preparing their cross-examina-tions of opposing witnesses. It was a crucial tool.

The federal courthouse in Sioux Falls was — and remains — a majestic structure, with three Romanesque stories of jasper pink quartzite and marble stairs leading to the third-floor courtroom. The courtroom's twenty-foot-high walls of oak panels were set off with gold-plated vent grills and enormous southern exposure windows, all connected by ornate lattice works which rimmed the room. Prospective jurors that late October morning found the courtroom quickly filling with anxious onlookers. As in Pierre, the mostly female crowd was so large it spilled into the corridor. The surprise of the morning came not in the form of a new star witness but in the announcement that the retrial would proceed without Ruth Kohler. Washington decided to try only Fern Sankey, the defendant against whom it had the strongest case. The government's decision to remove Ruth Kohler permitted the prosecution to focus solely on Fern's conduct.

It was a reasoned approach but also one Davenport and Laska no doubt welcomed: they too could focus the jury's attention solely on the more appealing of the defendants and the one with the adorable young children.

Jury selection stretched into midafternoon. After the first twelve names were called and the men seated, Davenport quizzed them as Fern Sankey sat at counsel's table, hands folded on her lap, intently following prospective jurors' responses to her lawyer's questions. Charlie Boettcher watched from the oak pews behind her.

The final jury was almost the opposite in geographical makeup from the Pierre jury. Eight were from western or central South Dakota — areas that had experienced the full fury of depression, drought, and dust: oil station attendants from Martin and Dupree, a rancher from Pedro, an Orient insurance agent, a Midland farmer, a Murdo carpenter, a Chamberlain bank examiner, and an Aberdeen shoe salesman. None lived within a hundred miles of Sioux Falls.

Late that afternoon, the old cowboy, George Philip, read jurors the lengthy indictment, then laid out what he expected the facts to show. It was vastly different from Eidem's Pierre opening. Gone were the pejoratives characterizing Fern Sankey as the archconspirator who drove her husband to crime. Philip's habit was to face the jurors, one hand in his hind pocket, the other punctuating his remarks, index finger directed at the jury, the defendant — wherever his subject took him. He employed simple, easily understood words delivered with striking authority so that no one who saw him operate in the courtroom forgot the experience.

Countering Philip's presentation, Davenport told the jurors they had to decide not whether Verne Sankey had kidnapped Charlie Boettcher but whether Mrs. Sankey had willingly participated. He reminded them of the legal presumption so prominent in the first trial — "What a wife does in the presence of her husband she does under his compulsion."

Davenport told jurors that although they would hear from many witnesses, "all evidence against Mrs. Sankey will come from the testimony of Gordon Alcorn, who we will show had quarreled with Sankey over the Boettcher ransom money and who had a distinct antipathy to Mrs. Sankey."

Davenport characterized Fern Sankey as an innocent farm girl, heartsick and constantly worried because her husband followed a life of crime. She had known nothing of the Boettcher plot until after the kidnapping occurred and could not have participated in its planning because she disliked Alcorn. Alcorn had, Davenport told jurors, referred to her as a "heifer," a remark she never forgot. Davenport turned the government's characterization of Fern Sankey back on Alcorn, characterizing him as a man vicious enough to kidnap a five-year-old girl. Alcorn was motivated, Davenport urged, by his quest for favorable government treatment for a pardon or early parole and his desire was to get even with Sankey for treating him unfairly in the ransom division.

With the issues framed for the jury, testimony began. This trial moved more briskly than the first, each party's attorneys more clearly ascertaining what could be accomplished with each witness. Witnesses quickly retraced testimony from the first trial; jurors heard seventeen government witnesses testify that first day; most testimony was brief.

On Wednesday afternoon, Gordon Alcorn took the stand. Armed with the Pierre trial transcript and given five months to prepare, Davenport first pummeled Alcorn's character, questioning in detail about how Alcorn and Sankey trailed five-year-old Ann Boettcher, intending to kidnap her. Davenport then parsed Alcorn's testimony, exposing for jurors evidence he had uncovered in the first trial — that Alcorn had never made his claims against Mrs. Sankey until her husband was dead, even though he had met often with prosecutors and bureau agents.

In nearly every instance Davenport impeached Alcorn's May trial testimony — how it had changed in ways that implicated Mrs. Sankey.

In an effort to blunt Davenport's claim that Alcorn had been willing to kidnap little Ann Boettcher, Philip elicited Alcorn's testimony that Mrs. Sankey had accompanied the men when they trailed the Boettcher child. The problem was that Alcorn had testified differently at Pierre, further weakening his credibility.

The defense called Ruth Kohler, Fern Sankey, and Harold Brown. Kohler's testimony was much better this time — brief, but touching all the key points. Fern Sankey looked weary as she softly answered Ben Laska's questions. The long months of agony were beginning to show. Fern again flatly denied participating in the kidnappings of either Boettcher or Haskell Bohn. In a low voice she told Laska that she had never had a confidential conversation with Gordon Alcorn in her life — had, in fact, never made any statements to him about a kidnapping. Yes, she recalled her husband driving to the ranch and returning to their Denver house with Gordon Alcorn, but when Alcorn left with Sankey on the night of the kidnapping she did not see him again until the Pierre trial.

George Philip's cross-examination of Fern Sankey was consistent with his style — direct and to the point. Did Fern deny that she had told former St. Paul police chief Dahill that she had been out in the automobile with her husband to deliver a ransom note in the Bohn case? She replied that she did not remember making such a statement. Did she deny telling bureau agent John Dowd that she had met Alcorn for the first time in Denver? "No," she replied. Had she told Omaha bureau chief Werner Hanni that she had convinced her husband to reduce the Bohn ransom from $35,000 to $12,000? Yes, she denied that she told Werner Hanni such a thing.

Why had the name "Sykes" been given to the Denver landlord when Sankey had rented the house? Philip asked. Fern responded that she did not know her husband had given that name and had later explained to the landlord it must have been a mistake. She *was* forced to admit that she had signed the name "Mae Young" on an application for gas and electricity service at Denver and that she used the name "Mrs. Moore" when she took a car to a Chicago service station in September 1933 but only because "Moore" was the name of her sister who lived in Chicago — and in whose name the car was titled.

There was a lot to explain. As Fern Sankey stepped down from the witness stand, a reporter noted that she "seemed to be in a daze . . . . her step wavered as she returned to her seat behind the attorneys."

The last witness was Harold Brown. There was little doubt that the thirty-four-year-old county prosecutor was an important endorsement of Fern Sankey's innocence. Brown was a plain and simple man, comfortable conversing with farmers and ranchers, Indians and town folk alike. He told jurors that while he was at the penitentiary he asked Gordon Alcorn whether "either . . . Mrs. Sankey or Mrs. Kohler, had anything to do with kidnapping." Alcorn replied matter-of-factly that neither woman had been involved. That was the last evidence jurors heard.

In closing, Laska barked that he "would not convict a dead cat on the evidence offered by the government against Mrs. Sankey." He asked, as he had in Pierre, why the government, who carried the burden of proving Mrs. Sankey's guilt, had not brought Pearce and Youngberg to court to hear *their* testimony. "A statement from them would exonerate Mrs. Sankey in three seconds." Laska mocked the prosecution's characterization of Alcorn as a reliable witness. "If Alcorn was on trial in this court today, the district attorney would pick [him] to pieces, but now that he is a witness for the government, Alcorn seems to have suddenly sprouted wings." It became difficult even for partisans to suppress smiles.

The jury got the case shortly after four on Friday afternoon and deliberated into the evening. At 8:55 P.M., they informed the bailiff they had reached a verdict. The tension became palpable as the court personnel reassembled. Anxious spectators shuffled back inside the courtroom. A pall hung heavily around the accused. Echo and Orville milled among the onlookers who filled the gallery.

When the words "All rise in honor of the jury" rang out, the jurors, solemn and worn, reentered the courtroom from the rear, single file, past the gallery of onlookers, past the attorneys, and past Fern Sankey. Multitudes of eyes searched jurors' countenances for any hint as to what verdict they had reached. After seating himself, Judge Wyman asked if the jury had reached a verdict. Foreman Frank Brady of Chamberlain rose with paper in hand and replied that it had. Marshal C. W. Robertson then approached the jury foreman, took the written decision from him, and handed it to the judge. After silently reading the verdict, the judge handed it to the court clerk, Roy B. Marker, who then audibly read words that echoed around the nation: "We the jury, duly assembled in the above matter to try the case of *United States v. Fern Sankey*, find the defendant not guilty."

The accused quivered with relief, then nearly collapsed. As her loved ones and friends thronged her, she clasped her hands together in thanksgiving. A reporter recreated the scene: "She pulled herself together and went over to the jurors and wrung the hand of each, almost overpowered by the emotion of her gratitude."

The trials of Mrs. Sankey had been among the longest criminal trials ever held in South Dakota's federal court. Jurors had voted four times to reach this decision. The first vote had been eight to four in favor of acquittal; the second ten to two, the third, eleven to a solitary holdout, who was finally swayed by the others to make it unanimous. Fern Sankey had now been tried three times for conspiracy to kidnap and walked out of the courtroom with no criminal record. The diminutive mother had beaten the State of Minnesota and now had given Cummings, Hoover, and Purvis their first defeat under the Lindbergh Law. She had done it during a period when the hysteria surrounding kidnapping had created a most unfavorable environment for a person charged with such a crime. In contrast to Hoover's earlier profile in the matter, he was noticeably silent, almost invisible.

All that mattered to Fern Sankey, though, was that she had won back her life, had been given a second chance. She told reporters she just wanted to go home.

15

They Who Lie in Wait

After the mortgage redemption period passed in early December 1934, Fern and Orville lingered around Gann Valley for a time. She survived as a WPA seamstress while Orville attended Gann Valley school. Echo stayed with Minnesota relatives, free from attention. Fern's relationship with the bachelor Mike Chopskie, her advisor and steadfast friend, had deepened into romance. It was reported that she was in love; but, for reasons lost to time, the relationship ended. It was clear to Fern that she and her children needed a fresh start to allow them an opportunity to extinguish the past or to at least neatly seam it up within the fabric of a new home, a new beginning. She and Orville left Buffalo County around 1935, settling in Seattle, where two of her sisters lived.

For the next lifetime, Fern Sankey labored long hours in draperies at Seattle's Bon Marche, dragging panels of the heavy fabric as she hemmed. It was hard, tedious work that took its toll on the slight woman. The modest pay allowed her and her son to survive. She never remarried.

Orville's memories of his Buffalo County days are hazy. He carries only the vaguest recollections of his father. Mike Chopskie was the only father figure Orville recalled. Decades later Orville recalled, "I kind of had my heart set on that he'd be my dad sometime." It never came to pass. Orville remained fatherless.

Echo Sankey had been a lovely child and grew into a lovely adult. She had seen and heard things no child should be exposed to; she had, for example, been in the car with Carl Pearce, Ruth Kohler, and Fern Sankey when Pearce gave Alcorn the clearance to release Charlie Boettcher and recover the ransom. But Echo had persevered, as though the innumerable bruises of her childhood had imbued her with deeper compassion and less judgment toward others. She conducted herself with character and dignity throughout her life, exhibiting a kind heart. She fell in love with and married a man who operated a pet salon, selling animal care items and providing grooming services. The two produced a daughter and worked alongside one another until his death in the 1980s. Throughout her life, Echo never spoke of the kidnappings and the ensuing trauma, even with her closest friends, except to admonish them to keep the events of those years from Orville.

Echo maintained a lifelong relationship with her South Dakota childhood friend, Carol Stephens. The two regularly corresponded through the years and periodically visited one another's homes despite the great distance separating them. They remained friends until Echo's death at age eighty in 1999.

Orville Sankey speaks with the soft tones of a gentleman so that one wonders if the demeanor he exhibits has its roots in his father's charm. He carries the manner of a man who has led a satisfying life, having served others in meaningful work and successfully raised three sons. After graduating from a Seattle high school, Orville chanced into a career as an occularist, hand-painting and custom-fitting artificial eyes for people who have lost theirs.

"I always felt that I was helping people," he says.

He has now passed the business on to his own son. Retired, Orville and his wife spend their days enjoying the grandchildren their three sons have produced. He has come a long way for a Depression boy whose father was Public Enemy No. 1.

Throughout the balance of her life, Fern Sankey dwelled quietly in humble circumstances. She grew passionate about baseball — perhaps the one thing the Sankeys shared with the Boettchers. She maintained enduringly loving relationships with her two children, both of whom lived nearby. In the end, Fern Sankey served her own prison term of sorts, bound to a wheelchair in her declining years. She died in 1994, having reached ninety-nine. By then, there was no one left to condemn or accuse her, no one even to recall the reasons one might do so. She had outlived her entire generation, her saga forgotten even by historians of the period, drawn to the glamorous, more accessible images of "Machine Gun Kelly," "Pretty Boy" Floyd, and Dillinger.

Although none of the juries who heard charges against her convicted her, Fern had in fact been far more involved in her husband's enterprises than she ever allowed. Her plaintive words to the Denver reporter after her March 1933 arrest rang hollow by the third trial's end: "There are thousands of others like me — just home wives. Our husbands . . . tell us nothing of their affairs. . . . They give us jewels, automobiles and new fur coats. We say thanks and never think to ask where the money came from."

She paid dearly for any transgressions, having endured earth's purest form of Hell during 1933 and 1934. She had been stripped of the sheen of the demure wife of a successful entrepreneur; jailed four times, totaling six months; denounced as a heartless plotter; witnessed her life laid bare in the national media; experienced agonizing separation from her children; staved off poverty; bore shame.

The Sankey family's West Coast anonymity was Fern's greatest reprieve. Few, if any, of her circle of nonfamily contacts there ever knew she had been married to America's No. 1 public enemy, that she had been charged with conspiracy to kidnap, that she thrice stood trial, and faced life in prison. Fern kept the truth from Orville, who was told that his father had been killed by a train. It was an honorable way to die. Orville was not aware even where his father was buried.

If Fern ever again mentioned the events of the Buffalo County years, no record of it remains. It was as if she took out her needle and thread and sewed the past closed inside impermeable fabric. One wishes to have been able to sit with her, even long years later and mine her memories, but it never happened. She bore them to her grave, lodged deep inside her bosom.

Historians still debate whether there was, in fact, a crime wave in the 1930s. Statistical data, such as it then existed, is inconclusive. What *is* clear is that an enormous number of crimes were perpetrated by inordinately few individuals. The spate of midwestern robberies in the late 1920s and early 1930s were largely the work of Bailey, Nash, Miller, Floyd, Kelly, the Barker-Karpis gang, the Barrows, and the Dillinger and Nelson gangs—perhaps as few as thirty men in all. Of the period's major kidnappings, Sankey and the Barker-Karpis gang each perpetrated two, and Kelly one. If there was a crime wave, it ended by 1935; by then virtually all the major midwestern outlaws had been either killed or captured.

The most indomitable enemy of the American people in 1933 was not the gangster but the Depression. Its lackeys and molls were poverty, alcoholism, and despair. The concept of "Public Enemy No. 1" held utility chiefly as a means to focus effort on eradicating the midwestern gangster. He was a highly visible target, considering the attention the press gave him. But once identified, he was a relatively easy enemy to vanquish.

All this is not to suggest the public enemy designation was without meaning. It provided a snapshot of sorts for posterity as to whom various local, state, and the federal governments considered the country's most important outlaw at a fixed moment. Despite Hoover's well-grounded objection that such a designation simply gave crooks something to aim for, the term proved a useful tool.

When in June 1934 Attorney General Cummings offered a government reward for Dillinger's death or capture, the public and press could not mistake whom Justice viewed as the country's new chief enemy. The government also exploited its pursuit of Dillinger and the others to promote its crime legislation. It used Sankey's capture, Dillinger's death, and the fate of their successors to demonstrate to Americans that government could enforce the nation's collective will, even against the wiliest and most dangerous desperadoes. Thus, in its own inimitable way, the public enemy concept became a crucial, if overlooked, component of the New Deal.

When the bureau had vanquished the relatively small band of midwestern gangsters, the crime spree, such as it was, largely ended. But it was chiefly through those pursuits that Hoover's band of youthful, law-trained agents — often inexperienced and ill-suited for the gun-toting roles they were forced to assume — transformed themselves into a symbol of law and order the entire world recognized and sought to emulate.

As quickly as the spate of bank robberies waned, the kidnapping epidemic — which ironically spiked following enactment of the Lindbergh Law — also subsided. The number of ransom kidnaps, after peaking at twenty-seven in 1933, slowed to a trickle. In 1939 there were only two. In 1963, the FBI claimed that it had solved all but two American ransom kidnaps since 1932.

The Sankeys' place in the history of 1930s crime lore, like so much else about the period, may be debated by thoughtful historians of the era. What is indisputable is that Verne Sankey was a trailblazer in the post–Lindbergh Law kidnapping epidemic. His abduction of Haskell Bohn was the first ransom kidnapping in America after the law's enactment, and his kidnapping of Charlie Boettcher was the first that involved a victim transported across state lines, following enactment. The Sankeys were the first to be charged under that law as well. Charlie Boettcher's kidnapping was the first the bureau actively investigated, and it was the first involving midwestern outlaws as such.

Finally, the short, round, affable Verne Sankey became the first person — and strictly speaking, the only person — ever identified by the Justice Department as America's "Public Enemy No. 1." Why, then, did Sankey fade from America's collective consciousness?

Several explanations offer themselves. Of the first four men designated — by either the government or the press — as America's Public Enemy No. 1, the others — Dillinger, Floyd, and Nelson — all went down in a blaze of gunfire, even though Dillinger returned no fire before his own killing and had himself meekly entered custody in Indiana before his celebrated breakout. Sankey resisted being taken alive, as well — but he had something different in mind from a shootout with the cops. Killing himself was a much more humane, if less dramatic approach. Also, Sankey's countenance simply did not conjure up images of a feared outlaw. He looked more like a haberdasher. The account of virtually everyone who knew him described Verne Sankey as pleasant-looking — not particularly attractive but a man who drew people to him because he had a likable, mild-mannered persona. His description fit no one's paradigm of a feared public enemy. Sankey suffered, too, from the lack of a colorful name or nickname.

Unlike Dillinger, Floyd, Nelson, and Karpis, Sankey eschewed the gangster image, save in banter with his closest compatriots. Like Harvey Bailey and Verne Miller, Sankey dwelled behind the veneer of respectability. Bailey and Miller each held memberships in more than one fashionable country club and, like Sankey, were Masons. In Sankey's case, though, it was more than a cover; it was entwined with who he understood himself to be. Sankey viewed himself as a family man who had committed unlawful acts, rather than as a crook who happened to have produced offspring.

In an interview Sankey granted while held in Sioux Falls, he told a reporter, "My life's mistake was asking $60,000 instead of 200 grand from Boettcher." It was a pathetic appraisal, one that utterly failed to acknowledge his real error — his choice to squander his abilities in a life of crime. It missed the mark in another way: Sankey was such an intractable gambler that no sum of money could ever have sufficed.

Sankey's notoriety in 1933 and early 1934 occurred partly because of the shocking crimes he committed, but also because he evaded capture so long and because of suspicions he was involved in the Hamm, Bremer, and Lindbergh abductions. Then, too, no other, more prominently known figure had come into the public's view as the bureau emerged to blunt crime's run. It is interesting to recall Dillinger's delivery into the custody of Crown Point jail authorities the same day agents grilled Sankey in Purvis's office a short drive away: on that day, the government hailed Sankey's capture, not Dillinger's, as that which had netted the country's chief enemy. It was when Dillinger subsequently posed for that picture with Prosecutor Estill and Sheriff Holley, and later escaped from Crown Point's confines, thereafter narrowly escaping bureau traps a few more times before his death four months later, that the joint efforts of Cummings, Hoover, and the nation's newspapers cast John Dillinger as the sum of all crime. With each successor to Dillinger's dubious mantle, Sankey's visage faded further from the public's consciousness.

Part of Sankey's modern-day anonymity is due also to the fact that so much of the research from the period is derived from FBI files garnered under the Freedom of Information Act. Records of the Sankey investigation have never surfaced in those files, although many separate regional files regarding him at one point existed.

Melvin Purvis considered Sankey significant enough to merit several pages in his memoirs. In them, Purvis observed:

> Sankey has sometimes been called the most intelligent of all the kidnappers; certainly my conversation with him would not lead me to contradict the statement. When I talked to him, he was . . . substantial-appearing and, to a degree, handsome. He did not look in the slightest like a criminal; he was forthright in speech and action; and he gave me no clue whatever to the events or combination of events which led him into crime. The fact remains that he was the master mind.

Purvis recalled that when he interrogated Sankey at the Chicago bureau, Sankey appeared relieved that the chase was finally over. "Only once did he become angry . . . [when] I asked him about [the Lindbergh abduction]. Sankey's temper flared. He looked at me with bitter, outraged eyes. 'I am a man,' he said. 'I'd kidnap another man. I'd never touch a baby.'"

Seventy years later, Doris Rogers Lockerman reflected:

> I remember [Sankey] well. . . . Not too many things have been written about Sankey [but] that doesn't minimize his significance. It is not that Sankey was not a pungent person in that time. I've made this observation in the past. Both [Verne] Miller and Sankey were not New York gangsters. They did not come from gang families. . . . My South

Dakota gangsters would easily be our neighbors and friends. We didn't look upon them, even when they were proven guilty, as public enemies. They had nice families. You have to understand that the Depression hit South Dakota and the Middle West terribly hard. It depleted the soil; it didn't rain. Things blew away. People were leaving homes to go to more opportunity.

Verne Sankey was a man with real friends who lived within the law, raised their families, attended church, paid their bills. He knew other gangsters only in the sense of his bootlegging connections.

After Sankey's death, his friends made excuses for his behavior or explained it away. Those excuses were products of sincere efforts to reconcile the contradictory images of the Verne Sankey they knew and the man billed as the country's chief public enemy. In fact, even sixty years later, locals from Gann Valley and Melville who knew the Sankeys harbored suspicions that the unindicted coconspirator in the Charlie Boettcher kidnapping was Charlie Boettcher himself, or that Vern Sankey was killed because he would not admit to kidnapping the Lindbergh baby. Old Sankey friend Raymond Bailey, Sr., at ninety-five, remembered Verne Sankey as a man with a heart who lived life with gusto, not as just a law-breaker. His version of the Boettcher case involved a bootlegging deal that had gone sour.

"Bottacher [*sic*] wouldn't pay him so Sankey and his two friends decided they're going to get that damn money some way. They kidnapped him."

There is no evidence to support that and similarly held theories, but Sankey's friends came by them honestly.

In the end, the Sankey saga holds its greatest fascination for what it informs us about the American experience of 1933–34 and how Americans — both ordinary and extraordinary — lived it. The story of Charlie Boettcher's kidnapping and the lives and times of the Sankeys and the Boettchers cannot be properly absorbed apart from the transfixing drama of the Depression, which remains, apart from the Civil War, America's defining epoch. The Depression challenged the character, the sinew, of men and women in ways ordinary times could not. The ordeal strengthened some, cracked others. It is hard to ignore that not only Sankey but innumerable others as well found a way out through suicide.

It is difficult to imagine Arthur Youngberg, Gordon Alcorn, or Carl Pearce as gangsters. They bore little resemblance to hardened criminals, as their prison records attest. Each of these affable, pliable Sankey lackeys had held good jobs before the Depression; none had ever been in trouble with the law. Yet as each found himself unemployed, Verne Sankey was able to induce him into Sankey's grandiose scheme.

The Depression provided Verne Sankey no similar excuses, though. In truth, he was more a product of the free-wheeling 1920s crime scene than a Depression-era outlaw. He was most often a gentleman when to be so served his interest, but he thrived on excitement and the bankroll that crime provided. His bent toward the dark side developed long before the Depression descended and it sprang from unrelated causes.

Les Trois Tours was completed in 1931; the following year, the Sankeys built their simple Buffalo County ranch home. Who could have foreseen that the Normandy chateau's massive beams would tumble down scarcely thirty years after they were put into place while the little ranch house still stands — now moved to its third foundation — even now carrying the echoes of children's voices shouting happily on the prairie.

Even the Sankey's South Emerson bungalow remains, little changed in its outward appearance from seventy years past. The irony continues in the Sankey and Boettcher descendants: no surviving descendant of the patriarch bears the Boettcher name while the Sankey name lives on in Orville's sons and grandchildren.

Conversely, there are today, even in Gann Valley and Kimball, few who know Verne Sankey ever lived; ask someone in Denver if they are familiar with the name Boettcher and many are — but what they know are the Boettcher Concert Hall or the Boettcher Foundation and its wonderful work. Few people today know that Charles Boettcher and his son, Claude, had a more profound impact on the state of Colorado, and on Denver itself, than almost any two other men. As the Good Book says, "There is no remembrance of men of old. . . . For the wise man, like the fool will not be long remembered; . . . both will be forgotten."[22]

The voices of 1933 are nearly all silent now. Few witnesses of its events survive as we move further and further away from those days. In the end, Verne Sankey was partially granted his wish to save his wife and children from the shame of his crimes. Dillinger, Floyd, Nelson, Karpis, and others, aided by their glamorous names and infamous deeds, unwittingly conspired to consign Verne Sankey, in death, to the purgatory of the unknown and unremembered. It was largely because of them that Orville Sankey's dad could meet the honorable fate of having been killed by a train. Today, no stone marks Verne Sankey's grave at Mount Pleasant Cemetery. His unmarked resting place serves as a metaphor for his forgotten life, the only surviving trace a slight depression in the grass above where his body lies.

Epilogue

Redemption

I admire people who turn dust into gold.
I'm trying not to turn gold into dust.
— CHARLES BOETTCHER HOFFMAN

Within a week of Fern Sankey's acquittal, the Department of Justice directed its attention to Ben Laska, contending that Laska knowingly accepted part of the Urschel ransom money from Bates for his legal fee. After an Oklahoma federal grand jury indicted Laska, he represented himself in the 1935 trial, defying the maxim that he who represents himself has a fool for a client. It did not go well: the jury found Laska guilty and the trial judge sentenced him to ten years in prison. In August 1936 Ben Laska entered Leavenworth Prison. The government paroled him in 1940, and President Truman pardoned him in 1947, restoring his right to practice in federal courts. But Laska sought the return of his Colorado state license before returning to the courtroom. With the support of former governors and federal judges, Laska pled for the right to again practice in Colorado's state courts. "I want to drop dead in the court room," he said. "My heart is a law book. I want it open before a jury when the time comes." But Laska's application for reinstatement to the Colorado Bar remained unheard for eight years. Then, one summer evening in 1948, after long years futilely spent trying to clear his name, Ben Laska swallowed a handful of sleeping pills. He left behind six suicide notes that expressed his anguish at not being reinstated. He was seventy-four years old.

Denver Post reporter Charles O'Brien, who doggedly covered Laska's trial, followed him to the grave two years later, suffering a fatal heart attack at forty-eight. In the end, the two stories that served as the hallmarks of O'Brien's career involved Ben Laska: the Boettcher kidnapping and Laska's own criminal trial. Among the luminous cast of honorary pallbearers at O'Brien's funeral were judges, congressmen, Denver's mayor, and Charlie Boettcher.

Laska's Sankey cocounsel, Holton Davenport, enjoyed a long and successful career after the two men parted ways. He established his own law practice in 1938, which grew into one of the state's largest and most prominent. He died suddenly in 1966 during a break in a deposition. Like Laska, he was seventy-four.

Harold Brown's law practice eventually resumed the routine of trying to solve problems for ordinary folks who often could not pay him. He loved the law, loved helping people — cowboys, Indians, townsfolk, whoever needed his help. In 1935, he moved to "paradise," a farm two miles east of town. When war broke out in Korea, he surrendered a son to the cause. Navy pilot Gerald "Sprig" Brown died when his plane crashed near an aircraft carrier. Nothing in Harold Brown's later career compared to those surreal days when the small-town prosecutor represented the nation's Public Enemy No. 1. By the time of his 1965 death, he could boast that he had fished every pond in Buffalo County.

The Sankeys left Buffalo County none too soon; things got worse before they got better. The drought dragged on incessantly. The year 1936 produced one of the paltriest crops on record. One July day that year the temperature reached a scorching 120 degrees, followed by eighteen straight days in which the high surpassed 100 in the shade (though there was no shade). What little vegetation the grasshoppers missed was "burned to a crisp." The Vierecks and their neighbors danced through it all, their last barn dance held in 1939. The old barn was placed on the National Register of Historic Places in the late 1990s. Even today, the ancient piano, covered with dust, still stands on the remnants of the barn's makeshift stage. In 1947, Herman turned the farm over to his son and lived on past ninety, dying in 1983.

Sankey crony Clarence Swartout never duplicated his feat of tractor sales from 1928. Bad crops, grasshoppers, and dust drove Dan Hathaway from his land shortly after Fern and Orville left the area. Otto Nelson sent five children to fight the Axis powers during World War II. First Lieutenant Norman Nelson and his crew died in a bomber attack over Germany in 1943.

Otto Nelson's good friend, Edwin Dye, ran the hotel through most of the Depression, for a time renting a room to Fern and Orville.

Mike Chopskie outlived all of his contemporaries. His life spanned six American wars, three devastating droughts, the Depression, and the collapse of the farm economy. In his later years, he whiled away hours at the card tables in Kimball's saloons. He finally succumbed in 1991, at the Veterans' Medical Center in Hot Springs, like Fern, having reached ninety-nine. He died without ever seeing Fern again.

Today, more than 80 percent of Buffalo County's two thousand residents are American Indians. The people remain poor. Indeed, the county's per capita income is one-fourth the national average, making it America's poorest, according to the 2000 Census.

In the years that followed the Sankey trial, the defense team's noble adversary, George Philip, proved himself an able U.S. attorney, serving a lengthy tenure, thanks in part to Roosevelt's four terms in office. Philip quipped, "I'm a friend of every man I've ever sent to prison" — an odd boast, but the stacks of letters he received from those he prosecuted attest to his compassion. One inmate wrote, "Dear Mr. Philip: It sure was nice of you to send me here." The inmate, who had offered testimony for the government in a case, was writing Philip to thank him for arranging his transfer from Alcatraz to Leavenworth. The author of the letter was unmistakably Gordon Alcorn.

George Philip's two sons served with distinction during the Second World War. United States marine major Robert Philip was killed in action in the South Pacific in 1943. Commander George Philip, Jr., a youthful James Stewart look-alike and Naval Academy graduate died in June 1945. After his death, the government commissioned the USS *George Philip* in his memory.

After his second son's war sacrifice, George Philip's health broke. When he died in March 1948, Wyman, Leo Flynn, and Tom Berry served as honorary pall bearers at his funeral.

In August 1935, Will Rogers and friend pilot Wiley Post, died in a plane crash near Point Barrow, Alaska. After Rogers's death, South Dakota governor Tom Berry was asked to replace Rogers's popular syndicated column with his own. Berry agreed to write it for a year but it quickly became obvious to him that he could not remain both politician and columnist. When the year was up, Berry surrendered the column.

After suffering defeat in his effort to secure a third term, the New Deal proponent later lost a run for the Senate and returned to West River, South Dakota, where he remained until his death in 1951.

If Berry was an ardent New Deal supporter, Homer Cummings was one of its chief architects. Cummings stayed six years on the job he had taken on an interim basis, longer than all but one of his predecessors. His twelve-point program established the federal government as a crime-fighting force.

It is striking that Homer Cummings's name means nothing to most Americans today. In 1933 and 1934, he was the most visible general in the war against the gangsters. Throughout 1933, the *New York Times* made more than twenty references to Cummings for every one to J. Edgar Hoover. The following year, it was six to one.

The man Cummings appointed as his assistant in charge of the criminal division of the Justice Department and the chief prosecutor of the War on Crime remained with the administration throughout Roosevelt's lifetime. In 1946, having orchestrated the prosecutions of the Sankeys, the Kellys, Bates, and Bailey, Joseph B. Keenan redirected his wrath from America's midwestern outlaws to Japanese war criminals. Keenan's no-nonsense verbal assaults on the international defendants in his role of chief international prosecutor recalled his 1933–34 vitriol. All twenty-five defendants whose cases were submitted to the international tribunal were found guilty.

Charlie Boettcher was the recipient of one of Judge Wyman's works of penciled artistry from the first Sankey trial. Charlie kept it in his scrap-book of the ordeal. The 1936 Frank Capra film, *Mr. Deeds Goes to Town*, contained a courtroom scene portraying a "pixilated" doodler judge eerily reminiscent of Wyman.

During the Second World War, the judge heard draft deserter and conscientious objector cases. Of the dozens of such defendants who paraded past his court through those years, he sentenced all but one to the maximum five years. Wyman hunted deer until a month before his December 1953 death at the age of seventy-nine.

"I'm afraid to go back to Alcatraz," Gordon Alcorn muttered after the October trial. Although he had earlier bragged of his friendship with Capone and Kelly, he now expressed fear for his life. Alcorn acknowledged that his cooperation with the federal government had won him a promise from prosecutors to help get him out of Alcatraz and back to Leavenworth. Before he left the state, authorities informed Alcorn that through George Philip's efforts, the government had granted the transfer.

Alcorn later claimed someone other than law enforcement must have found a substantial sum of the ransom money at the ranch and had not turned it in to authorities: "A part of the money was hidden in a bin at the ranch," Alcorn disclosed. "As far as I know nobody ever got this money." Alcorn had a point. As much as sixty-six hundred dollars remained unaccounted for — five thousand dollars of Alcorn's share and sixteen hundred dollars of Youngberg's.

Alcorn's account sounded similar to Arthur Youngberg's remark that four thousand dollars had been placed in a stovepipe inside the grain bin of a barn at the Sankey ranch. Both statements bring to mind the time

Youngberg was brought back to South Dakota under guard to help locate the buried ransom on the farm. The press reported the strange sojourn he and federal officers took through a cemetery near the ranch, the report wildly speculating that Youngberg might be providing evidence of a killing.

Decades later, a Sioux Indian woman named Vera Call Him passed a twenty-dollar bill at a local grocery store. It was an old bill from the thirties. At first, the grocer thought little of it, but when she appeared again the next day with another, suspicious, he contacted authorities. Eventually, the woman led them to a grave in the St. Peter's Episcopal Church Cemetery, about a mile from the Sankey ranch. She said she had been planting flowers alongside the grave of a loved one, when she uncovered the money. It was the last of the ransom money recovered.

After the October trial, Birdie disappeared. Her promise to wait for Alcorn proved too great a commitment. If she wrote or visited him after December 1934, no record of it remains.

Alcorn proved to be an industrious inmate. He maintained a friendly attitude and kept a nearly spotless record inside the walls. A 1945 Leavenworth report stated that Alcorn "has always seemed utterly ashamed of [the kidnapping]." The prison staff considered him a good candidate to succeed on the outside.

Beginning in October 1936, Alcorn's mother and siblings instituted a campaign to earn his release and deportation to Canada. In a series of impassioned epistles, they won the support of the Boettchers and George Philip, but their efforts were in vain. Washington was loathe to release Alcorn for fear it would send the wrong message to other potential kidnappers. Mrs. Alcorn and her children pressed their crusade into 1940. Ray Robinson had been recently released from Stillwater with little fanfare. Alcorn's mother, by then alone with two sons in the war effort, related this fact to Charlie Boettcher, who had actually gotten to know Gordon Alcorn, the men having met twice while waiting to give testimony. Alcorn had apologized to Charlie, and the pair had talked at length about events during Charlie's captivity.

Finally, in August 1949, Gordon Alcorn walked out of prison after serving fifteen years of a life sentence. He wrote Claude to thank him. "If

it would not has [*sic*] been for your kindness in recommending my release I doubt if I would of ever obtained my freedom." Alcorn could
never return to Melville. Even though his family welcomed him back
into its fold, he was unwilling to inflict on them the burden of his presence there. He found work with British American Oil Company in Winnipeg, where he labored with boilers as a stationary engineer. It was a
good occupation, one he pursued for the rest of his working life, but he
had passed from youth to middle age in prison and remained to the
world a desperate criminal, guilty of the vilest of crimes. Neither the
appellation nor the disgrace ever left him.

In the late 1960s, Alcorn moved to Kitamat, a small community in
British Columbia, where he worked in an aluminum smelter. In time, he
fell gravely ill and died alone in a Vancouver rooming house in 1982.

Arthur Youngberg's prison stay was briefer than Alcorn's and Pearce's —
two concurrent terms of sixteen years. When they opened Alcatraz, the
Justice Department reserved a bed for Youngberg. He arrived there, like
Alcorn, in September 1934, but in 1938 federal officials transferred him
back to Leavenworth, concluding that he was not Alcatraz material. The
institutional staff at Leavenworth sized him up well, noting that he, too,
was to some degree, "a victim of circumstances," a cooperative inmate
and not at all a vicious criminal. Youngberg was paroled on July 15,
1943, having served ten years of his sentence.

Carl Pearce suffered the cruelest fate of the three. Although Pearce had
played a minor role in Charlie Boettcher's abduction, he paid dearly for
telling the Justice Department, in effect, to take a hike. His prison record
showed that his war injury had caused him to suffer "psychoneurosis,
hysterical type, severe," which became exaggerated when he was agitated. Pearce was not psychotic but he tended to come apart emotionally
whenever his routine was adjusted.

The prison kept Pearce in the neuropsychiatric ward, away from the
general population, where he worked quite well a few hours a day as a
clerical worker. He was a useful aide to the medical staff in that limited
role, on his own schedule, working alone. Leavenworth's chief medical

officer, who had befriended Pearce, recommended clemency in May 1938, expressing fear that the progressive nature of Pearce's condition would make it extremely difficult for him to readjust to civilian life if he were incarcerated much longer. The recommendation was denied. Pearce was not paroled until late in 1944; by then he was forty-eight years old and broken.

A month after Fern Sankey's acquittal, on November 27, 1934, "Baby Face" Nelson engaged bureau agents in a bloody shootout near Barrington, Illinois, in which two agents were killed. Nelson was shot seventeen times but managed to escape in a bureau car. His body was discovered the next day lying alongside the St. Peter cemetery in Skokie, Illinois. The *New York Times* reported three men — all kidnappers — as heirs apparent. One of the trio was Alvin Karpis; another, his partner, Dock Barker.

Despite being wrongly convicted for Urschel's abduction, Harvey Bailey could see that it was not so much the system's injustice that accounted for his circumstances, as his own choices. Though Bailey spent decades spurning moralists' entreaties to repent his wrongdoing, he eventually reached the conclusion that a free man must be guided by that very morality he had so long rejected. It was not just a change of thinking — it was a change of heart.

Bailey was baptized a Roman Catholic, solemnly resolving, "I may starve but I'll never steal again." He was finally released from prison in 1965 and spent his remaining years working quietly as a carpenter, finally succumbing at age ninety-one in 1979, having outlived nearly every crook and cop he ever knew, save an apparently unrepentant Alvin Karpis, who died later that same year.

Ironically, both Melvin Purvis's failures and his successes doomed his bureau career. Hoover remained disgusted over the major gaffes under Purvis's watch and even more vociferously opposed the attention Purvis garnered over other bureau agents — and even himself. Hoover's unrelenting harassment drove Purvis from the bureau in 1935. Purvis thereafter pursued a variety of promotional activities before reestablishing his South Carolina law practice. He twice sought congressional aide positions. Each time Hoover undermined his efforts. He died in 1960 at his home of a gunshot to his head, reportedly by the gun his fellow agents had given him as a retirement gift.

Purvis's secretary, Doris Rogers — later Doris Lockerman — also left the bureau in 1935, together with her future husband. They were, essentially, additional Hoover casualties. Another agent made a comment one evening after hours that was disparaging of Hoover, which Allen Lockerman refused to repeat to Hoover's top assistant, Harold Nathan. The next day, Doris recalled, Lockerman — who had participated in the attempted capture of Verne Miller and Dillinger's killing — was "reassigned to, of all places, Butte, Montana. It was a banishment." Both Agent Lockerman and Doris left the bureau.

In 1935 Doris Lockerman wrote a series of articles for the *Chicago Tribune* on Public Enemies, beginning with Verne Sankey, followed by Dillinger. Lockerman eventually became a prominent Atlanta attorney and Doris accepted a post with the *Atlanta Journal*, in time serving as its women's editor. Eventually, the *Atlanta Constitution* hired her away, where she became the first female associate editor of a major southern newspaper.

In 1945 an error-riddled article appear in *The Investigator*, an FBI publication, that rewrote the Boettcher investigation to give the bureau credit for identifying Sankey as the culprit, apart from the work of Denver police. It made for interesting fiction; strikingly, the story did not mention Melvin Purvis.

If Charlie and Anna Lou Boettcher knew any real joy in their marriage before the kidnapping, they seldom experienced it thereafter. Charlie never spoke of the kidnapping in the presence of his daughters, yet its effects were all around them. He had iron bars installed on the windows of *Les Trois Tours*, and a direct telephone line from the upstairs bedroom area to the police station. Claudia was a young woman before it dawned on her that not everyone had such a life. As Charlie's daughters grew, the most prominent figure in their lives was their governess, Nelia Reynolds, who cared for Claudia from birth until she left home for boarding school. Reynolds was, it turns out, under the employ of Claude, who expected her to provide full reports of Charlie's activities. Charles's drinking progressively worsened, creating added pressures on the family's life and undoubtedly eroding opportunities to exercise meaningful control over family enterprises.

Anna Lou, emotionally delicate by nature, had been devastated by Charlie's lengthy captivity while near to term with her second child. Her life thereafter, despite the blessings her children brought her, was filled with discontent. Reflecting, years later, her daughter Claudia sensed that Anna Lou would have been happier marrying back in Helena and raising a family out of the intense limelight. Claude and Edna retained expectations of the role Charlie and Anna should take in community activities, but Anna Lou had neither the inclination nor the temperament. Even if she had, Charlie's drinking did not permit him to maintain such a role.

One September day in 1941, thirty-seven-year-old Anna Lou Boettcher went to her bedroom, donned her nightgown, then put a pistol to her head and pulled the trigger. The story headlined both Denver newspapers, each attributing her act to poor health. The truth was different: Anna Lou had been facing almost incessant pressures from Claude on the one hand and from her mother on the other concerning a pressing family matter. She had begun to drink excessively, hoping to blunt her emotional pain, but it only sent her further into despondency. Anna Lou's body was cremated. Two days later, the family held a private funeral at *Les Trois Tours*, the dream home Claude had built for her and Charlie fifteen years earlier.

Following Anna Lou's death and the bombing of Pearl Harbor in December that year, Charlie enlisted in the Army Air Corps as a matériel officer. He attained the rank of major but his alcoholism wreaked havoc on his service career and the army issued him a medical discharge. On his return to civilian life, he joined the Civil Air Patrol, in 1949, heading the Colorado wing.

Charlie eventually compiled an impressive résumé, serving on various family company boards and as chairman of the Boettcher Foundation.

His civic and social involvement was equally prominent: New York's Yale Club, the Denver Country Club, and a host of others. It made for a great obituary, but the reality was that Charlie found little fulfillment in life. Even after the war, his grandfather, then in his nineties, still maintained a much closer bond with Claude than Charlie could claim.

After his return from the war, Charlie fell in love with Lee Wylie, a part-Cherokee jazz singer. Charlie wanted to marry Wylie but she would not live in the mansion because Anna Lou had died there. When the couple found a house they liked, Anne and Claudia, then about sixteen and eleven, balked at the move. In the end, Charlie terminated the relationship with Wylie. Not long after, he married the recently widowed Mae Scott Foster, with whom he spent the remainder of his life. The two traveled widely, frequenting their Hawaiian property, often in the company of Charlie's daughters.

The family patriarch's body finally wore out in July 1948, at the age of ninety-six. He was among America's least-known magnates. Reporters dug into their files, and uncovered a late interview in which the failing old man had offered: "The young man who wants to go into business should consider hardware. Axes and hammers don't go out of style like so many things."

Fanny, from whom he was estranged over the last three decades of his life, outlived him by four years. Fannie proved her own financial capabilities after the separation. She took her several-hundred-thousand-dollar share from the couple's separation and invested wisely so that, at her death, it had grown to nearly $5 million despite her own considerable philanthropic efforts, for which she scornfully resisted publicity. The intelligent but difficult woman spent the last decade of her life in the old Grant Street mansion, "attended only by servants with whom she quarreled constantly." She lived out her life largely in seclusion, a distant figure to her own few great-grandchildren, one of whose most pungent recollections of her was her brutally bad breath, likely a symptom of poor dental hygiene.

As time passed, Charlie and Mae spent less and less time at *Les Trois Tours*. The last straw was a 1950 incident in which a car ran a red light and struck the house. "That's it," he told his family. "We're moving. It's not safe here any more." Charlie and Mae moved into the ninth-floor suite Charlie's grandfather had occupied at the Brown Palace. Two years later, Charlie sold *Le Trois Tours* for fifty thousand dollars.

Claude and Edna reveled in their societal and business roles through the vicissitudes of Charlie's tumultuous life and Anna Lou's tragic death. Edna remained Denver's unchallenged society leader and, at least according to *Life* magazine, its best-dressed woman. When she traveled to London in June 1934 between the Sankey trials, she had an audience with King George and Queen Mary at the Court of St. James. The year Anna Lou took her life Edna entertained the Duke and Duchess of Windsor at the Boettchers' fabulous Florida estate.

Claude and Edna's focus, tight as it was on social and civic affairs, left little time for matters of the heart or quiet times with their family. Claudia remembered her grandfather as a reproachful man. A trip to their Eighth Avenue mansion seemed less like a visit to Grandpa's and Grandma's than a command performance. Edna, who had no children of her own, merely tolerated kids generally, an attitude that extended to her husband's grandchildren.

Edna's best friends were her jewels. A woman established in Floridian society encountered her bedecked in ostentatious diamonds in the afternoon sun and commented that Florida society women refrained from wearing diamonds in the daytime. Edna returned the volley with little effort: "When I didn't have them I didn't wear them in the daytime, either."

Late in his life, Claude Boettcher reflected, "I've come to understand the only real satisfaction in life is work." In Claude's declining years, arthritis affected his hips and cataracts interfered with his vision, but underlings trekked daily to the mansion for briefings and his decisions. Even then, Charlie addressed his father as "Sir" and deferred to his judgment on a wide variety of subjects.

In June 1957 Claude died in the mansion at Eighth Avenue and Logan. At his death, he was reputedly Colorado's wealthiest man and among the nation's richest, with assets — including corporate assets he controlled — estimated by the *Rocky Mountain News* to approach $1 billion. The following year, Edna suffered a stroke and died at the mansion. One of "old Denver's" most sophisticated couples and its most philanthropic, had passed from the scene.

The family's charitable foundation gave the mansion, along with some one thousand articles of art and furniture, to the state of Colorado. Today it serves as the governor's mansion.

Claude's crowning achievement and legacy is the Boettcher Foundation, which he established together with his father and son in the late Depression with an initial gift of $17 million. Dedicated solely to charitable, religious, and educational causes within the state of Colorado, the Boettcher Foundation has grown into one of the state's largest charitable institutions, with an endowment exceeding $200 million.

At Claude's death, Denver's *Rocky Mountain News* wrote:

> His son, Charles II, whom he loved fiercely if not tenderly, presented
> him with a challenge he never quite conquered. That was because
> Charles II, the son, was a fuller and more perceptive man in the ways
> of other men than his father. In death, the restrictive father may have
> given the son some belated freedom.

It is true that Charlie was more perceptive than his father regarding other people. He knew and understood frailty and failure in a way his father and grandfather never could. While it brought him no success in the business world, it allowed him a measure of compassion his father did not know.

Whatever freedom Charlie experienced with his father's passing, though, was by then little consolation. His last years were marked by a series of health maladies — diabetes, heart troubles, a spinal ailment — all complicated by years of incessant drinking. Shortly after his father's death, he finally admitted himself to Houston's Menninger Clinic and overcame his addiction, but by then his health was gone. Charlie Boettcher died in San Francisco of a heart attack, in April 1963.

By the time Charlie died, the mansion his father had built as a gift for his only son was in decline, symbolic of the ruins of Charlie and Anna Lou's marriage. It was eventually abandoned, then vandalized. Over time it developed a reputation as a haunted house, perhaps because of Anna Lou's suicide there, perhaps because, in its crumbling state, it looked creepy. Teenagers dared one another to spend an hour in the mansion at night.

Two months after Charlie Boettcher died, *Les Trois Tours* was finally razed. The stone-arch doorways, the decorative brick chimney, the ornate ceiling too high even for vandals to destroy, were visible to the public for a few days. Then it was all reduced to rubble and carted away.

After Charlie's death, no one remained to carry forward the Boettcher name. Charlie had handed the baton of family legacy onto daughters of the fourth generation who would be far less visible, but happier and more productive, than he had been.

Tall, strikingly attractive Claudia Boettcher shocked Denver high society when she enrolled at the University of Colorado; no one guessed that this product of Denver's preeminent family, whose own parents had attended Vassar and Yale, would condescend to attend Colorado's flagship public university. Claudia Boettcher, however, did not fit neatly into anyone's mold.

She studied music at the University of Colorado and fell in love with fellow music major, Le Roy Hoffman. When the pair announced their engagement, the news jolted her father: it was not that he questioned Hoffman's character or his social status — although the latter caused Claude some concern. Charlie's dismay stemmed from the fact that his precious daughter was marrying a South Dakota farmer who had grown up only a short distance from Verne Sankey's boyhood home. It took awhile to warm to the idea.

The Denver press hailed the couple's exchange of vows as Denver society's most fashionable June wedding. The *Post*'s coverage included a nearly full-page wedding day photograph of the dazzling bride. After the wedding, Hoffman embarked on a career as a professional soloist. He performed in premier concert halls across the nation and around the world — touring Europe with the Vienna Academy Choir and performing at Carnegie Hall in New York, with the Denver Symphony, and in Austria with the Salzburg Opera Company. When Claudia returned to Denver for family visits, the *Post* usually noticed, often carrying her photograph alongside a brief story. In October 1956, Claudia gave birth to a son, Thurn, the surname of Le Roy's maternal grandparents. A second son followed three years later, whom the couple named Charles Boettcher Hoffman.

As much as Le Roy loved to perform his heart tugged him homeward to the family farm outside Eureka, South Dakota, population twelve hundred. Claudia consented to the move and the young Hoffmans gave up touring for rural life. When Le Roy later got the urge to tour again, Claudia quickly ended the discussion. "If you think I'm going to freeze out here on the prairie alone with the kids while you tour Europe, you're dreaming." So Le Roy deferred, raising corn, oats, alfalfa, livestock — and two sons.

The description of Charlie Hoffman's father, Le Roy, as a farmer is a bit of a misnomer. In reality, he was something of a renaissance man — well read, talented, and interested in a wide range of subjects. Forfeiting his performing career to raise a family in his home community, Le Roy immersed himself in South Dakota politics. He was elected to the South Dakota Senate and in 1978 sought the Republican nomination for governor, losing in a tough primary. Le Roy died in 1980.

The couple's sons both graduated from Eureka's public high school, each in classes of around fifty students. Thurn then graduated from the prestigious Colorado College — to which, his mother proudly notes, he gained admission without the school knowing of the Boettcher connection. After college, Thurn embarked on a New York City acting career. Charlie Boettcher Hoffman attended South Dakota colleges and today devotes his efforts to raising and selling registered black Angus livestock on the farm he grew up on, where he and his wife raised three talented and athletic children. His goal is to develop one of the nation's finest registered black Angus herds.

Charlie is an immediately disarming and engaging conversationalist.

"I admire people who come from tough circumstances and make something of their lives, turn dust into gold," he said, reflecting on his family heritage. Then he laughed: "I'm trying not to turn gold into dust." People around Eureka know of the family's storied past only in the vaguest of ways; they know Charlie's dad was active in state politics and once toured the world as a concert soloist but have little knowledge of the Boettchers simply because Charlie and his family did not make an issue of it.

Although Charlie Hoffman has himself traveled widely, he is thoroughly a South Dakotan. On a normal day, even in public, he might wear a worn western shirt, the T-shirt visibly tattered around the collar. He is a big man with a robust handsomeness reminiscent of South Dakota pioneers, with a well-groomed mustache.

"People here are some of the greatest people in the world," Charlie said.

His German blood fits in well in the Eureka community known for its German ethnicity. In spite of his South Dakota roots, Charlie has one latent ambition that would take him out of state. "My dream, some day," he said, "is to spend six months a year in Denver on the board of the Boettcher Foundation to share in the good work of the organization. That's my aspiration."

After Le Roy's death, Claudia married a lawyer-lobbyist who worked the U.S. Senate; when he died, she returned to the Denver area. Today she chairs the board of the Boettcher Foundation.

Claude had a strong sense of obligation that governed his life, which led him to establish the foundation. "My grandfather and his father felt that the family had prospered here," Claudia recalled, "and they thought it was their duty to give back to the state." So whatever faults Claude possessed, Claudia credits Claude as the charitable entity's initial driving force. "God Bless him for starting the Foundation."

Claudia's memories of her great-grandfather, Charles, are much different.

"He was quite gracious to us," she said. "He enjoyed seeing his great-grandchildren. In my memory, he was a wonderful gentleman."

Ann Boettcher Ohrel possesses her mother's beauty and physical stature as well as some of her natural reserve. Five years Claudia's senior, Ann was thirteen when her mother took her life; her memories of the kidnapping and of her mother are, even today, too painful for her to talk about. Unlike her parents who were Episcopalian but rarely attended church, Ann joined her husband's Catholic faith when married and remains an active member. She diverged from her parents in another way:

she abstains from alcohol. For more than fifty years Ann successfully raised and bred riding horses, first Tennessee Walkers and then Spanish and Portuguese lineage animals.

One might well wonder what would become of a person who had lived Claudia Boettcher's childhood — chauffeured to school and church; heir to a fortune; the daughter of tragically matched parents. It is difficult to reconcile that child of privilege with the balanced, grounded person Claudia Boettcher has become. When asked how she accounts for the person she is today, Claudia paused, then said, "I think it was South Dakota. I learned to live around ordinary people. That's the backbone of this country, after all — the middle class. Lord preserve us if it's the wealthy."

Claudia's years on the Dakota prairie forged a bond between her and the people of her adopted state that continues today, though she lives in a Denver suburb near the foundation. She is active in her Congregational church and passionately follows the travails of the Colorado Rockies.

"My father introduced me to baseball — the Class A Denver Bears — when I was a teenager. Most of the happy times I remember in his company revolved around Bear games," Claudia recalled. She also frequents Nuggets and Broncos games.

Claudia's bond to the state and its people remains intact and she frequently returns to the Eureka area. "I still consider South Dakota my home," she said. "I love Eureka. I always did."

"In a [small] town," she said, "everyone takes part. You don't find that in the cities. I have very good friends there and we still have lunch together when I go back. The people of the state are so real. They're not phonies. They work hard. They live responsible lives."

The lives of Charlie Boettcher and Verne Sankey — oddly entwined by the events of 1933 and shaped by the South Dakota prairie and its people — offer poignant character portraits. On one level, excessive materialism and its effects played tragic roles in each of their lives. Their generation produced no happy endings. Perhaps that accounts for the gratification one experiences when considering the productive, fulfilling lives led by the generation that succeeded them — lives driven not by the pursuit of wealth but by the satisfaction of raising a loving family, engaging in honest labor, and improving the lives of those around them. In this, the progeny of these men have, in no small sense, redeemed their family heritage and, indeed, enhanced it. They are people we can relate to, even if our father was neither a Depression-era millionaire nor Public Enemy No. 1.

Author's Note

I have endeavored to write the definitive history of Verne Sankey and the Charlie Boettcher kidnapping, without embellishment. Whenever words are attributed to a character, those words were really spoken; when mannerisms are described, they were observed by one who documented them. I alone take responsibility for any weaknesses the text contains, or blanks, which to your disappointment, remain unfilled in the account of these strikingly fascinating people. These are the results of my own limitations.

One of the chief reasons the name Verne Sankey has lingered in such obscurity despite the renaissance of the early-thirties crime figures is that, unlike most of the others, for whatever reason, no Verne Sankey files survive, or at least none have been catalogued by the Federal Bureau of Investigation. The explanations for this vary and require some understanding of how bureau records were then preserved. The modern bureau, really then only in its infancy, had regional offices that served as the repository for all reports generated by a crime investigated out of its geographical area. Even investigations on the case performed by agents in other regions were funneled to the originating regional office. In the case of the Verne Sankey investigation, that office was most likely the Salt Lake City bureau office. The process of archiving files, however, was not yet then perfected. Particularly when the suspect was dead, it was likely given a low priority, as the bureau geared up its efforts to pursue Dillinger, Floyd, Nelson, and the others.

What documents and photographs I was able to glean from the FBI came not from my Freedom of Information request, but from chance. Longtime family friend and retired FBI agent, Greg Stevens, also a Kimball native, shared my interest in Verne Sankey, and offered assistance. After Greg learned that my FOI search had yielded no documents, he went to the office of an acquaintance, John Fox, the FBI's historian, about the dilemma. As he sat in Fox's office explaining who Verne Sankey was, Fox recalled that he had just seen the Sankey name in a box of uncataloged documents and photographs in his office. There, stacked among documents on the Barker-Karpis gang and the Bremer kidnapping, were documents and photographs of Sankey. I am appreciative of the time and insight into the FBI of the period that Dr. Fox provided, and also for permission to publish the Sankey photographs.

As a whole, my research yielded scant Justice Department records. The marked exception, fortunately, proved to be the National Archives' preservation of the federal court files of Fern Sankey's two trials, which provided a wealth of documents relating to the investigation of her husband and his cohorts, as well.

Newspapers, of course, served as crucial sources for my research, publications ranging from the *New York Times* to the *Gann Valley Chief*. They were loaded with information, but, predictably, often told more than they knew. Any effort relying heavily on such sources necessarily requires careful scrutiny, and often corroboration, of accounts, before authenticating them. Frequently, accounts appeared that were outlandish, and unsubstantiated by other reputable sources — or disproved by later events. The *Denver Post* covered the Boettcher kidnapping so thoroughly that at times its sheer aggressiveness led to overreporting. That said, this publication was also the most valuable to my work because of that same thoroughness.

The oral interviews granted to me by nonagenarians Leo Flynn, Louis Hurwitz, Harry Konechne, Leon Chmela, Doris Rogers Lockerman,

Dureene Petersen, and Betty Champagne were especially pleasurable and enlightening. They provided me moving accounts of a time now three generations removed but still strikingly recalled. The photographs made available by the Colorado Museum of History, from the *Denver Post* archives, were a special find and extremely useful. At the University of Oklahoma Press, acquisitions editor Kirk Bjornsgaard has provided steady, devoted support and is always cheerful. Thanks, too, to Steven Baker, manuscript editor, and to freelance copyeditor Jack Rummel, whose incisive comments and suggestions were unfailingly apt. Thank you to Greg Stevens for answering questions about the FBI and for agreeing to read and comment on an early version of the manuscript.

I wish also to thank the Honorable Lawrence Piersol, federal judge for the District of South Dakota, who now presides in the courtroom once overseen by Judge Wyman, for graciously agreeing to read the manuscript and for providing thoughtful, productive comments.

I must also acknowledge the Melville Historical Society and the staff who published the remarkable Buffalo County history books, for their enthusiastic help in answering questions and providing information. I wish to thank John and Kelly Alcorn for background information concerning their uncle and great-uncle, Gordon Alcorn.

My telephone interviews with Orville Sankey revealed a kind and gentle man, not particularly desirous of attention, but nonetheless, exceedingly polite. I am deeply grateful for his warm-hearted cooperation and information.

While I was in the latter stages of writing this book, Bryan Burrough's *Public Enemies: America's Greatest Crime Wave and the Birth of the FBI, 1933–34* was released, a superb book that codified much of the history of crime in 1933 and 1934 and proved very useful. I also found particularly helpful William Helmer and Rick Mattix's work, *Public Enemies: America's Criminal Past, 1919–1940*; Paul Maccabee's *John Dillinger Slept Here: A Crook's Tour of Crimes and Corruption in St. Paul 1920–1936*; Clyde Calahan and Byron Jones's *Heritage of an Outlaw*; and Earnest Alix's *Ransom Kidnapping in America, 1874–1974: The Creation of a Capital Crime*.

I am indebted to my old acquaintance, and Eureka, South Dakota, native, Steve Smith, for connecting me with his boyhood friend, Charlie Boettcher Hoffman, which in turn allowed me the opportunity to meet with Claudia Boettcher Merthan, first in a series of telephone conversations, then in a visit to her home, which she so graciously opened up to me.

I cannot adequately express my deep gratitude to the Boettcher family, and in particular, to Claudia Boettcher Merthan, for her extreme kindness and candor throughout this process. The details of the kidnapping and of her family's often fascinating history, though not always flattering, were willingly and frankly shared. I am particularly indebted to Mrs. Merthan for allowing me unfettered access to the Boettcher family's voluminous archives, painstakingly assembled, likely by Claude and Charlie Boettcher's longtime personal secretary, Mrs. Ruth Brown. These documents, filling eight large, bound volumes, made for fascinating reading. Without them and the extensive Boettcher color movie footage from the 1930s, much of the flavor of the Boettcher investigation and of the Boettcher men, would have been missed.

Notes

Abbreviations

DP   *Denver Post*

NYT   *New York Times*

RMN   *Rocky Mountain News*

AL   *Sioux Falls Argus Leader*

NA   National Archives

Citations to a work consist of the author's surname as it appears in the bibliography.

Chapter 1

4   *Until he outran them*: *Greeley Daily Tribune*, Mar. 2, 1933; DP, Feb. 10, 1934.

4   *Raccoon coat, diamond rings*: *Melville Advance*, Nov. 13, 1996.

4   *Verne Sankey's birth place and ancestry and move to near Wilmot*: Plaintiff's Exhibit 44, United States District Court for the District of South Dakota, Central Division, Pierre; Record Group 21; National Archives; Docket Number 586 (hereafter cited as NA, *U.S. v. Sankey et al.*); U.S. Census Records, 1905, South Dakota, Cards 2216-2219, 2226.

4   *Farms, homes, and businesses*: Mills, 3, 6.

4   *Verne Sankey's arrival in Wilmot*: U.S. Census Records, 1905, South Dakota, Cards 2216-2219, 2226. *Verne was about nine on arrival in the Wilmot area around 1900.* Ibid., Card 2216.

5   *Sankey as a youth*: *Wilmot Enterprise*, Feb. 15, 1934.

5   *Verne Sankey's marriage to Fern Young*: Roberts County, South Dakota Register of Deeds Marriage License records; Roberts County, SD, Homestead Township Map, Summit Township, South Dakota Archives.

5   *Around the time of their marriage*: *Wilmot Enterprise*, Feb. 1, 1934; *Melville Advance*, Nov. 13, 1996. These sources indicate Sankey arrived in Melville as early as 1910. Sankey's marriage license, however, indicates that he was a resident of Wilmot at the time of his March 1914 wedding.

5   *"We have yet to meet"*: *Wilmot Enterprise*, Feb. 15, 1934.

5   *Canada railroad job*: *Wilmot Enterprise*, Feb. 1, 1934.

5   *Sankey began as a lowly watchman*: *Winnipeg Tribune*, Feb. 1, 1934.

5   *Sankey's railroad pay*: *Wilmot Enterprise*, Feb. 15, 1934.

6   *Melville in 1914*: City of Melville, www.city.melville.sk.ca.

6   *On good nights, he spent lavishly*: *Melville Advance*, Nov. 13, 1996.

6   *Sankey's height*: South Dakota State Penitentiary records show his height at only five feet, four and a half inches tall. Plaintiff's Exhibit 44, *U.S. v. Fern Sankey et al.* Other records list Sankey's height as around five feet, seven inches.

6   *Sankey's build and hat*: Boettcher family personal papers, Wanted Poster of Verne Sankey, issued Mar. 21, 1933.

7   *Betty Champagne quote*: *Melville Advance*, Nov. 13, 1996; confirmed in author interview, Betty Champagne.

7   *Trainman disarmingly soft-spoken and fun*: Author interview, Betty Champagne; *Winnipeg Tribune*, Feb. 1, 1934.

7   *Some fellow rail workers witnessed a braggadocio*: Boettcher family personal papers, Carroll Report to Robert L. Stearns, 4, with cover letter dated Aug. 15, 1933.

7   *Sankey and his lifestyle and liquor hauling*: *Melville Advance*, Nov. 13, 1996.

7   *Sankey's Melville home*: Author interviews, Marj Redenbach and Betty Champagne.

7   *On Sankey in Melville and his bootleg activities*: *Melville Advance*, Nov. 13, 1996.

8   *"You couldn't admire"*: Author interview, Betty Champagne.

8   *Sankey often took Echo with him on bootlegging trips*: author interviews, Marj Redenbach and Betty Champagne.

8   *Sankey smuggling liquor*: DP, Feb. 3, 1934.

8   *The dray horses bet*: *Melville Advance*, Nov. 13, 1996.

8   *Commodities market losses nearly broke him*: DP, Feb. 3, 1934.

9   *Lost virtually all his profits*: Ibid.

9   *Sankey slipping out of a North Dakota town*: *Melville Advance*, Nov. 13, 1996.

9   *Story of Clint Head's dying teenage daughter and quote*: Ibid.; author interview, Marj Redenbach.

9   *"Women in Melville used to hate the sight"*: *Melville Advance*, Nov. 13, 1996.

9   *Particularly lucrative trade in Denver*: DP, Mar. 8, 1933.

9   *Work absences from Canadian railroad*: Ibid.

9   *"He operated two big Nash cars"*: *Melville Advance*, Nov. 13, 1996.

10   *Sankey's Denver business*: DP, Mar. 8, 1933.

10   39Sankey's solitary conviction: AL, Feb. 9, 1934.

10   *Craze for miniature golf*: *Winnipeg Tribune*, Feb. 1, 1934.

10   *Sankey's sweetheart in Winnipeg*: Boettcher family personal papers, United States Postal Inspector Report of Aug. 9, 1933, at 2, 4; *"You get to know a man"*: *Winnipeg Tribune*, Feb. 1, 1934.

10   *Sankey's card game in Winnipeg*: *Winnipeg Tribune*, Feb. 1, 1934.

11   *The account of the Regina robbery taken from*: *Melville Advance*, Nov. 13, 1996.

11   *Sankey's departure from Canada and arrival in Kimball*: *Kimball Graphic*, Mar. 9, 1933; *Winnipeg Tribune*, Feb. 1, 1934.

11   *Bought 320 undeveloped acres*: Buffalo County Register of Deeds real estate records. Throughout this book the terms "farm" and "ranch" will be used in referring to Sankey's South Dakota land. The press generally used "ranch," while Sankey and those around him called it a "farm." South Dakotans, then and today, generally refer to a grain and livestock operation as a farm. The term "ranch" describes an operation primarily devoted to grazing cattle.

11   *Land bought at $14 an acre*: Buffalo County Real Estate records.

11   *Sankey land and house and their remoteness*: Taken from county maps of existing roads, the author's own traversing of the land, and *Kimball Graphic*, Mar. 9, 1933; author interview, Leon Chmela.

11   *Sankey raised 75 head of beef*: *Java Herald*, Feb. 8, 1934.

12   *Sankey's drinking*: DP, Mar. 14, 1933; *his relationship with neighbors*: *Kimball Graphic*, Mar. 9, 1933, and author's recollection of conversation with Kimball barbers, Leo and Hubert Herrlein, who knew Sankey.

12   *"Honesty is the best policy"*: DP, Feb. 7, 1934.

12   *"I sure am a lucky devil"*: Ibid., Mar. 7, 1933.

12   *Observation by Sankey neighbors and gunfire at the ranch*: *Kimball Graphic*, Mar. 9, 1933.

13   Account of Vayland bank robbery: *Miller Press*, Oct. 6, 1932, and Mar. 16, 1933.

13   *Sankey's relationships in Gann Valley area*: AL and *Kimball Graphic*, both Mar. 9, 1933.

14   *Alcorn was born in the tiny Saskatchewan village of Welwyn*: Much of the background of Gordon Alcorn, and the circumstances surrounding his decision to come to South Dakota, discussed in this section was discovered in a statement he gave bureau agents in Chicago on Feb. 2, 1934, and other government records from Leavenworth and Alcatraz. Alcorn's statements to bureau agents will be referred to as NA, Alcorn

Statement, Feb 2, 1934. The balance of his prison records will be referred to as NA, Alcorn Prison Records. The prison records of Arthur Youngberg and Carl Pearce will be cited as NA, Youngberg Prison Records, and NA, Pearce Prison Records, respectively. All are found in National Archives Record Group129. AL, Feb. 10, 1934, also contains some information on Alcorn, but portions are sadly inaccurate.

15   *Youngberg and Alcorn assumed their duties*: NA, Alcorn Statement, Feb. 2, 1934.

15   *Arthur Youngberg's background and demeanor*: NA, Youngberg Prison Records.

16   *The night of the 1932 Congregational Church Christmas program*: Author interview, Carol Stevens. Stevens remembered the event, although did not provide the year.

17   *Carl Pearce's background*: NA, Pearce Prison Records.

18   *Alcorn-Youngberg fight and Alcorn's subsequent departure from the ranch*: NA, Alcorn Statement, Feb. 2, 1934; NA, Alcorn Prison Records.

18   *Ransom amount*: DP, May 13, 1934.

Chapter 2

19   *Account of the Boettcher abduction*: Taken from NA, Alcorn Statement, Feb. 2, 1934, 2–3, except when cited otherwise. While it is almost certain that the Boettchers were at the Brown Palace, based on the description and location of the hotel, its name was not specifically mentioned.

19   *Account of the men's stop at the Sankey residence*, with minor paraphrasing: AL, May 14, 1934.

20   *Charlie Boettcher's early life within the Boettcher family*: RMN, June 17, 1979.

20   *Claude decided he did not enjoy competition from within his own family*: Author interview, Claudia Boettcher Merthan.

20   *Charlie Boettcher's passion for baseball*: Author interview, Claudia Boettcher Merthan.

21   *An elaborate Helena wedding*: Author interview and correspondence, Claudia Boettcher Merthan.

21   *On Anna Lou's social role and anti-Prohibition involvement*: DP, Feb. 13, 1933.

21   *On Les Trois Tours*: Ibid., June 20, 1963.

22   *Charlie Boettcher's reported friendship with Charles Lindbergh*: New York Journal and New York Evening Post, both articles appearing Feb. 13, 1933; San Francisco Examiner and New York Daily News, both articles appearing Feb. 14, 1933, RMN, Sept. 18, 1941. Neither of Charlie Boettcher's daughters was aware of this widely reported relationship.

22   *Charles Boettcher II held*: DP, Feb. 13, 1933.

23   *The sequence of events in Charlie Boettcher's abduction*: Ibid.
23   *The kidnapping and dialogue*: Ibid.; Humphreys, 32.
23   *The ransom note*: NA, *U.S. v. Sankey et al.*, Plaintiff's Exhibit 8. The ransom note is reproduced without editing, and letters throughout this book are presented as written, without any attempt to identify misspellings or grammatical errors.
24   *On actions after the kidnapping, the arrival of police, and description of the kidnappers*: RMN, Feb. 13, 1933; Humphreys, 33–34.
24   *Chief Clark's comments to the press*: RMN, Feb. 13, 1933.
24   *Immortalized on the silver screen*: Powers, 16.
25   *On suspicions of Capone cousin Allegretti*: DP, Feb. 13, 14, 1933; NYT, Feb. 15, 1933.
25   *On police search and bootleggers' quoted response*: NYT, Feb. 18, 1933.
25   *On Capone's reported income from the illegal sale of alcohol*: McWilliams, pt.4, 9;
25   *On Vine-glo*: Ibid., 10.
25   *On changing public sentiments toward Prohibition*: Literary Digest, Nov. 18, 1933.
25   *Vigilante forces*: DP, Feb. 13, 1934.
25   *Governor Johnson quotes*: Ibid.
25   *Colorado's kidnapping law*: Ibid. Only Georgia had such a light maximum sentence.
26   *The Colorado Legislature rushed a bill*: DP, Feb. 22, 1933; Alix, 195.
26   *The Klan's resurgence*: Goldberg, 3–10, 53–54.
26   *Stapleton's election and Candlish's appointment*: Ibid., 29–33.
27   *Klan supported gubernatorial and Senate winners*: Ibid., 70–83.
27   *The Klan's demise*: Ibid., 84–116.
27   *On Claude's and Charlie's homes*: DP, Feb. 15, 1933.
28   *On the Boettchers jail visit and* Denver Post *quote*: Ibid.
28   *Police investigation of Charlie's activities*: Ibid.; NYT, Feb. 17, 1933.
28   *Director of Bureau of Investigation thrust his agency*: NYT, Feb. 15, 1933.
28   *On Bureau's early years*: Theoharis et al., 6–12.
29   *On Bureau activities*: Ibid.
29   *Discussion of Harlan Stone's findings when he came to Justice, his decision to hire J. Edgar Hoover, and the immediate positive changes Hoover instituted in the Bureau*: From Curt Gentry's well-written work, 124–32, and Theoharis et al., 11, 332.
29   *On Walsh and Hoover*: Gentry, 153.
30   *On Hoover's lack of legal authority to enter Boettcher kidnapping case*: Alix, 79.
30   *Pared to about three hundred agents*: Theoharis and Cox, 126; Theoharis et al., 14.

Chapter 3

31 *Accidents resulted*: DP, Feb. 17, 1933.

31 *Letter from the egg woman*: Boettcher family private papers, letter from Elizabeth Fisher, dated Mar. 6, 1933.

31 *"I know how I"*: Ibid., letter from E. E. Thompson, Greensboro, NC, dated Feb. 26, 1933.

32 *"I am a Half-orphan"*: Ibid., letter from N. B. Gafford, Commerce, TX, dated Mar. 10, 1933.

32 *"Now Dear Mr. Boettcher"*: Ibid., letter from Sister M. Gratiana, O. S. F., St. Mary's Hospital, Emporia, Kansas, dated Apr. 6, 1933.

32 *Claude's quandary*: DP, Feb. 18, 1933.

32 *Investigation focused more intensely on Denver's mob-affiliated culprits*: Ibid.

32 *Seven suspects had been jailed*: Ibid., Feb. 14–19, 1933.

33 *Account of Charlie Boettcher's kidnapping and trip to ranch*: NA, Alcorn Statement, Feb. 2, 1934; DP, Feb. 13 and Mar. 2, 1933.

33 *Account of Boettcher at the ranch in Youngberg's custody and Youngberg's exchange with Sankey*: DP, Mar. 2 and May 28, 1933.

34 *"Swore he would die"*: Ibid., Feb. 11, 1934.

34 *"Don't give those bulls"*: Ibid.

34 *Contents of Sankey's letter delivered through Rev. Dagwell*: NA, U.S. v. Sankey et al., Plaintiff's Exhibit 9a.

34 *Sankey bought a 1932 Ford Model 18 V-8*: Exhibit 50; NA, Alcorn Statement, Feb. 2, 1934, 5.

35 *Account of Joe Roma's death and investigation*: DP and NYT, both Feb. 19, 1933.

35 *Armstrong's orders to arrest known police characters*: DP, Feb. 19, 1933.

36 *"I have received many"*: RMN, Feb. 20, 1933.

36 *Claude's early life*: Ibid., June 10, 1957; Bean, 66. *Denver's First Citizen*: Humphreys, 33.

36 *Claude's education and marriages*: Boettcher Foundation Website at http:///boettcherfoundation.com

37 *Claude's stature*: DP, June 16, 1957.

37 *Claude's attitude toward work*: RMN, June 7, 1956.

37 *Edna's societal stature and "pull the smart set out"*: Ibid., Sept. 3, 1947, and May 6, 1948.

37 *On Edna Boettcher*: Author interview, Claudia Boettcher Merthan.

38 *Sankey's reply to Claude's open letter to kidnappers*: NA, U.S. v. Sankey, Plaintiff's Exhibit 19.

38 *"Since Sunday"*: DP, Feb. 21, 1933.

39 *Clark's unwarranted optimism*: RMN, Feb. 27, 1933.

39 *Denver police had little experience investigating kidnap-for-ransom*: DP, Feb. 13, 1933. In January 1932, a Denver man had been held for fifty thousand dollars, but when the money was not paid he was released. The ringleader shot himself rather than face prison.

Chapter 4

40   *"We have always been happy"*: *New York Journal*, Feb. 15, 1933.
41   *Anna Lou's stress*: DP, Feb. 27, 1933; RMN, Sept. 18, 1941.
41   *Anna Lou's interoceanic interview*: RMN, Feb. 16, 1933.
41   *"Sankey thought his South Dakota ranch"*: DP, May 10, 1934.
41   *"Miles make no difference"*: Ibid., May 13, 1934.
42   *"Upon the return of my son"*: NYT, Feb. 24, 1933.
42   *"If the abductors of my son"*: RMN, Feb. 23, 1933.
42   *Claude received twenty notes*: Ibid.
42   *"I am going no place at no time"*: Ibid., Feb. 25, 1933.
42   *Promptly and secretively*: Ibid.
43   *The* Denver Post's *editorial*: DP, Mar. 1, 1933.
43   *Rogers's comments on Al Capone*: Joseph Carter, 226–27.
43   *"You are never going to correct the crime situation"*: Lowenthal, 414.
44   *"If you are agreeable"*: NA, *U.S. v. Sankey et al.*, Plaintiff's Exhibit 18.
44   *Neighbors would likely become suspicious*: NA, Alcorn statement, Feb. 2, 1934.
44   *Pearce returned to Denver*: This account of the delivery of Charlie Boettcher and pickup of the ransom is taken largely from accounts of Alcorn's trial testimony in DP, May 14, 1934.
45   *Charlie Boettcher at the drugstore*: Ibid., Mar. 2, 1933.
45   *People flood the drugstore*: Ibid.
45   *Chief Clark arrived late*: RMN, Mar. 2, 1933.
46   *"Sixteen days and nights"*: DP, Mar. 2, 1933.
46   *O'Brien's background*: Ibid., Sept. 3, 1950. *Boettcher interview claim*: Ibid., Mar. 2, 1933.
46   New York Times *telephone interview of Charlie*: NYT, Mar. 2, 1933.
46   *Charlie Boettcher's return home*: DP, Mar. 2, 1933.
46   *Anna Lou's condition leading up to Charlie's release*: Ibid., Feb. 26, 1933.
47   *Reporters broke the news to Anna Lou*: RMN, Mar. 2, 1933.
47   *"I'm back and don't worry"*: DP, Mar. 2, Ibid.
47   *She leapt to her feet*: Ibid.
47   *"Fate was cruel to the Lindberghs"*: Ibid.
47   *"I met every obligation"*: Ibid.
47   *"As long as I live"*: NYT, Mar. 2, 1933.
47   *Claude pulls a gun on reporters and quote*: DP, Mar. 2, 1933.
48   *Police error*: RMN, Mar. 2, 1933.
48   *Account of the exchange of gunfire with Brighton police*: DP, Mar. 2, 1933.
48   *Bullets pierced the Ford's windshield*: NA, Alcorn Statement, Feb. 2, 1934.
49   *Sankey felt Claude had violated his promise*: DP, Feb. 2, 1934.
49   *Denver police search of roads out of city*: RMN, Mar. 2, 1933.
49   *Encountered Greeley police officers*: Greeley Daily Tribune, Mar. 2, 1933.
49   *Bureau agents confiscated ransom notes*: DP, Mar. 4, 1933.
49   *Claude's $25,000 reward*: Ibid., Mar. 5, 1933.

50   *Charlie slipped the tape off his eyes*: NYT, Mar. 8, 1933.
50   *His attention to detail*: Ibid.; DP, Mar. 2, 1933.
50   *The subject of conversation*: RMN, Mar. 3, 1933.
50   *"Hunted by the police"*: Ibid.
50   *"The authors of the Arabian nights"*: NYT, Mar. 10, 1934.
50   *Charlie's cigarette burn accidental*: DP, Mar. 8, 1933.
50   *Myth of the airliner flying overhead*: Ibid., Mar. 2, 1933.
50   *Into the Dakotas*: NYT, Mar. 3 and 4, 1933.
50   *The "three Georges" trek to Dakota*: *Kimball Graphic*, Mar. 9, 1933; see also DP, Mar. 7, 1933, which refers to O'Donnell's first name as John.
51   *On problems with law enforcement and safe cities*: Maccabee, 60.
51   *Last train robbery by horse*: Callahan and Jones, 159.
51   *"First in everything"*: DP, Mar. 2, 1933. The paper's own front page characterized the *Post* as "The Best Newspaper in the U.S.A."
52   *"Another scoop"*: Ibid., Mar. 2, 1933.
52   *Charles Boettcher, conducting "business as usual"*: Ibid., Mar. 2, 1933.
53   *Charles Boettcher's background*: Has been told well in Geraldine Bean's biography and various articles on his life. Taken from Bean generally and from "Leadville's Last," *Time* 52 (May 12, 1948): 15; RMN, June 17, 1979; and DP, Nov. 23, 1947.
53   *World-class tightwad*: *Time*, "Leadville's Last," 52 (May 12, 1948): 15.
53   *Brown Palace's valet fees excessive*: Ibid.
53   *"I didn't have a rich father"*: Author interview, Claudia Boettcher Merthan.
54   *Monopoly first sold in 1933*: www.Monopoly.com.
54   *Walsh traveled to Havana*: AL, Mar. 2, 1933.
54   *Body returned by train*: Ibid., Mar. 8, 1933.
54   *Chief Clark issued his standard pronouncement*: DP, Mar. 5, 1933.
54   *Questioning gangsters*: Ibid., Mar. 6, 1933.
55   *Alcorn's return to the ranch*: This account taken largely from NA, Alcorn Statement, Feb. 2, 1934.
55   *Information the Ellsworths and Miss Fletcher gave to police*: Boettcher family personal papers, Apr. 9, 1934, letter from Mayor's Reward Commission to Mayor Begole; and DP, Mar. 8, 1933.
55   *Police brought pearce in for questioning*: DP, Mar. 8, 1933.
55   *Pencil drafts of the ransom notes*: Ibid. Mar. 7 and 10, 1933.
55   *Fern Sankey's account tracked her sister's*: Ibid.
56   *Pearce's interrogation and "Sankey showed me"*: Ibid., Mar. 8 and 9, 1933.
56   *Pearce was the driver*: NA, Alcorn Statement, Feb. 2, 1934.
56   *Sankey obtained a copy*: DP, Mar. 10, 1933. This was likely the Mar. 3 edition, issued the day police interviewed the Ellsworths and Miss Fletcher, the headline of which announced that the hunt for the kidnappers had extended to the Dakotas.
56   *"I got nervous" and "Never mind. They'll never find"*: Ibid., Mar. 10, 1933.

56 *Laska defended Locke*: RMN, June 3, 1948; Goldberg, 32.
56 *"Sure she can talk"*: AL, May 15, 1934.
57 *Laska's background*: RMN, June 3, 1948.
57 *Professor B. Laska*: *Colorado Springs Gazette*, June 18, 1935.
57 *Laska at law school*: RMN, June 3, 1948.
57 *A hostile witness offered testimony*: Ibid., June 10, 1939.
57 *"Don't get these bootleggers off"*: Goldberg, 32.
57 *Laska got the message*: Ibid., 99.
57 *The Jewish Laska even joined*: Ibid., 109.
58 *Merelyn Kohler described its remote location*: DP, Mar. 7 and 8, 1933.
58 *The trek of the "three Georges"*: NYT, Mar. 8, 1933; *Kimball Graphic*, Mar. 9, 1933.
58 *Rifles from Kimball*: *Kimball Graphic*, Mar. 9, 1933.
59 *Sankey was a "good guy"*: AL, Mar. 9, 1933.
59 *"Pounced on the gang's lair"*: DP, Mar. 8, 1933.
59 *Arrival at the Sankey ranch*: Ibid.
59 *"Ringleader Caught in Boettcher Plot"*: NYT, Mar. 8, 1933.
59 *Youngberg's initial statements to authorities*: DP, Mar. 8, 1933.
59 *Youngberg slashed his throat*: *Kimball Graphic*, Mar. 9, 1933.
59 *Hoped to keep Youngberg's arrest secret*: NYT, Mar. 8, 1933.
60 *"He may be a kidnapper"*: DP, Mar. 8, 1933.
60 *"I never seen him in my life"*: NYT, Mar. 9, 1933.
60 *Youngberg's accent confirmed for Boettcher*: Ibid.
60 *Telegram from Winnipeg*: DP, Mar. 10, 1933.
61 *Account of Youngberg's confession*: Ibid.
61 *"Charlie was a good guy"*: Ibid.
61 *Sankey as the official bootlegger of the Denver 400 and denial by Boettchers*: Ibid., Mar. 8, 1933.
61 *Many began to arm*: Ibid., Mar. 4, 1933.
62 *Hoover's press release*: Ibid., Mar. 8, 1933.
62 *Elkhorn*: Several early articles referred to Sankey's associate as Gordon Elkhorn, rather than Alcorn.

Chapter 5

63 *News story of the father finding the dead pig*: NYT, Mar. 29, 1933.
64 *One in four American wage earners*: Shannon, 6; *"Ill-housed, ill-clad, ill-nourished"*: Lowitt and Beasley, preface.
64 *Central Park cave*: Burns.
64 *Bankers bolstered prices*: NYT, Oct. 25, 1929, as quoted in Shannon, 2, 3.
64 *$9 billion losses*: NYT, Oct. 29, 1929, as quoted in Shannon, 4.
64 *Market's tailspin continued*: Shannon, 74.
64 *More than five thousand banks closed*: Ibid., 72.
65 *Elderly lady lost her life savings*: Ibid., 83–84.
65 *Farmers' situation*: Ibid., 16, 17.

65   *Typical farmer earning less than entry-level industrial worker*: Ibid., 17.
65   *Crops sometimes went unharvested*: Ibid., 26–27.
65   *Poverty amid plenty*: Ibid., 26–37.
65   *"They promised me a chicken in the pot"*: Ibid., 27.
65   *"A woman with five children"*: AL, Dec. 8, 1932. The store manager's response was that "if she had the nerve to do it, I guess I have heart enough to let her get away with it — this time."
65   *Defiance of warnings about soil erosion*: Shannon, 31; Lauber, 46.
66   *Land allotted to the settlers not enough*: Shannon, 31.
66   *Ruth's salary cut*: AL, Mar. 13, 1933.
66   *Salaries*: Britten and Brash, at 26.
66   *Appealed a tax assessment*: RMN, Oct. 4, 1938.
67   *Sankey's Denver acquaintances and quotes*: DP, Mar. 8, 1933.
67   *On Sankey's Denver home and Bible verse*: Ibid.
68   *Account of Sankey hideout*: Ibid., Mar. 9, 1933.
68   *Repeal prohibition to permit sale of 3.2 beer*: Ibid., Mar. 15, 1933.
68   *Claudia's birth*: Ibid., Mar. 8, 1933.
68   *Boettcher hospitalization*: RMN, Mar. 12, 1933.
68   *Charlie Boettcher incident with motorist*: Ibid., Mar. 21, 1933.
68   *On Boettcher death threats*: DP, Feb. 27 and Mar. 23, 1933.
69   *Potential tax liability*: Ibid., Mar. 30, 1933.

Chapter 6

70   *"In the Republican platform at Cleveland"*: Joseph Carter, 173.
70   *Roosevelt's election and assassination attempt*: NYT, Mar. 5, 1933. Guiseppe Zangara murdered Chicago mayor Anton Cernak in the attempt; Cernak died on Mar. 6. Zangara was executed fourteen days later. AL, Mar. 6 and 20, 1933.
70   *Hitler's rise and action taken*: AL, Mar. 24, 1933.
70   *Bank holidays*: Ibid., Mar. 5 and 10, 1933.
71   *Homer Cummings appointed as interim replacement*: Gentry, 155.
71   *Hoover impressing Cummings*: Ibid., 55–156.
71   *Sankey as the first of the famous Depression-era gangsters*: Alix, 79–80.
71   *On Bohn investigation*: DP, Mar. 17, 1933.
72   *Cummings as an astute politician and on gangster movies*: Theoharis et al., 267–68.
72   *Drive against movies*: Ibid., 268.
72   *Catholics pledged to boycott movies*: Ibid.
72   *Expanded federal crime-fighting role*: Theoharis, 121.
72   *Twelve-point program*: Ibid.; 122.
73   *"Super police force"*:Ibid.
73   *Gann Valley population*: Author interview, Hugh Sedgewick.
74   *Temperature extremes*: Ruffner, 893. The information in this relating to Buffalo County is taken almost exclusively from the informative vol-

umes on Buffalo County History published in 1985 and 1999, Krog et al. and Sinkie et al.

74 *The blizzard of 1888*: AL, Dec. 26, 2004.
74 *Land thick with rattlesnakes*: Krog et al., 208.
74 *Anthrax*: Ibid., 205.
74 *On typhoid*: Brule County Historical Society, 562.
74 *The Keithahns*: Krog, 69–70; Sinkie, 144.
74 *Gann Valley's businesses*: Krog et al., 60–72.
75 *No potable running water*: Ibid., 70–71, 250.
75 *Gann Valley's banks*: Ibid., 70.
75 *On Buffalo County sheriffs Nelson and Klindt*: Ibid., 199, 281.
75 *Buffalo County Giant and his exploits*: Sinkie, 77.
76 *Sankey's distribution of ransom*: NA, Alcorn Statement, Feb. 2, 1934.
76 *Division and hiding of ransom*: DP, Apr. 2, 1933.
76 *Sankey prevailed on his older brother*: DP, Mar. 13, 1933.
76 *Sankey's stay in Minneapolis*: RMN, Mar. 10, 1933.
77 *"Arrived here O.K. everything fine" (Sankey letter to Fern and kids)*: U.S. *v. Fern Sankey et al.*, Plaintiff's Exhibit 47.
78 *Alcorn in Chicago*: NA, Alcorn Statement, Feb. 2, 1934.
78 *Sankey's return to ranch to dig up loot*: AL, Feb. 11, 1934; Mar. 11, 1933, and NA, Alcorn Statement, Feb. 2, 1934. This is an amalgamated account based on separate statements Sankey made to an unnamed Justice official and to a cellmate, and on Alcorn's version provided to bureau agents.
79 *Sankey's timing was exquisite*: DP, Feb. 11, 1934.
79 *"There are thousands of others like me" (Fern Sankey interview)*: Ibid., Mar. 8, 1933.
80 *Bohn kidnapping*: DP, Mar. 17 and 20, 1933.
80 *Robinson's confession and involvement with Sankey in Bohn case*: Ibid., Apr. 1 and 3, 1933.
80 *Fern's alleged involvement in the Bohn case*: Ibid., Mar. 28, Apr. 10, and May 25, 1933.
80 *Grand jury indictments*: Ibid., Mar. 29, 1933.
81 *Most-hunted fugitives*: RMN, Mar. 8 and 9, 1933; DP, July 18, 1933.

Chapter 7

82 *Lack of coordination in Lindbergh kidnapping investigation*: Gentry, 161.
82 *"I might know"*: DP, Apr. 2, 1933.
83 *Alcorn's marriage*: NA, Alcorn Statement, Feb. 2, 1934.
83 *Nettie Roma posted his bond*: DP, Mar. 8, 1933.
84 *Sankey's holdup of Alcorn*: Taken from two accounts, both by Alcorn, given eight days apart: NA, Alcorn Statement, Feb. 2, 1934, and AL, Feb. 10, 1934.
84 *The last time the pair spoke*: Actually the two were jailed next to each

other for several days in early Feb. 1934. It is conceivable that they exchanged limited conversation while under constant guard, but if so, there is no documentation of it.

85 *Claude Boettcher's payment to Youngberg and discovery of buried ransom*: Boettcher family personal papers, May 6, 1933, letter from Robert Stearns to Claude Boettcher; DP, May 2, 7, and 22, 1933.

85 *Sankey goes back for Youngberg's share*: DP, Feb. 10, 1934.

85 *Youngberg's discussion with authorities*: Ibid., May 7, 1933.

85 *Gleason to guard ranch*: Boettcher family personal papers, May 6, 1933, letter from Stearns to Claude Boettcher.

85 *Ransom allegedly hidden in stovepipe*: DP, May 20, 1933.

85 *Youngberg takes bureau agents through cemetery*: Ibid., May 22, 1934.

86 *Digging at the ranch*: Boettcher family personal papers, billing statements of Chopskies, and letter from Gleason to Stearns, May 26, 1933.

86 *Boettcher and government investigators work*: Boettcher family personal papers, George Carroll Report, with cover letter to attorney Robert Stearns, dated Aug. 15, 1933; May 6, 1933 letter from Stearns to Claude Boettcher; and May 20, 1933 letter from Ray Barger to Stearns.

86 *Kimball-area residents on national stage:* Verne Miller and Verne Sankey were not the only men of that period associated with Kimball to make their mark. Another was Edward William Alton Ochsner, born there in May 1896. Wilds and Harkey, 8, 1–15, generally. Ochsner while viewing an autopsy as a medical student, observed an unusual phenomenon, one, the supervising surgeon explained, he might not again see: the deceased's exposed cancerous lung. The mentor's prediction proved mistaken, but it tilled the soil for one of the most significant medical discoveries of the twentieth century. Ibid., 177.

In 1936, then president of Tulane University's prestigious Department of Medicine, Ochsner witnessed nine separate cases of carcinoma of the lung in a span of six months. On investigation, he found that each of the patients had been heavy smokers who had developed the habit during the World War. Ibid., 177–78. In 1939, with the help of his protégé, Dr. Michael DeBakey, who himself became a world-renowned cardiovascular surgeon, Ochsner confronted the medical establishment by publishing a controversial article in the journal *Surgery, Gynecology, and Obstetrics*, urging that a link existed between cigarette smoking and lung cancer. Ibid., 177; see also *Ochsner Journal* 4, no. 1: pp. 48–52. The medical profession greeted Ochsner's conclusion with notable disdain and more than a little ridicule. Wilds and Harkey, 178–87. It took decades for him to be fully vindicated. Today he is remembered as a pioneer concerning the risks posed by cigarette smoking. Wilds and Harkey, 250–51.

86 *Miller's 1920 election*: *Evening Huronite*, Nov. 3 and 4, 1920.

86 *Miller's Stutz Bearcat*: Author interview, Kenneth Larsen.

86 *Miller's bootlegging raids enforcing Prohibition*: Brad Smith, 31.

87   *Miller's St. Paul arrest*: Ibid., 36, 37.
87   *Miller eventually pled guilty*: South Dakota State Archives, State Penitentiary Inmate Files, Verne Miller.
87   *He became a player*: Brad Smith, 39–42.
87   *Speculation about Verne Miller and Sankey forming a kidnapping racket*: DP, Sept. 21. 1933.
88   *The line of Oklahoma outlaws*: Callahan and Jones, 8–9.
88   *The last U.S. train robbery executed on horseback*: Ibid., xiv.
88   *Nash imprisonment*: Ibid., 159.
88   *Bailey's career*: Haley, 3–5.
88   *A whopping $2.8 million*: Helmer, 165. Bailey's biographer quotes him as stating that, although he planned the heist and later helped exchange the funds, he was not there at its execution. Ibid., 34–51, 84.
88   *Bailey an unknown*: See Ibid., xi.
88   *Bailey's legitimate sojourn and reentry into robbery with Holden and Keating*: Ibid., 71–85.
89   *These men were, more than any other group*: See, e.g., Helmer, 172–225; Haley, 34–142, generally.
89   *Robbery of Ft. Scott bank*: Helmer, 175.
89   *Bailey's arrest*: Haley, 102–22; Helmer, 182.
89   *Bailey's escape:* Haley, 102–22.
89   *Bureau pursuit of Nash*: Unger.
89   *Sankey sighting*: DP, May 21, 1933.
90   *Fissure between the bureau and Denver police*: Ibid.
90   *Youngberg's guilty plea*: Ibid., May 7 and 29, 1933.
90   *Youngberg's and Pearce's sentencing and quotes*: Ibid., May 27, 1933.
90   *Youngberg's sentence*: Ibid., May 27 and 28, 1933.
91   *"I will rot in jail"*: Ibid., May 28, 1933.
91   *Pearce's words as he was led away to prison*: Ibid., June 3, 1933.
91   *Youngberg's mistake as to his sentence*: Ibid., May 28, 1933.
91   *O'Brien's characterization of Youngberg*: Ibid., May 7, 1933.
92   *Youngberg's interview*: Ibid., May 28, 1933.
92   *Fern wept through the sentencing*: Ibid., May 27, 1933.
92   *Fern Sankey faces Bohn charges*: Ibid., May 25, 1933.
92   *Fern's tearful farewell and quote*: DP and RMN, both dated May 29, 1933.
92   *Fern gave Evelyn $290*: DP, May 29, 1933.
93   *Case against Fern Sankey for Bohn kidnapping*: Ibid., June 14–16, 1933.
93   *Laska's letter from Verne Sankey*: Ibid., June 10, 1933.
93   *First day of Bohn trial*: Ibid., June 14, 1933.
94   *Fern's questioning during Bohn kidnapping trial proceedings, jury outcome, and Fern's quotes*: Ibid., June 15, 16, 1933.
95   *Verne Sankey as a suspect in Hamm kidnapping and coverage of Sankey contact with Laska through Echo Sankey, including quotes of Fern Sankey and Laska*: Ibid., June 17, 1933.

95   "*Boys, I am a Jew*": Ibid., Sept. 19, 1933.
96   *Sankey's bullet-riddled car at Ramsey County Courthouse*: Ibid., June 17, 1933.
96   *Barker-Karpis gang and its role in Hamm's kidnapping and Dunn as Henry Sawyer's friend*: Burrough, 36.
96   *Brown leaked crucial information*: Ibid., 37.
96   *Hot Springs police connection to underworld*: Callahan and Jones, 60–74.
97   *Frank Nash's capture*: Ibid., 75–76.
97   *On Lazia's influence*: McCullough, 200.
97   "*You know the rules*": Callahan and Jones, 78.
98   *Account of the Union Station massacre*: Ibid., 80–87.
98   "*No time, money or labor will be spared*": Wallis, 322.
98   *Cummings pledge*: NYT, June 17, 1933.

Chapter 8

113   *Sixty bank robberies*: Helmer, 179–99.
113   *Rogers quote*: Joseph Carter, 224.
113   *Six ransom kidnappings*: Alix 81.
114   *Dahill questions Fern Sankey*: DP, May 15, 1934.
114   "*A very fortunate and comfortable day*": AL, July 14, 1933.
114   *The twenty-nine-year-old Purvis*: Theoharis et al., 350.
114   *Slightly built, a little more than five feet*: Summers, 67–72; Burrough, 65–66. Gentry (70) claims Purvis was only five feet tall; Burrough that he was five foot, seven inches.
114   *Purvis had recently transferred to Chicago*: Author interview, Doris Rogers Lockerman.
114   *Purvis's style, manner, and mode of transportation*: Burrough, 66.
115   *Sankey as Hamm and Factor kidnappings suspect, and Dan "Tubbo" Gilbert's role in case*: DP, June 17 and July 3, 1933; Burrough, 66–67.
115   "*What do you mean a ham?*": Burrough, 67.
115   *Hamm said his captor resembled Verne Sankey*: DP, June 19, 1933.
115   *Purvis's announcement of "an ironclad case"*: Burrough, 67.
115   "*A splendid piece of work*": Ibid.
115   *Juries unaware of Gilbert's mob affiliation*: Ibid., 66–67.
116   *Five days later*: Gentry, 158.
116   "*Conduct the nation-wide warfare*": Ibid. In 1935 the agency became known as the Federal Bureau of Investigation. Theoharis et al., 14. For simplicity, it will continue to be referred to here as "the bureau."
116   Newsweek, *then in its inaugural year*: Gentry, 158.
116   Collier's *article*: Ibid., 158–59.
116   "*Now we'll call you 'Machine Gun Kelly'* ": This and other background on Kelly taken from: Barnes, 206–21.
116   *She followed the Boettcher kidnapping*: Ibid., 221.
117   *A few days later, President Roosevelt*: AL, Aug. 2, 1933; Alix, 193–94.

117 *Gus Jones's background and role in Urschel kidnapping investigation*: Burrough, 53–55, 83–89. As Burrough points out, Hoover later hailed Jones's interview as a masterpiece of detective work, but had Jones and his associates listened to a lowly Fort Worth detective's repeated entreaties to investigate the Kellys, the task would not have been nearly so difficult or drawn out.

117 *Bailey's arrest*: Haley, 133.

117 *Kelly had given Bailey ransom money*: Helmer, 190.

117 *Bailey a wanted gunman*: Haley, xi, 133.

117 *Joseph B. Keenan involved in the case*: Ibid., 137.

118 *The press portrayed Bailey*: Ibid., 140.

118 *"Sittin' in the jailhouse"*: DP, Aug. 17, 1933.

118 *"Without specific desire"*: Haley, 138.

118 *Account of Bates in Denver jail and Armstrong quote*: DP, Aug. 17, 1933.

119 *Bates; Kelly in Denver, and "Oh, what a terrible looking man"*: Ibid., Aug. 19, 1933.

119 *Kelley's supposed sighting in Denver*: Ibid., Aug. 17, 1933; Burrough, 93–94.

119 *"Like Bates and the other"*: DP, Aug. 19, 1933.

119 *Keenan's quote and Bates's response*: Ibid., Aug. 24, 1933.

120 *"I'm not like some bank robbers"*: Helmer, 49.

Chapter 9

121 *The June heat spell*: Gann Valley Chief, June 8, 22, 1933.

121 On *Fern Sankey's arrival at the Minnehaha County Jail*: AL, June, 28, 1933.

122 *Fern Sankey's background*: U.S. Census Records, 1905, South Dakota, Cards 2053, 2131.

122 *Background of Day and Christopherson quote*: AL, May 1, 1988.

122 Argus Leader's *quote of Fern's reunion with Echo*: Ibid., July 6, 1933.

122 *Gann Valley benefactors meet her bail*: NA, *U.S. v. Sankey et al.*; Bail Bond, July 19, 1933.

122 *Mike Chopski as surrogate parent for Sankey kids*: Author interview, Orville Sankey.

123 *"The turkeys have been laying eggs"*: DP, June 4, 1933.

123 *Carroll's investigation at the Sankey farm*: Boettcher family personal papers, George Carroll Report, with cover letter to attorney Robert Stearns, Aug. 15, 1933.

123 *Reward claimants*: DP, June 29, 1933.

123 *On Ellsworth shooting*: Ibid., July 31, 1933.

123 *Ellsworth's beating*: Ibid., Sept. 16, 17, 1933.

124 *Insurance statistics on suicide*: Britten and Brash, 26; National Center for Health Statistics for 1932–33.

124 *On suicidal thoughts during the Depression*: McElvaine, 175. A Federal

Emergency Relief Administration investigator reported in 1934 that almost all of her clients had expressed to her that they had considered suicide.

124 *Suicide stories*: AL, Oct. 7, 1933 and Oct. 5, 1934, respectively.
125 *On Major League attendance*: Wolff et al., 7.
125 *Laska's defense of Bates and quotes*: DP, Sept. 19, 1933.
126 *Harold Nathan alerted Melvin Purvis*: Burrough, 124.
126 *Kelly's capture*: Ibid., 131, 132.
126 *Evidence against Bailey was circumstantial*: Haley, 166–73.
126 *Urschel sentences*: www.fbi.gov., Urschel kidnapping file; Helmer, 191.
126 *Kellys' conviction and sentencing*: Helmer, 191–97.
127 *On the McGee conviction and quote*: Alix, 84; DP, June 4, 1933.
127 *Lynching as intimidation against blacks*: See James Allen, 26–28.
127 *In Opelousas, Louisiana*: AL, Sept. 27, 1933.
127 *San Jose mob*: Ibid.
127 *California governor's quote*: Alix, 95, 96.
127 *St. Joseph lynching*: AL, Nov. 29, 1933.
128 *Photographs of lynching*: James Allen, see, e.g., images 30, 31, 54, 57, and 79.
128 *Eventually Sankey dropped at least $10,000*: DP, Feb. 4, 1934.
128 *Sankey and female companion*: Ibid., Feb. 1, 1934; NA, Alcorn Statement, Feb. 2 1934.
128 *Helen Mattern's real name*: Boettcher family personal papers, Apr. 9, 1934, letter from Reward Committee to Denver Mayor Begole.
128 *Fern's Chicago visit*: RMN, Feb. 1, 1934; DP, May 14, 1934.
129 *Sankey bought toiletries with some of the ransom*: DP, Apr. 19, 1934.
129 *Verne Sankey as desperate farmer*: Chicago Daily Tribune, Feb. 1, 1934.
129 *Data on South Dakota's population trends*: Johansen, 8–14 and 26–46.
130 *Fully 39 percent*: Schell, 292.
130 *Analyzing sheriff's deeds*: The information on sheriff's deeds was garnered from a study of the records of the Buffalo County Register of Deeds throughout the 1920s and 1930s.

Chapter 10

131 *Tip on Sankey in Chicago and as Lindbergh kidnapping suspect*: DP, Oct. 7, 1933; Feb. 1, 1934, respectively.
132 *Mayor's reward committee*: Boettcher family personal papers, September 21 letter from Mayor to Committee; DP, Sept. 18, 1933.
132 *Average laborer earned*: Britten and Brash, 26.
132 *Committee's recommendation for reward apportionment*: Boettcher Family personal papers, Committee's letter of Oct. 6, 1933 to Mayor.
132 *Claude engaged Walter Byron*: Boettcher Family personal papers, Mar. 9, 1933, statement from Byron and Claude's responsive letter.
132 *George Carroll shadowed Sankey family members*: Boettcher family per-

sonal papers, George Carroll statement of billing to Claude Boettcher, payment date Aug. 4, 1933.

133   *Claude's investigative efforts and attorneys:* Boettcher family personal
papers, and various statements.

133   *Sheriff Rasmussen's letter:* Boettcher family personal papers, Aug. 19,
1933, letter from sheriff to Claude Boettcher.

133   *On information the Boettchers supplied to the bureau:* Boettcher family
personal papers, letters to bureau agents Werner Hanni, dated Aug.
26, 1933, and to Val Zimmer, dated Aug. 16, 1935, and letter from
John A. Dowd, SAC of Salt Lake City bureau office to Claude Boettcher in acknowledgment of documents provided.

133   *Gibbs in Algona:* Ibid. George Carroll Report to Robert Stearns, with
cover letter dated Aug. 15, 1933.

134   *Facts of Gibbs at Sankey ranch:* DP, Feb. 11, 1934.

134   *Gann Valley fire:* Krog et al., 53.

134   *Background on Doris Rogers and events of that day:* Burrough, 150–52;
author interview, Doris Rogers Lockerman.

134   *The aftermath of Miller's escape:* Taken largely from Burrough, 150–
152.

134   *It was Verne Miller's nude body:* AL, Nov. 30, 1933.

135   *Pastor F. E. Lochridge spoke: Evening Huronite,* Dec. 6, 1933.

135   *"A raging dust-storm":* AL, Nov. 12, 1933.

135   *The first of sixty dust storms: Daily Capital Journal,* May 24, 1934.

136   *Cloudburst caused massive flooding:* Krog et al., 53.

136   *Sheriff's sale:* Buffalo County Register of Deeds records, Dec. 17,
1934, Book 10 of Deeds, p. 446.

136   *Sankey family survival during summer and fall of 1933:* Author interview, Dureene Petersen.

136   *Dureene Petersen's background and comments:* Ibid.

137   *Cowboy governor Tom Berry and his walk, and background on farm unrest:*
Lowitt and Beasley, 85; "Milestones," *Time* (Nov. 12, 1951). Even
Rogers was struck by the resemblance. The similarities were striking:
he was folksy, direct, plain, and humorous. Rancher Berry quickly
became known as South Dakota's "Cowboy Governor." He spoke to
the student body at the University of South Dakota: "You don't get
brains at college," he quipped. "You either have 'em when you come
here or you don't. If you have 'em, the professors can polish 'em up for
you and you can get a permanent wave. If you don't have 'em your [*sic*]
wasting your own time and your folks money. I hope that you won't
learn so much here you won't have room to learn anything after you
get out of college." Dalthorp, 57–60.

137   *In the spring of 1933, Congress also established the Federal Emergency
Relief Administration:* The background of the Federal Emergency Relief Administration and Lorena Hickok has been taken from Lowitt

and Beasley's useful compilation of Hickok's letters to Harry Hopkins, xvii–xxi.

137   *His first investigator, Lorena A. Hickok*: Hickok was born in Wisconsin in 1893, but as a young child she moved with her family to the dusty settlement of Bowdle, in northern South Dakota, from which her father practiced his trade as a traveling butter maker. Her home life was abysmal; her father beat her routinely. When her mother died, the father told fourteen-year-old Lorena to hit the road. After a few failed attempts at college, she caught on with the *Minneapolis Tribune* in 1917. The job did not last, but her interest in journalism took hold, and eventually she landed a position with the Associated Press. On an assignment to cover the Democratic candidate's wife in the 1932 presidential campaign, she met Eleanor Roosevelt, and, over the course of the campaign, they formed an intimate friendship. Ibid., xxv–xxxv.

137   *From there she wrote to Hopkins*: Quotes from Hickok's report offer fascinating firsthand depictions of South Dakota conditions in the fall of 1933. I have taken the following quotations from Hickok's letters from Lowitt and Beasley, 83–85.

138   *Further Hickok observations and quotes*: Ibid., 90–93.

138   *Echo's journey to Chicago*: DP, Feb. 1, 1934.

139   *Childhood recollections of Echo and her father*: Author interview, Carol Stephens.

139   *Fern's suspicions about Roy Gibbs, culminating in her ordering them and Ruth to leave the ranch*: DP, Feb. 11, 1934.

Chapter 11

140   *Identify the city's most heinous criminals*: See Powers, 23; Helmer, 298.

140   *Public enemies list*: Helmer, 295.

140   *It has been frequently written*: See, e.g., Theoharis et al., 273.

140   *Movie G-Men and the Public Enemies list*: Ibid. The term was popularized, as well, by the 1931 movie *The Public Enemy*, which starred James Cagney.

141   *Justice Department informally identified Dillinger as Public Enemy No. 1*: Gentry, 172; Girardin and Helmer, 288–89. The FBI website, www.fbi.gov., also suggests as much in its history of Dillinger and the bureau. Certainly John Dillinger plays an enormous role in its own telling of bureau history.

141   *FBI Ten Most Wanted list*: Gentry, 172; see also FBI's own recitation of the history of the Ten Most Wanted list, found at *www.fbi.gov*.

141   *Keenan's announcement that Public Enemy No. 1 had been captured*: *Chicago Daily Tribune*, Feb. 1, 1934.

142   *Gibbs's undercover work*: Largely from DP, Feb. 11, 1934.

143   *One paper contained Ruth's photograph*: NYT, Jan. 4, 1934.

143   *"I never got any letters from him"*: Ibid.

143   *Kinkead's suspicions of Sankey involvement in Lindbergh abduction*: DP, Jan. 3, 1934.

144   *Sankey caught the attention also of Colonel Norman Schartzkopf*: Ibid., Feb. 1, 1934. Colonel Schwarzkopf was the father of the general bearing the same name, who led coalition forces that liberated Kuwait in the 1990–91 Iraqi war.

144   *Hoover's concession that kidnapping had increased*: Ibid., Jan. 6, 1934.

144   *Roosevelt urged Congress to adopt Cummings's twelve-point plan*: Theoharis and Cox, 126.

144   *Bremer's abduction*: AL, Jan. 24, 1934.

145   *Sankey on a bus*: Ibid., Feb. 4, 1934.

145   *Authorities would eventually learn*: Maccabee, 184.

145   *Brown leaked information to the gang*: Ibid., 186–87.

145   *Hoover ordered the Sankey manhunt intensified*: DP, Jan. 22, 1934.

145   *Routinely stopped for a shave, haircut, massage, or other tonsorial treatment*: Ibid., Feb. 1, 2, 1934; RMN, Feb. 2, 1934.

146   *Remove the moles*: Chicago Daily Tribune, Feb. 1, 1934;

146   *Sankey appeared at the barbershop*: DP, Feb. 11, 1934; NYT, Feb. 1, 1934.

146   *Tip that Sankey frequented Mueller's barbershop*: DP, Feb. 7, 1934.

146   *Sankey vowed he would never be taken alive*: Ibid., Feb. 1, 2, 1934.

146   *Agents and policeman monitor the barbershop*: Ibid.

146   *The plan was that police and bureau agents would take Sankey at the barbershop*: Ibid.

147   *Agents had not gotten law degrees to be shot*: Author interview, Doris Rogers Lockerman.

147   *Agents slept in caskets*: Alston Purvis, 86.

147   *The account of events leading up to Sankey's capture are pieced together from several source articles*: DP, Feb. 1, 7, and 11; NYT, Feb. 1, 1934.

148   *"We knew [Sankey] had sworn"*: DP, Jan. 31, 1934.

148   *"America's Public Enemy No. 1"*: Ibid.

148   *"This means the end of the man"*: Ibid., Feb. 1, 1934. The *Chicago Daily Tribune* quoted Keenan as follows: "America's public enemy No. 1 has been captured." Feb. 1, 1934.

148   *Keenan's statement set off a buzz*: Many assumed this meant Sankey was implicated in the Lindbergh case: DP; *Chicago Daily Tribune*, Feb. 1, 1934.

148   *"We will question him"*: DP, Jan. 31, 1934.

148   *"He had no chance"*: Ibid.

149   *"And to think"*: Ibid., Feb. 1, 1934.

149   *What agents found when they raided Sankey's apartment, and statements by and about Helen Mattern*: Ibid.

150   *Verne Sankey's unmailed letter to Claude*: Ibid., Feb. 2, 1934. The letter indicates that Sankey had likely not sold liquor directly to the Boettchers.

151   *Solved twenty kidnappings since March 1933*: Ibid., Feb. 1, 1934.

151   *Lifted Bremer family spirits:* NYT, Feb. 2, 1934.
151   *Cullen article suspecting Sankey in Bremer kidnapping:* DP, Feb. 1, 1934. The same day the bureau captured Sankey, a Chicago jury deliberated over the fate of the Touhy gang, on trial for the alleged kidnapping of John Factor, alias Jake the Barber. Even as it tried the Touhy gang, the Justice Department continued to explore Sankey's potential involvement with the Touhys. Ibid., Feb. 2, 1934. The Touhy gang's defense to the charge — that Factor was actually kidnapped by the Capone Gang — proved false, a fact almost certainly unknown to the Touhy gang themselves. The truth, which would not be revealed for years, was far worse: Factor had not likely been kidnapped at all. The jury deadlocked; the court declared a mistrial. Prosecutors retried Touhy and his gang less than two weeks later, this time obtaining their conviction. Helmer, 208; Burrough, 67–68, citing *USA ex. rel. Roger Touhy v. Joseph E. Ragen,* U.S. District Court, No. District of Illinois, Eastern Division, No. 48C448, Opinion of Court.
151   *Suspicions concerning Sankey's involvement in Lindbergh baby abduction:* DP, Feb. 1, 1934.
151   *Kinkead trip to Chicago to interview Sankey:* Ibid.
151   *Police took Sankey to bureau offices:* Ibid.
151   *Purvis and his agents interrogated him:* Ibid., Feb. 2, 1934; AL, Feb. 1, 1934. Purvis himself questioned Sankey until about 1:30 in the morning. Ibid.
152   *Purvis's personal secretary, Doris Rogers:* Author interview, Doris Rogers Lockerman; *Chicago Tribune,* Oct. 12, 1935.
152   *Chicago Bureau interrogation procedure under Purvis with Lockerman quotes:* Author interview, Doris Rogers Lockerman.
152   *Purvis normally delegated questioning:* Author interview, Doris Rogers Lockerman; AL, Feb. 1, 1934.
153   *Sankey was sad:* DP, Feb. 1, 1934; *Chicago Tribune,* Oct. 12, 1935.
153   *"I decided that I could improve":* AL, Feb. 9, 1934.
153   *Purvis interview of Sankey:* Purvis, 120–23.
153   *Purvis doubted Sankey was involved in Lindbergh case:* RMN, Feb. 2, 1934; see also Purvis, 122. *"A courageous overthrow":* Chicago Tribune,* Feb. 4, 1934.
153   *Brown informed South Dakota authorities:* NYT, Feb. 2, 1934.
154   *South Dakota's kidnapping law:* South Dakota Revised Code of 1919, Section 4046.
154   *Beyond question that Sankey trial should be in Denver:* DP, Feb. 1, 1934.
154   *Dillinger's return from Arizona: Chicago Tribune,* Jan. 31, 1934; NYT, Feb. 2, 1934. There had been some question about whether it was appropriate to hold the cagey robber at Crown Point. The state penitentiary offered a more secure setting with presumably better-trained guards, but county sheriff Lillian Holley, who was filling out the term

in office of her husband, who had been killed in the line of duty, assured the state that Dillinger could be contained in her state-of-the-art jail. Others shared the sheriff's confidence. As Dillinger was jailed, syndicated crime reporter Jack Lait wrote: "In all my experience with desperados in custody, I have never seen such elaborate precautions as are functioning here to prevent a possible rescue of John Dillinger, the cop-killer and double jail-breaker." DP, Feb. 1, 1934.

154   *Dillinger's early life, prison sentence, and resumption of life of banditry*: NYT, July 23, 1934; Powers, 187–89.

154   *Dillinger's bank robbery résumé*: NYT, July 23, 1934; Girardin, 271–76.

155   *Dillinger pose and Sankey photo*: NYT, Feb. 1, 1934.

155   *Reasons for trying Sankey in South Dakota*: AL, Feb. 4, 1934.

156   *"Closely guarded by federal operatives"*: DP, Feb. 2, 1934.

156   *"[Sankey] had a car to himself"*: Purvis, 122. U.S. marshal's concern: *Chicago Tribune*, Feb. 4, 1934.

156   *"It seemed incredible"*: DP, Feb. 2, 1934.

157   *Jack Lait news report and quotes*: Ibid.

Chapter 12

158   "Shaved and apparently refreshed": DP, Feb. 2, 1934.

159   *"It is doubtful"*: AL, Feb. 2, 1934.

159   *Ten U.S. deputy marshals and guards*: Ibid.

159   *Gorder article on Public Enemy No. 1*: Ibid.

159   *Sankey did not remain in the county jail long and had spent only one day in jail in his life*: Ibid.

160   *"They are shooting at us, already"*: Ibid.

160   *Preference over all other federal cases*: Ibid., Feb. 3, 1934.

160   *"We're not going to take any chances"*: DP, Feb. 2, 1934.

160   *Purvis in Sioux Falls*: AL, Feb. 2, 1934.

160   *When federal officials marched Sankey*: Ibid.

161   *"Uncle" Mike Chopskie reprised his earlier role*: Ibid.

161   *Judge Wyman increased Fern's bond*: Ibid.

161   *"Mrs. Sankey has not attempted to leave"*: Ibid.

161   *"Mrs. Sankey, who looks no more than 30"*: Ibid., Feb. 3, 1934.

162   *Alcorn's arrest*: DP., Feb. 2, 3, 1934.

162   *"I'm awfully sorry"*: Ibid., Feb. 3, 1934.

163   *"That's great"*: NYT, Feb. 3, 1934.

163   *"I wouldn't put anything past him"*: DP, Feb. 2, 1934.

163   *"Sioux Falls had the eyes"*: AL, Feb. 2, 1934.

163   *Authorities parked Alcorn*: Ibid., Feb. 3, 1934.

163   *"I had a swell time"*: DP, Feb. 4, 1934.

163   *"This is the funniest experience"*: Ibid.

163   *"Not so tough"*: Ibid., Feb. 4.

163   *Sankey's flattened mood*: Ibid., AL, Feb. 3, 4, 1934.

164 *"If I find that my husband" and "I'm still for Verne"*: DP, Feb. 3, 1934.
165 *Stories circulated*: Ibid., Ibid., Feb. 5, 1934.
165 *Those around him attributed Sankey's morose mood*: AL, Feb. 4, and Feb. 9, 1934.
165 *"Alcorn is a swell fellow"*: Ibid., Feb. 4, 1934.
165 *Brown made it clear his role was advisory*: Ibid., Feb. 5, 1934.
165 *Proposal to dismiss charges against Fern*: DP, Feb. 9, 1934.
165 *Government's trial efforts and Keenan's instructions*: AL, Feb. 3 and Feb. 5, 1934.
166 *Their first move was to publicly separate Fern's guilt*: Ibid., Feb. 3, 1934.
166 *"There is no doubt whatever"*: Ibid., Feb. 7, 1934.
166 *"I have not been interested in preparing any defense"*: Ibid.
166 *Prosecutors decided to move briskly*: Ibid.
167 *Administration rejoiced*: Ibid., Feb. 8, 1934.
167 *As the days of Verne Sankey's solitary confinement passed*: This account of Sankey's death is amalgamated from the DP and AL accounts of Feb. 9 and Feb. 10, 1934. On Harold Alcorn's background: Author interview, John Alcorn.
170 *Hoover's comments on Sankey's death*: DP, Feb. 9, 1934.
170 *Reactions of Alcorn, Charlie Boettcher, and others*: Ibid.
171 *"Vern Sankey couldn't take it"*: Ibid.
171 *"Verne Sankey has kept his word to 'beat the law'"*: Ibid.
171 *Ben Laska saw something more than fear*: Ibid.
171 *"Pour eviter toute possibilite qu'ils ne se pendent"*: AL, Feb. 12, 1934.
171 *Sankey's suicide*: Ibid., Feb. 9, 1934.
172 *"One of the most dastardly"*: Ibid.
172 *Sankey's funeral arrangements*: DP, Feb. 12, 1934.
173 *"Our Service is Within the Means of All"*: Sioux Falls Telephone Directory, 1934.
173 *Background on the funeral*: AL, Feb. 12, 1934.
174 *Background on the Sankey pallbearers*: Taken largely from Krog et al., 183–84, 227–29, 251–52, 263–64.
174 *At Mount Pleasant Cemetery*: AL, Feb. 12, 1934.

Chapter 13

175 *"I really feel more sorry"*: Ibid., Feb. 10, 1934.
176 *Wyman reduces Fern's bond*: Ibid.
176 *Holton Davenport filed letters of administration*: Buffalo County Probate #502, Estate of Verne R. Sankey.
176 *Just under $2,500.00*: Boettcher family personal papers, September 20, 1937, letter to Claude Boettcher from the law firm of Lewis & Grant.
176 *The petition listed as assets*: Petition for Letters of Administration, Probate #502.

177   *A sheriff's deed would issue*: Buffalo County Office of the Register of Deeds, 10 of Deeds, 466.

177   *Alcorn becomes the government's new key witness*: DP, Apr. 1, 1934.

177   *Fern Kohler's bail*: NA, *U.S. v. Sankey et al.*, Bail Bond, Apr. 2, 1934.

177   *"I warned him the first thing"*: Helmer, 49.

177   *"Shoot [his] way out"*: NYT, Mar. 4, 1934.

177   *His guards were sufficiently confident*: Ibid.

178   *Account of Dillinger and Nelson's Sioux Falls robbery*: AL, Mar. 6, 1934; Burrough, 244–246.

178   *"Sold the neckties"*: DP, Feb. 23, 1934.

178   *April 1934 reward allocation*: Boettcher family personal papers, Apr. 9, 1934 letter from the reward committee to Mayor Begole; DP. Apr. 22, 1934.

178   *Gibbs's reward and divorce petition*: DP, Apr. 22, 24, 1934.

179   *Ellsworth family woes and accident*: Ibid., Apr. 25, 1934.

179   *As the Boettcher kidnapping trial approached, bureau agents pursuing John Dillinger*: It is difficult to improve on the incisive recitation Burrough provides of the Little Bohemia raid. The version of it appearing here comes from that source at 292–322.

180   *"Well, they had Dillinger surrounded"*: Ibid., 324.

180   *Davenport was a New England native*: The background on Holton Davenport came largely from an interview with his partner, Louis Hurwitz, a study of Davenport's published opinions, and the following article: AL, May 1, 1988.

180   *South Dakota's Supreme Court decided seventeen cases*: Westlaw Reports of South Dakota Supreme Court Decisions.

181   *"I think in all Lee Wyman's years"*: Author interview, Louis Hurwitz.

181   *Some of the war's bloodiest battles*: Sandburg, 288–89.

181   *It was a memorable welcome*: Author interview, Leo Flynn.

182   *In 1928 Hoover appointed Wyman*: The background on Judge Wyman is, except where otherwise cited, taken from Peggy Teslow's useful work on South Dakota's federal court judges, at 40–46.

182   *"Possessed an innate sense"*: Teslow, 42–43.

182   *"Any damn fool can know"*: Author interview, Leo Flynn interview.

182   *Wyman's reputation*: Author interview, Louis Hurwitz.

182   *Discussion of Wyman's doodling habit*: Teslow, 42–43; Author interview, Leo Flynn.

183   *"Send names of men who have been good jurors in your courts"*: Teslow, 46.

183   *Defense counsel's request for a meeting with the sisters*: DP, May 6, 1934; and AL, May 9, 1934.

183   *Gordon Alcorn's troubles and concessions to Alcorn*: DP, May 9, 1934.

183   *May 10 dust storm*: *Daily Capital Journal*, May 11, 1934.

183   *Dust on the president's desk*: Lauber, 15.

184   *Spectators packed*: DP, May 10, 1934; AL, May 11, 1934; *Daily Capital Journal*, May 12, 1934.
184   *"Tears or hysteria"*: DP, May 11, 1934.
184   *"Highly improper," and Laska's problems during jury selection*: Ibid. Accounts of the trial present an interesting case in perspective. The *Denver Post* tended to focus on Laska's involvement in the trial, while The *Argus Leader* highlighted the role of Holton Davenport, son-in-law of its publisher.
184   *The jury makeup*: AL May 11, 1934.
184   *Eidem's opening statement*: DP, May 11, 1934; see also Ibid., May 9, 1934.
185   *"Now look here, Mr. Laska"*: *Daily Capital Journal*, May 11, 1934; AL, May 11, 1934.
185   *Late in the afternoon on May 10*: DP, May 11, 1934.
185   *Early trial witnesses*: AL, May 11, 1934.
185   *Alcorn's trial testimony*: DP, May 12, 1934.
185   *Alcorn's depiction of the Sankeys and planning of the kidnapping*: DP, May 13, 14, 1934; NYT, May 14, 1934.
187   *Alcorn's prior statement to bureau agents*: NA, Alcorn Statement, Feb. 2, 1934.
188   *Davenport's cross-examination of Alcorn*: NYT, May 14, 1934; AL, May 14, 1934.
188   *When Davenport reminded Alcorn*: DP, May 15, 1934.
188   *Hanni's testimony*: AL, May 15, 1934.
188   *"The old lady wants us to turn Bohn loose"*: DP, May 16, 1934.
189   *Account of Fern Sankey's testimony*: Ibid.
189   *Account of Ruth Kohler's testimony*: Ibid.
190   *Account of Harold Brown's testimony*: Ibid.
190   *Account of closing arguments*: AL, May 17, 18, 1934; DP. May 17, 1934.
191   *Judge Wyman's instructions from memory*: NA, *U.S. v. Sankey et al.*, judge's jury instructions. See also Teslow, 43.
192   *Account of jury deliberation, outcome, and posttrial quotes*: AL, May 18, 1934.

Chapter 14

193   *The demise of Bonnie and Clyde*: Helmer, 213.
193   *Dillinger as America's chief at-large criminal*: NYT, June 24, 1934.
194   *Dillinger's death and Floyd as Public Enemy Number One*: Ibid., July 23, 1934; Wallis, 328.
194   *Background on George Philip and quotes, except where otherwise noted*: *Rapid City Journal*, Mar. 15, 1948.
194   *George Philip's biographical sketch of Scotty Philip*: South Dakota Historical Collections, 20:356–406.
194   *About Scotty Philip's bison*: The foundation livestock for the bison that

roam South Dakota's Custer State Park today originated from Scotty Philip's herd.

194 *Philip barely got his law office opened*: Bison-bull fight story is taken from South Dakota Historical Collections, 20:409–30.

194 *Philip's service on various state commissions*: As had Wyman, George Philip also served on the South Dakota Cement Plant Commission. *Rapid City Journal*, Mar. 15, 1948.

195 *Threats on Gibbs's life, new evidence from Gibbs, and his untimely death*: NYT, Oct. 12, 1934.

195 *"There's a fox, shoot him"*: RMN, Oct. 13, 1934; see also DP, Oct. 12, 13, 1934.

196 *The inquest panel concluded*: DP, Oct. 16, 1934.

196 *Gibbs's estate fight*: Ibid., Oct. 13 and 19, 1934.

196 *"Life of the party"*: AL, Oct. 20, 1934.

196 *Floyd's death and Richetti's capture*: NYT, Oct. 23, 1934.

196 *Justice Department announced a new premier Public Enemy*: Ibid.

196 *Hauptmann's arrest and consultation with Laska*: AL, Oct. 25, 1934; RMN, June 3, 1948.

197 *Mostly female crowd was so large*: AL, Oct. 25, 1934.

197 *Washington decided*: Ibid., Oct. 22, 1934; see also DP, May 20, 1934.

197 *Jury selection at retrial*: AL, Oct. 22, 1934.

197 *Charlie Boettcher watched from the oak pews*: Ibid.

197 *Composition of jury*: Ibid., Oct. 24, 1934.

197 *George Philip's opening statement*: Ibid., Oct. 23, 1934.

198 *Philip's mannerisms and presentation*: Rapid City Journal, Mar. 15, 1948.

198 *Davenport's opening statement and quotes*: DP, Oct. 23, 1934.

198 *Heartsick and constantly worried*: AL, Oct. 23, 1934.

199 *Alcorn's testimony*: Ibid., Oct. 25, 1934. It is clear that Davenport still did not have Alcorn's February 2, 1934, statement to bureau agents, in which Alcorn gave a thorough account of the kidnapping and events before and after, yet did not mention any role played in it by Fern Sankey. Davenport had, however, asked Alcorn at the first trial if, while Verne Sankey was alive, he ever told bureau agents that Fern had been involved. Alcorn admitted that he had not done so, but decided to tell them of her involvement after his mother urged him to tell the whole truth. DP, Oct. 25, 1934.

200 *Defense witnesses Kohler, Fern Sankey, and Brown*: AL, Oct. 26, 1934.

200 *Laska's closing argument*: Ibid., Oct. 26, 27, 1934.

200 *"A statement from them would exonerate Mrs. Sankey"*: Ibid., Oct. 27, 1934.

201 *Fern Sankey's reaction to the verdict*: RMN Oct. 27, 1934.

Chapter 15

"These men lie in wait for their own blood; they waylay only themselves!": Proverbs 1:18 (New International Version)

202   *Fern and Orville Sankey in Gann Valley and Echo in Minneapolis after trial and the move west*: Author interviews, Dureene Petersen and Orville Sankey; RMN, Oct. 27, 1934, Apr. 8, 1934.

202   *Fern Sankey's new life*: Author interview, Orville Sankey. It is not clear when Echo rejoined her mother and brother.

202   *On Orville Sankey's remembrances of childhood, later life, and quotes*: Author interviews, Dureene Petersen and Orville Sankey; RMN, Oct. 27, 1934, and Apr. 8, 1934. It is not clear when Echo rejoined her mother and brother.

203   *Echo in the car the night Boettcher was released*: DP, May 14, 1934.

203   *On Echo Sankey's later life and her admonishment to keep the kidnapping events from Orville*: Author interviews, Carol Stephens, Doreene Petersen, and Orville Sankey.

203   *Orville Sankey on his life*: Author interview, Orville Sankey.

204   *Fern Sankey's later life and death*: Author interview, Orville Sankey.

204   *"There are thousands of others"*: DP, Mar. 28, 1933.

204   *Fern kept the truth from Orville*: Author interview, Orville Sankey.

205   *The role of a relative few in the spate of bank robberies*: Burrough, 543, and cast of characters, following xiv.

206   *Public Enemy No. 1 designation as aspect of the New Deal*: See Ibid., 543; Theoharis et al., 12–15; Powers, 32.

206   *Decline in number of kidnappings*: Alix, 123, 169, 191.

206   *In 1963, the FBI claimed that it had solved*: Ibid., 121.

206   *Charlie Boettcher's kidnapping was the first the bureau actively investigated*: Ibid., 79.

207   *Sankey as a Mason*: Boettcher Family Personal Papers, George Carroll report to Robert Stearns, 4, with cover letter dated Aug. 15, 1933.

207   *"My life's mistake"*: DP, Feb. 4, 1934.

208   *"Sankey has sometimes been called"*: Purvis, 117, 118. Purvis's otherwise interesting account is riddled with inaccuracies, such as Sankey's age, the circumstances of the decision to take Charlie Boettcher, and other less significant facts. Purvis also states, incorrectly, that Fern Sankey was present at the ranch while Boettcher was held there.

208   *"Only once did he become angry"*: Ibid., 121, 122.

209   *Doris Rogers Lockerman's reflections*: Author interview, Doris Rogers Lockerman.

209   *Myths about Sankey's role in the Boettcher kidnapping and cause of his death*: Carol Stephens's and Lloyd Marten's recollections of common belief about the kidnapping in Gann Valley, Author interviews, Carol Stephens and Lloyd Marten.

209   *"Bottacher [sic] wouldn't pay him"*: Melville Advance, Nov. 13, 1996.

210   *Sankey ranch house now on its third foundation*: Author interview, Leon Chmela.

211   *As the Good Book says*: Ecclesiastes, 1:11, 16 (New International Version).

Epilogue

212   *The bureau's version of Laska's conduct*: www.fbi.org, 1935 Bureau report of Urschel kidnapping.

212   *Laska pardoned*: RMN, June 3, 1948.

213   *Laska quotes and death*: Ibid.

213   *Charles O'Brien's death*: DP, September 3, 1950

213   *Honorary pallbearers at O'Brien's funeral*: Ibid., September 5, 1950.

213   *Davenport established his own law practice*: AL, May 1, 1988.

213   *The facts of Harold Brown's life after the Sankey trial*: Krog et al., 148.

214   *Heat wave of 1936*: Ibid., 54.

214   *Viereck history*: Ibid., 263–64; Sinkie et al., 65–66; Author interview, Ruth Viereck.

214   *Nelson history*: Krog et al., 227–28; Sinkie et al., 188–90.

214   *Edwin Dye history*: Krog et al., 61, 159; author interview, Dureene Petersen.

214   *Mike Chopskie's death*: Burial permit, Office of the Brule County Register of Deeds; author interviews, Judy Busack and Orville Sankey.

214   *Buffalo County Census data*: U.S. Census Bureau data, 2000.

214   *"I'm a friend of every man I've ever sent to prison"*: AL and *Rapid City Journal*, both Mar. 15, 1948.

215   *Deaths of Philip's sons and commissioning of ship*: *Rapid City Journal*, Mar. 15, 1948; www.navysite.de.

215   *Berry asked to replace Rogers's syndicated column*: Dalthorp, 59, 60.

215   *Cummings's efforts*: Taken in part from an article written by the FBI's historian, John Fox: Fox, 6.

215   *NYT references to Cummings and Hoover*: NYT Index, 1933 and 1934.

216   *Joseph B. Keenan's later life and the Japanese war trials*: www.oasis .harvard.edu. Keenan, Joseph Berry, 1888–1954.

216   *The judge heard draft deserter and conscientious objector cases*: Author interview, Leo Flynn; Teslow, 43–46.

216   *Wyman's later life and death*: Teslow, 47–48; Author interview, Leo Flynn.

216   *Alcorn's deal with prosecutors, ransom, and quotes*: AL, Oct. 20, 29, 1934.

217   *Account of the money found in Vega cemetery*: Author interviews, Dureene Petersen, Lloyd Marken, and John Mayer. The exact amount recovered is unclear. Petersen and Marken recalled that it was $5,000.

217   *Birdie's disappearance and "has always seemed utterly ashamed"*: NA, Alcorn Prison Records.

217   *Letter-writing effort on Alcorn's behalf*: Boettcher family personal papers, various letters from Alcorn's mother to Claude and others, and their responses.

217   *Washington was loathe to release Alcorn*: Ibid., Apr. 3, 1937 letter from Robert H. Turner to Charles Boettcher II.

217   *Letter-writing effort on Alcorn's behalf and meetings*: Ibid., letters from

Alcorn's mother and siblings to Claude and his responses; DP, Mar. 22
and May 15, 1934.

218 *"If it would not has [sic] been for your kindness"*: Ibid., letter from Gordon Alcorn to Claude Boettcher, Sept. 12, 1949.

218 *Gordon Alcorn's later life and death*: Author interview, John Alcorn.

218 *"A victim of circumstances"*: NA, Youngberg Prison Records.

218 *Youngberg was paroled*: Ibid.

218 *Pearce prison diagnosis*: NA, Pearce Prison Records; Compilation of Reports made by Chief Medical Officer, Leavenworth Prison.

219 *Pearce's prison employment, support from staff, and his eventual release*: NA, Pearce Prison Records; Boettcher family personal papers, various correspondence between Lillie Knight and Charlie Boettcher.

219 *Nelson shoots federal agents and is killed*: NYT, Nov. 29, 1934.

219 *Bailey's later life and "I may starve but I'll never steal again"*: Bailey, 202.

219 *Having outlived nearly every crook*: Ibid.; Burrough, 1–3, recounts Karpis's later life and portrays a bitter, defiant man.

220 *Purvis's later life and death*: Theoharis et al., 350; Gentry, 174–76.

220 *Doris Lockerman's later life*: Author interview, Doris Rogers Lockerman.

220 *1945* Investigator *article*: Penny, 1–4.

221 *On Charlie after the kidnapping and governess Nelia Reynolds*: Author interiew, Claudia Merthan.

221 *Reflections on Anna Lou Boettcher's later life and Charlie's drinking*: Author interview, Claudia Boettcher Merthan.

221 *Anna Lou Boettcher suicide*: RMN and DP, Sept. 18, 20, 1941; author interview, Claudia Boettcher Merthan.

222 *Charlie's social and civic activity and later life*: RMN, Apr. 16, 1963; Author interview, Claudia Boettcher Merthan.

222 *Charlie's romance with Lee Wylie, later marriage, and travel*: Author interview, Claudia Boettcher Merthan; RMN, Apr. 16, 1963.

222 *Charles Boettcher's death and "The young man who wants to go into business"*: Time, "Leadville's Last," July 12, 1948.

222 *Fanny's death*: DP, Nov. 10, 1952.

222 *Fannie took her several-hundred-thousand-dollar share*: Ibid., Nov. 16, 1947, and Nov. 20, 1952; Bean, 196.

222 *"Attended only by servants"*: DP, Nov. 26, 1947; Bean, 200.

222 *A distant figure to her own few great-grandchildren*: Author interview, Claudia Boettcher Merthan.

223 *"That's it. We're moving"*: Ibid.

223 *Charlie and Mae moved into the ninth-floor suite*: Ibid.; DP, June 20, 1963.

223 Edna as Denver's society leader and best-dressed woman: RMN, Sept. 3, 1947, and May 6, 1948.

223 *Edna with royalty*: DP, June 10, 1957.

223   *She merely tolerated children generally; a visit to Claude and Edna like a command performance*: Author interview, Claudia Boettcher Merthan.
223   *The role of jewelry in Edna Boettcher's life*: Ibid.
223   *"I've come to understand" and declining health*: RMN, June 7, 1956.
223   *Charlie addressed his father as "Sir"*: Author interview, Claudia Boettcher Merthan.
223   *Claude's death and the value of his estate*: DP, June 10, 1957; RMN, June 11, 1957.
224   *Edna's death*: RMN, June 17, 1979.
224   *Gift to the state of Colorado of the Claude Boettcher mansion and furnishings*: DP, Dec. 25, 1959.
224   *Claude's crowning achievement*: Ibid., May 2, 1999.
224   *Boettcher Foundation endowment*: Author interview, Claudia Boettcher Merthan.
224   *Claude's obituary regarding his relationship with his son*: RMN, June 13, 1957.
224   *Charlie Boettcher's death*: Ibid., Apr. 16, 1963.
225   *Mansion's decline and vandalism*: Ibid., May 24, 1961.
225   *Teenagers dared one another; razing of the mansion*: DP, June 20, 1963.
225   *Tall, strikingly attractive Claudia Boettcher*: Author interview with Denver resident, Lyn Spenst.
225   *Charlie's concerns about Claudia marrying a South Dakotan*: Author interview, Claudia Boettcher Merthan.
225   *Claudia's marriage*: DP, June 6, 1954.
225   *Hoffman's career as a professional soloist*: Author interview, Claudia Boettcher Merthan; RMN, Apr. 3, 1961.
226   *Le Roy Hoffman's decision to end touring*: Author interviews, Charles Boettcher Hoffman and Claudia Boettcher Merthan.
226   *Le Roy Hoffman as a Renaissance man; Claudia and Le Roy's children*: Author interview, Claudia Boettcher Merthan.
227   *People around Eureka*: Author interview, Steve Smith.
227   *Charlie Hoffman's appearance, quotes, and his German blood*: Author interview, Charles Boettcher Hoffman.
227   *Quotes of Claudia Boettcher Merthan*: Author interview, Claudia Boettcher Merthan.
228   *Ann Boettcher Ohrel's life*: Ibid. Ann declined to be interviewed for this book.
228   *Claudia's comments on South Dakota, her transformation, her father, and her work with the Boettcher Foundation*: Ibid.

Selected Bibliography

Archival Sources

Boettcher Family Personal Papers
Buffalo County, South Dakota
   Clerk of Courts Records
   Register of Deeds Records
Federal Bureau of Investigation Files
   Pretty Boy Floyd and Kansas City Massacre. FBI file No. I. C. 62-28915.
      Barker-Karpis Gang; John Dillinger; Baby Face Nelson.
Federal Bureau of Investigation website, www.fbi.gov.
National Archives and Records Administration, Washington, D.C, Record
   Group.
South Dakota State Prison Inmate Files, South Dakota Archives, Pierre.

Published Primary Sources

Hamlin, William G. *100 Years of South Dakota Agriculture 1900–1999.* Sioux
   Falls: South Dakota Agricultural Statistics Service, 2000.
Johansen, John P. *Population Trends in Relation to Resources Development in
   South Dakota.* Brookings: Rural Sociology Department, Agricultural
   Experiment Station, South Dakota State College, 1954.
South Dakota Historical Collections. Vols. 20 and 23. Pierre: State Histor-
   ical Society, 1940.
South Dakota Revised Code of 1919. Prepared and annotated by John B.
   Hanten et al. Pierre: Hipple, 1919.
South Dakota State Census Records.

Books, Articles, and Films

Agee, James, and Walker Evans. *Let Us Now Praise Famous Men*. Boston: Houghton Mifflin, 1941.

Alix, Ernest Kahlar. *Ransom Kidnapping in America, 1874–1974: The Creation of a Capital Crime*. Carbondale, IL: Southern Illinois University Press, 1978.

Allen, Frederick Lewis. *Since Yesterday: The 1930s in America*. New York: Harper and Row, 1939.

Allen, James. *Without Sanctuary*. New York: Twin Palms, 2000.

Barnes, Bruce. *Machine Gun Kelly: To Right a Wrong*. Perris, CA: Tipper, 1991.

Bean, Geraldine. *Charles Boettcher: A Study in Pioneer Western Enterprise*. Boulder, CO: Westview Press, 1976.

Behr, Edward. *Prohibition: Thirteen Years that Changed America*. New York: Arcade, 1996.

Britten, Loretta, and Sarah Brash, ed. *Hard Times, The 30s*. Alexandria, VA: Time-Life Books, 1998.

Brule County Historical Society. *Brule County History*. Pierre, SD: State Publishing, 1977.

Burns, Ken. *Jazz* (a film). PBS, 2001. Also see http://www.pbs.org/jazz/time/time _ depression.htm.

Burrough, Bryan. *Public Enemies: America's Greatest Crime Wave and the Birth of the FBI, 1933–34*. New York: Penguin, 2004.

Callahan, Clyde C., and Byron B. Jones. *Heritage of an Outlaw*. Hobart, OK: Schoonmaker, 1979.

Carter, Jimmy. *An Hour before Daylight: Memories of a Rural Boyhood*. New York: Simon and Schuster, 2001.

Carter, Joseph. *Never Met a Man I Didn't Like: The Life and Writings of Will Rogers*. New York: Avon Books, 1991.

Clarens, Carlos. *Crime Movies, An Illustrated History, From Griffith to the Godfather and Beyond*. New York: W. W. Norton, 1980.

Cooper, Courtney Ryley. *Ten Thousand Public Enemies*. Boston: Little, Brown, 1935.

Crowther, Bosley. *The Great Films, Fifty Golden Years of Motion Pictures*. New York: G. P. Putnam's Sons, 1967.

Dalthorp, Charles, ed. *South Dakota's Governors*. Sioux Falls, SD: Midwest-Beach, 1953.

English, T. J. *Paddy Whacked*. New York: Regan Books, 2005.

Fox, John. "Homer Cummings' National War on Crime." *The Investigator* (May 2001): 6–7.

Gallagher, Hugh Gregory. *FDR's Splendid Deception*. New York: Dodd, Mead, 1985.

Gentry, Curt. *J. Edgar Hoover: The Man and the Secrets*. New York: W. W. Norton, 1991.

Girardin, G. Russell and William J. Helmer. *Dillinger: The Untold Story*. Bloomington: Indiana University Press, 2005.

Goldberg, Robert Alan. *Hooded Empire: The Ku Klux Klan in Colorado*. Urbana: University of Illinois Press, 1981.

Haley, I. Evetts. *Robbing Banks Was My Business*. Canyon, TX: Palo Duro Press, 1973.

Hall, Burt L. *Last Roundup*. Pierre, SD: The Reminder, 1954.

Hamilton, Floyd. *Public Enemy No. 1*. Dallas: Acclaimed Books/International Prison Ministry, 1978.

Helmer, William, with Rick Mattix. *Public Enemies: America's Criminal Past, 1919–1940*. New York: Checkmark Books, 1998.

Hillenbrand, Laura. *Seabiscuit: An American Legend*. New York: Ballantine Books, 2001.

Horan, James D. *The Desperate Years*. New York: Bonanza Books, 1962.

Humphreys, Ray. "The Inside Story of Denver's $60,000 Boettcher Abduction." *Startling Detective Adventures* 10 (June 1933): 30–37.

Karpis, Alvin, as told to Robert Livesey. *On the Rock: Twenty-Five Years in Alcatraz*. New York: Beaufort Books, 1980.

Karpis, Alvin, with Bill Trent. *The Alvin Karpis Story*. New York: Loward-McCann and Geohegan, 1971.

Krog, Bertha, et al., ed. *History of Buffalo County, 1885–1935*. Chamberlain, SD: Register-Lakota Printing, 1958.

Lamb, Brian. *Who's Buried in Grant's Tomb? A Tour of Presidential Gravesites*. New York: PublicAffairs, 2000.

Lauber, Patricia. *Dust Bowl: The Challenge of the Great Plains*. New York: Coward-McCann, 1958.

Lindell, Lisa. "No Greater Menace." *Colorado History Magazine* 10 (2004): 37–56.

Lowenthal, Max. *The Federal Bureau of Investigation*. New York: William Sloane, 1950.

Lowitt, Richard, and Maurine Beasley, ed. *One Third of a Nation: Lorena Hickok Reports on the Great Depression*. Urbana, IL: University of Illinois Press, 1981.

Lusk, Robert D. "The Life and Death of 470 Acres." *Saturday Evening Post* 211 (August 13, 1938): 5–6, 30–34.

Maccabee, Paul. *John Dillinger Slept Here: A Crook's Tour of Crimes and Corruption in St. Paul 1920–1936*. St. Paul: Minnesota Historical Press, 1995.

Malone, Bill C. *Country Music, U.S.A.* Austin: University of Texas Press, 1968.

Maquis Who's Who. *Who Was Who in America: With World Notables*. Vol. 5. *1969–73*. St Louis: Von Hoffman Press, 1973.

McCullough, David. *Truman*. New York: Simon and Schuster, 1992.

McElvaine, Robert S. *The Great Depression: America, 1929–1941*. New York: Times Books, 1984.

McWilliams, Peter. *Ain't Nobody's Business If You Do: The Absurdity of Consensual Crimes in a Free Country*. Los Angeles: Prelude Press, 1998.

Mills, Rick W. *The Milwaukee Road in Dakota*. Hermosa, SD: Battle Creek, 1998.

New York Times. *The New York Times Index: A Book of Record*. New York: New York Times Company, 1933.

———. *The New York Times Index: A Book of Record*. New York: New York Times Company, 1934.

Nash, Jay Robert. *Citizen Hoover: A Critical Study of the Life and Times of J. Edgar Hoover*. Chicago: Nelson-Hall, 1972.

Nickel, Steven, and William J. Helmer. *Baby Face Nelson: Portrait of a Public Enemy*. Nashville, TN: Cumberland House, 2002.

North, Mark. *Act of Treason: The Role of J. Edgar Hoover in the Assassination of President Kennedy*. New York: Carrol and Graf, 1991.

Ochsner Journal 4, no. 1: 48–52.

Penny, Eileen M. "Boettcher Kidnapping." *The Investigator* (September 1945): 1–4.

Pohlman, Ralph. Point of View: Small Town Boy Makes Bad. See also www.stouffvilleonline.com/editorial.php?editoriallD=24.

Potter, Claire Bond. *War on Crime: Bandits, G-Men, and the Politics of Mass Culture*. New Brunswick, NJ: Rutgers University Press, 1998.

Powers, Richard Gid. *G-Men, Hoover's F.B.I. in American Popular Culture*. Carbondale: Southern Illinois University Press, 1983.

———, ed. *Secrecy and Power: The Life of J. Edgar Hoover*. New York: Free Press, 1987.

Purvis, Alston W., with Alex Tresniowski. *The Vendetta: FBI Hero Melvin Purvis's War against Crime, and J. Edgar Hoover's War against Him*. New York: PublicAffairs, 2005.

Purvis, Melvin. *American Agent*. Garden City, NY: Doubleday, Doran, 1936.

Reddig, William M. *Tom's Town: Kansas City and the Pendergast Legend*. Philadelphia: J. P. Lippincott, 1947.

Reeves, George S. *A Man from South Dakota*. New York: E. P. Dutton, 1950.

Rodgers, Richard, ed. *100 Hundred Best Songs of the 20's and 30's*. New York: Harmony Books, 1973.

Ruffner, James A., et al. *Climates of the States*. Detroit: Gale Research, 1978.

Ruth, David E. *Inventing the Public Enemy: The Gangster in American Culture, 1918–1934*. Chicago: University of Chicago Press, 1996.

Sandburg, Carl. *Abraham Lincoln: The Prairie Years and the War Years*. 1 vol. New York: Harcourt, Brace, & World, 1954.

Schell, Herbert S. *History of South Dakota*. Lincoln: University of Nebraska Press, 1961.

Shannon, David A. *The Great Depression*. England Cliffs, NJ: Prentice-Hall, 1960.

Sinkie, Juanita, et al., ed. *History of Buffalo County*. Vol.3. *1985–2000*. Chamberlain, SD: Register-Lakota Printing, 1999.

Smith, Brad. *Lawman to Outlaw: Verne Miller and the Kansas City Massacre*. Bedford, IN: JoNa Books, 2002.

Smith, Rex Alan. *The Carving of Mount Rushmore.* New York: Abbeville Press, 1985.

Steele, Phillip W. *Outlaws and Gun Fighters of the Old West.* Gretna, LA: Pelican, 1998.

Sullivan, William, with Gill Brown. *The Bureau: My Thirty Years in Hoover's FBI.* New York: W. W. Norton, 1979.

Summers, Anthony. *Official and Confidential: The Secret Life of J. Edgar Hoover.* New York: G. P. Putnam's Sons, 1993.

Teslow, Peggy J. *History of the United States District Court for The District of South Dakota.* Minneapolis, MN: West, 1991.

Theoharis, Athan G., and John Stuart Cox. *The Boss: J. Edgar Hoover and the Great American Inquisition.* Philadelphia: Temple University Press, 1988.

Theoharis, Athan G., et al. *The FBI: A Comprehensive Reference Guide.* New York: Citadel Press, 1988.

Thomas, Tony. *A Wonderful Life: The Films and Career of James Stewart.* New York: Citadel Press, 1988.

Touhy, Roger, with Roy Brennan. *The Stolen Years.* Cleveland: Pennington, 1959.

Unger, Robert. *The Union Station Massacre: The Original Sin of J. Edgar Hoover's FBI.* Kansas City: Andrews McMeel, 1997.

Waite, Arthur Edward. *A New Encyclopaedia of Freemasonry.* New York: Weathervane Books, 1970.

Wallis, Michael. *Pretty Boy: The Life and Times of Charles Arthur Floyd.* New York: St. Martin's Press, 1992.

Watkins, T. H. *The Great Depression: America in the 1930s.* Boston: Little, Brown, 1993.

———. *The Hungry Years: A Narrative History of the Great Depression in America.* New York: Henry Holt, 1999.

Wilson, P. W. *"America's New 'Public Enemy No. 1' Arrested." Literary Digest* 117, no. 6 (February 10, 1934): 38.

Wilson, P. W., with Robert Livesey. *On the Rock.* Don Mills, Ontario: Musson/ General, 1980.

Wolff, Rick, et al. *The Baseball Encyclopedia.* 8th ed. New York: Macmillan, 1990.

Interviews

John Alcorn, Regina, Saskatchewan.
Kelly Alcorn, Saskatoon, Saskatchewan.
Judy Busack, Chamberlain, South Dakota.
Betty Champagne, Melville, Saskatchewan.
Leon Chmela, Kimball, South Dakota.
Leo P. Flynn, Milbank, South Dakota.
John Fox, FBI, Washington, D.C.

Charles Boettcher Hoffman, Eureka, South Dakota.
Louis R. Hurwitz, Fontana, Florida.
Harry Konechne, Kimball, South Dakota.
Kenneth Larsen, Huron, South Dakota.
Doris Rogers Lockerman, Atlanta.
Lloyd Marken, Reliance, South Dakota.
John Mayer, Pukwana, South Dakota.
Claudia Boettcher Merthan, Denver.
Dureene Petersen, Gann Valley, South Dakota.
Melvin Rank, Gann Valley, South Dakota.
Marj Redenbach, Melville, Saskatchewan.
Orville Sankey, Seattle, Washington.
Hugh Sedgewick, Gann Valley, South Dakota.
Steve Smith, Chamberlain, South Dakota.
Lyn Spenst, Denver.
Carol Stephens, Gann Valley, South Dakota.
Gregory Stevens, Westminster, Maryland.
LaDean Swoboda, Kimball, South Dakota.
Ruth Viereck, Kimball, South Dakota.
Vernetta Wolfe, Miller, South Dakota.

Index

Bohn, Haskell, 39, 71, 79
Bohn kidnapping: and F. Sankey, 79–
80, 92–93; and Lindbergh Law,
39; and Ray Robinson, 80, 92, 93,
188; and V. Sankey, 71, 83, 87
Bonnie and Clyde, 71, 193
Bootlegging, 7–8, 9–10, 25, 61, 83
Bremer, Adolf, 144
Bremer, Edward G., 144, 151, 166–
67
Bremer kidnapping, 144, 145, 151,
166–67
Brighton gunfight, 48–49
Brown, Harold: as alibi for Sankey,
153–54; and Gann Valley, 13, 75;
later life and death of, 213; as
Sankey's adviser, 165, 166; trial
testimony of, 190, 200
Brown, Thomas, 96, 145
Brisbane, Arthur, 171
Buffalo County, S.Dak., 73, 75
Bungalow on South Emerson (Den-
ver), 16, 55, 67, 210
Burns, William J., 29
Byron, Walter, 132

Caffrey, Ray, 97
Camp Charles, 27, 30
Camp Claude, 27, 30
Candlish, William, 26
Capone, Al ("Scarface"), 24–25, 43,
140, 196
Cardin, Nettie B., 161
Carlson, Roy (Sankey pseud.), 34
Carr, Ralph, 55, 90
Carroll, George, 50–51, 58
Champagne, Betty, 6, 8
Chicago Crime Commission, 140–
41
Chopskie, Andrew, 59, 86
Chopskie, Mike: as caretaker of
ranch, 86, 123; later life and death
of, 214; and romance with F. San-
key, 202; and Sankey children,

122, 161, 169, 202; Sankey neighbor, 59; at Sankey's funeral, 174
Christopherson, Fred C., 122, 163
Clark, Albert T.: at CBII's release,
45–46; and letter from V. Sankey
to F. Sankey, 77; optimism of, 38–
39, 54; on Sankey's suicide, 170;
at scene of Boettcher kidnapping,
24, *104*; and Three Georges, 58;
and Youngberg, 60
Clark, William E. (pseud.). *See* Sankey, Verne
Coors, Adolph, 41
Crime, escalation of, 113–14, 119–
20, 144
Cullen, Thomas F., 153–54
Cummings, Homer: attorney general appointment, 71; federal
authority extended by, 72–73;
and Hoover appointment, 116;
and "Ten Most Wanted List,"
141; twelve-point plan of, 144,
193, 215–16; and Union Station
Massacre, 98; and Youngberg's
fruitless search, 85

Dagwell, B. D., 33–34
Dahill, Thomas, 113, 151
Davenport, Holton: background of,
180–81, 213; and retrial of
F. Sankey, 198–99; and Sankey-
Kohler trial, 190–91; as Sankeys'
lawyer, 165, 168, 176, 197
Day, Charles M., 122
Day, Dorothy, 180
Dempsey, Jack, 143, 145
Denver Post: ad placed by Claude,
34; courthouse scene description,
27–28; and criticism of Denver
police, 42–43; on ordeal of CBII,
45–46; on Sankey's suicide, 170–
71; scoop on CBII's release, 51–
52; Youngberg interview in, 91–
92

Depression era: anecdotes of, 63–
65; and crime, 26, 71, 87–89,
210; mortgage foreclosures during, 129–30, 136–37; repeal of
prohibition during, 25, 68; and
resentment of Boettcher wealth,
66, 68–69; stock market crash
in 1929, 64; and suicides, 124,
210; as true Public Enemy No. 1,
205
Dillinger, John: background of, 154;
and Crown Point jail, 154, 177,
208, 255n; death of, 193; escape
at Little Bohemia, 179–80; photo
described with prosecutor and
sheriff, 154–55, 208; as Public
Enemy No. 1 in 1934, 141, 193,
205
Donney, Mrs. (Denver neighbor),
66–67
Drought conditions, 65–66, 129–
30
Dunn, William, 96
Dye, Edwin, 174, 214

Earhardt, Beth, 10
Eidem, Olaf, 160, 184–86, 190,
192, 194
Eisenhand, Edward, 67–68
Ellsworth, Frances, 55, 123, 132,
178–79
Ellsworth, William, 55, 83, 122–23,
178–79
Estill, Robert, 154–55
Evans, Ellsworth, 180

Factor, John ("Jake the Barber"),
115, 254n
Farmers, desperate conditions for,
65
Farm-ranch in South Dakota, *105,
106*; and buried money, 92; designation as farm or ranch, 237n;
design of, 67–68; mortgage

foreclosure on, 129–30, 136,
177; purchase of land for, 11;
and Youngberg, 15–16, 18, 33,
59
Farnsworth, Charles, 58
FBI (Federal Bureau of Investiga-
tion): and avoidance of shootouts,
146–47; background of, 28–29;
and Boettcher kidnapping, 28, 30,
61–62, 89–90; ridicule of, 116.
See also Hoover, J. Edgar; Purvis,
Melvin
Feinberg, J. C., 123
FERA (Federal Emergency Relief
Administration), 137
*Fern Sankey, United States v. See
United States v. Fern Sankey*
Fischer, Carrie, 146
Flemina, Elizabeth, 17
Fletcher, Lucille, 55
Floods, 135–36
Floyd, Arthur ("Pretty Boy"), 71,
97, 141, 193–94, 196, 204
Flynn, Leo, 181
Foreclosures, mortgage, 129–30,
136–37

Gangsters, Depression era, 71, 87–
89
Gann Valley, S.Dak., 11, 73–75
Gibbs, Calista Kohler (Mrs. Roy),
133, 139, 142, 178, 195, 196
Gibbs, Roy, 133–34, 142–43, 178,
195–96
Gilbert, Dan ("Tubbo"), 115
Gillis, Lester. *See* Nelson, "Baby
Face"
Gilmore, Frank, 168
Gleason, Dan, 85
G-Men (film), 140
Gorder, P. O., 158–59, 175
Grant, James ("Bruce"), 132
Great Depression. *See* Depression
era